SYSTEMIC RISK, INSTITUTIONAL DESIGN, AND THE REGULATION OF FINANCIAL MARKETS

Systemic Risk, Institutional Design, and the Regulation of Financial Markets

Edited by
ANITA ANAND
Faculty of Law
University of Toronto

OXFORD
UNIVERSITY PRESS

OXFORD
UNIVERSITY PRESS

Great Clarendon Street, Oxford, OX2 6DP,
United Kingdom

Oxford University Press is a department of the University of Oxford.
It furthers the University's objective of excellence in research, scholarship,
and education by publishing worldwide. Oxford is a registered trade mark of
Oxford University Press in the UK and in certain other countries

First Edition published in 2016

Published in the United States of America by Oxford University Press
198 Madison Avenue, New York, NY 10016, United States of America

British Library Cataloguing in Publication Data
Data available

Library of Congress Control Number: 2016958837

ISBN 978–0–19–877762–5

This book is dedicated to my dear parents,
Dr SV Anand and Dr SD Ram,
for their endless love and support.
My gratitude to them is similarly endless.

Preface

Following the recent financial crisis, regulators have been preoccupied with the concept of systemic risk in financial markets. They believed that such risk could cause the markets they oversee to implode. At the same time, they demonstrated—and continue to demonstrate—a limited inability to develop and implement comprehensive policies to address systemic risk. This inability is due not only to the indeterminacy inherent in the term 'systemic risk' but also to existing institutional structures. Because of their existing legal mandates, it is difficult for regulators to monitor and regulate systemic risk across an entire economic system and across borders. These two concepts—defining risk and developing appropriate institutional structures—constitute the foundation for this book and the chapters that follow.

In particular, this book is a collection of papers that explores the related concepts of systemic risk and institutional design of financial markets: in other words, what is the problem and what can be done about it? The chapters focus on regulation that can be devised and implemented to respond to systemic risk. They examine the design of countries' financial systems and, in particular, respond to the following questions: How should systemic risk be regulated? What should be the role of the central bank, banking authorities, and securities regulators? Is a 'twin peaks' approach optimal? Should countries implement a macroprudential regulator? If not, how is macroprudential regulation to be addressed within their respective legislative schemes? What policy mechanisms can be employed when developing regulation relating to financial markets?

This book aims to foster discussion of these questions in its examination of systemic risk, institutional design, and financial market regulation. It addresses both domestic and international approaches to regulation and develops an approach to examining the conceptual legal and institutional frameworks within which financial market regulators operate. The book explores not only problems of regulatory coordination within national systems because of fragmented mandates, but also parallel problems across national systems given that systemic risk has increasing cross-border dimensions.

Our project contributes to a deep literature, much of which predates the financial crisis, relating to systemic risk and macroprudential regulation. Previous authors usefully examine the challenge that financial market regulators face in attempting to quantify stress in financial systems.[1] But there is more analysis to be undertaken in terms of the legal and institutional architecture in place across economic systems. In particular, the question of whether this architecture lends itself to the regulation of systemic risk warrants deeper analysis following the most recent financial crisis.

In Chapter 1, Anita Anand, Michael Trebilcock, and Michael Rosenstock analyse macroprudential regulation and supervision from an institutional perspective at the national and international levels across developed countries. They argue that systemic risk has evolved to include macroprudential risk, and further, that it has evolved to extend beyond the formal commercial banking sector to include the shadow banking sector and the cross-border dimensions of the phenomenon. They call upon regulators to play a proactive role in overseeing this new conception of systemic risk. In particular, they call for more integration and coordination among regulators in light of the dangers posed by systemic risks that can span across jurisdictions and borders. To this end, they favour an approach to regulation under which financial markets are regulated according to certain regulatory objectives that are specified in the applicable legislation, including macroeconomic stability.

In Chapter 2, Steven L Schwarcz persuasively argues that, because systemic shocks are inevitable, regulation should be designed not only to try to reduce those shocks but also to protect the financial system against their unavoidable impact. This could be done, he explains, by applying chaos theory to help stabilize the financial system. While chaos theory is typically used to address engineering system complexity, it can also inform financial system complexity. One aspect of chaos theory is deterministic chaos in dynamic systems, which recognizes that the more complex the system, the more likely it is that failures will occur. Thus, the most successful systems are those in which the consequences of failures are limited. Schwarcz argues that there are at least two ways that financial regulation could accomplish this: by ensuring liquidity to systemically important firms and markets, and by requiring those firms and markets to be more internally robust.

Dan Awrey contends in Chapter 3 that the relationship between institutional design and the promotion of regulatory objectives, such as financial stability, is poorly understood. He argues that the institutional structure of financial regulation is particularly important in advancing the objective of

[1] In the economics field, several books—both monographs and edited collections—address systemic risk in financial markets. These books, mainly addressing systemic risk from an international and global perspective, include: Prasanna Gai, *Systemic Risk: The Dynamics of Modern Financial Systems* (OUP 2013) and Jean-Pierre Fouque and Joseph A Langsam (eds), *Handbook on Systemic Risk* (CUP 2013).

financial stability because many of the potential sources of financial instability transcend the historical distinctions between 'banking', 'securities', and 'insurance' which have often served as the blueprints for the institutional structure of financial regulation. To the extent that it serves to enhance (or impede) effective information flow and coordination, the institutional structure of financial regulation can thus be understood as playing a significant role in advancing (or undermining) the objective of financial stability. Given this important role, Awrey argues, the institutional structure of financial regulation should recognize the realities of the law's influence on financial stability.

In Chapters 4 and 5, respectively, Roberta Romano and Edward M Iacobucci address another problem: what happens when regulation designed to respond to financial crises is overly burdensome and costly to implement? Romano argues that the protracted rule-making experience of the Dodd-Frank Act, with its 'off-the-rack solutions', augurs in favour of sunsetting because the stakes for interested parties would be lowered, and hence lobbying less intense and prolonged, if regulation had to be reassessed and put to a legislative vote at a future date. In her view, sunsetting and regulatory experimentation are the best tools to mitigate the perils that arise when one is 'regulating in the dark', since they improve the quality of decision-making by providing a mechanism for evaluating and remedying regulatory errors.

Iacobucci offers an alternative view of sunsetting. He argues that it is not clear why greater information accumulation pushes for sunsetting and why, in particular, the default rule used by regulators should be the pre-crisis legislation rather than the crisis legislation. Rather than only considering pre-crisis and crisis legislation (i.e., as alternatives), Iacobucci proposes a third alternative. This alternative, a variation on the sunset clause, conceives of neither the pre-crisis legislation nor the crisis legislation as the default rule. Rather, an alternative piece of reform, undesirable to all parties, is automatically enacted if legislative consensus is not reached. This alternative captures the possibility of improved law-making in light of better information, while also creating a strong counterweight to legislative inertia.

In Chapter 6, Weitseng Chen addresses China's 'rush' to internationalize the Renminbi, the country's national currency. Chen argues that, regardless of whether or not the liberalization of its financial markets was premature, the necessary macroprudential policies attendant on such liberalization were left aside. Because the aggressive internalization of the Renminbi called for what Chen refers to as 'pro-cyclical' policies—that is, policies that make capital easy to secure—Chinese policy-makers overlooked the 'counter-cyclical' policies on which macroprudential regulation is built. In this way, China underestimated certain systemic risks—risks that were expressed, in part, by the volatility in Chinese equity markets in 2015. In this chapter, Chen discusses the unique aspects of Chinese capital markets, including the prevalence of its shadow banking system, which has exacerbated the problems posed by its international financial policies. To mitigate the systemic risks created by these policies, Chen recommends that China reform its domestic institutions by enacting macroprudential regulation.

In Chapter 7, Rosa M Lastra points out that the ability of central banks during the recent financial crisis to act as lenders of last resort in order to provide financial institutions with emergency liquidity assistance posed economic, legal, and political challenges. In particular, the systemic risks of such crises require *ex ante* laws that set out clear procedures by which central banks can provide emergency liquidity assistance to troubled institutions, but at the same time, these laws must give central banks the flexibility to act in a manner appropriate to the specific circumstances of the crisis. Here, disciplined cost-benefit analysis helps mitigate some of the moral hazards otherwise posed by such intervention. While flexibility and speed are essential, this legal framework must also establish adequate *ex post* accountability. Given that systemic risk is not delineated along national—but international—lines, solutions to the regulation of systemic risk require thinking outside the boundaries of purely national law.

As is clear from this brief overview of the chapters, this book examines the importance of designing regulatory institutions so that they can more effectively regulate systemic risk. In addition to regulating systemic risk, the book focuses on macroprudential regulation and supervision in developed and developing market economies. This book will be useful for academic law researchers who study financial system design and systemic risk. For those involved in policy-making, the book will be informative given the increased focus on macroprudential regulation as the broad policy framework within which systemic risk is to be addressed. Woven throughout the chapters that follow is the concept of macroprudential risk: can it be regulated and, if so, which particular regulatory tools make such regulation possible?

The Group of Thirty, an international group of leading representatives from the private and public sectors and academia, declared that 'macroprudential policy is concerned not only with systemic risk but also with developing the appropriate responses to those risks in order to strengthen the financial system and avoid similar crises in the future'.[2] The focus is on 'the interconnectedness of financial institutions and markets, common exposures

[2] The Group of Thirty, 'Enhancing Financial Stability and Resilience: Macroprudential Policy, Tools, and Systems for the Future' (October 2010) <http://group30.org/images/uploads/publications/G30_EnhancingFinancialStabilityResilience.pdf> accessed 10 March 2016.

to economic variables, and procyclical behaviors [which] can create risk'.[3] But it is impossible to develop a policy relating to macroprudential regulation without understanding the institutional framework in place in a given country. The papers included in this book will prove extremely useful in laying the legal and institutional groundwork for macroprudential regulation and the implementation issues that arise with respect to this issue.

In the 2013 *Handbook of the Economics of Finance*, Markus Brunnermeier and Martin Oehmke persuasively argue that while there has been an explosion of literature regarding financial bubbles and crises, many important research questions remain. In identifying issues of particular importance, the authors cite the following questions, which in their view, require further research: what macroprudential tools should financial market regulators and central banks deploy? How effective is macroprudential regulation and how does it interact with monetary policy? These are questions with relevance to law. It makes little sense to discuss the role of macroprudential regulation post-crisis without reference to the legal rules and mandates within which regulators act. This is a gap that this book seeks to fill.

This book evolved from a conference by the same name held at the University of Toronto's Faculty of Law in September 2014. I then began inviting a number of additional contributors to join the project in order for the book to have an international focus. I thank Edward M Iacobucci, Roberta Romano, Steven L Schwarcz, Michael Trebilcock, and Michael Rosenstock for attending the initial conference and Dan Awrey, Weitseng Chen, and Rosa M Lastra for agreeing to join our project thereafter. It has been an absolute pleasure to work with you through the project.

I thank the Social Sciences and Humanities Research Council of Canada and the Torys Fund at the University of Toronto for providing financial support. I thank Krupa Kotecha for her tireless assistance in editing the citations and keeping the inflow and outflow of edited chapters organized. I also thank Andrew Mihalik for stepping in to assist and for doing an excellent job towards the end of the project. Finally, I extend deep appreciation to my colleague and dear friend, Michael Trebilcock, for his continuous guidance not only with respect to this project but also throughout my academic career.

Anita Anand
February 2016

[3] Macroprudential regulation does not seek to remove economic shocks, but it does aim to identify and address a financial system's exposure to such shocks *ex ante*, so that they can be addressed and the market's ability to resist such shocks can be established: ibid 17.

Table of Contents

List of Abbreviations

ABCP	asset-backed commercial paper
ABS	asset-backed security
AIIB	Asian Infrastructure Investment Bank
APA	Administrative Procedure Act
APRA	Australian Prudential Regulatory Authority
ASIC	Australian Securities and Investment Commission
BIS	Bank of International Settlements
CCMR	Cooperative Capital Markets Regulator
CCP	central counterparty
CDO	collateralized debt obligation
CDS	credit default swap
CFPB	Consumer Financial Protection Bureau
CFR	Code of Federal Regulations
CFTC	Commodity Futures Trading Commission
CG	Comptroller General
CRA	credit rating agency
CRA	Congressional Review Act (as used in Chapter 4)
CSE	Consolidated Supervised Entities
CSRC	China Securities Regulatory Commission
CTRF	contingent term repo facility
DPA	deferred prosecution agreement
DWF	discount window facility
EBA	European Banking Authority
EC	European Commission
ECB	European Central Bank
EESA	Emergency and Economic Stabilization Act
EIOPA	European Insurance and Occupational Pension Authority
ELA	emergency liquidity assistance
ESA	European supervisory authority
ESCB	European System of Central Banks
ESM	European Stability Mechanism

ESMA	European Securities and Markets Authority
ESRB	European Systemic Risk Board
FCA	Financial Conduct Authority
FCAC	Financial Consumer Agency of Canada
FDIC	Federal Deposit Insurance Corporation
FDICIA	Federal Deposit Insurance Corporation Improvement Act of 1991
FLS	Funding for Lending Scheme
FMU	financial market utility
FOMC	Federal Open Market Committee
FPC	Financial Policy Committee
FRB	Federal Reserve
FSA	Financial Services Authority
FSB	Financial Stability Board
FSOC	Financial Stability Oversight Council
GCC	German Constitutional Court
GSE	government-sponsored enterprise
HMT	Her Majesty's Treasury
HUD	Department of Housing and Urban Development
ILTR	indexed long term repo
IMF	International Monetary Fund
IOSCO	International Organization of Securities Commissions
ISDA	International Swaps and Derivatives Association
LOLR	lender of last resort
MBS	mortgage-backed securities
MMOU	Multilateral Memorandum of Understanding
MOU	memorandum of understanding
NAIC	National Association of Insurance Commissioners
NCA	national competent authority
NCB	national central banks
NSR	new systemic risk
OCC	Office of the Comptroller of the Currency
OMO	open market operation
OMT	Outright Monetary Transaction
OSFI	Office of the Superintendent of Financial Institutions
OSHA	Occupational Safety and Health Association

OTC	over-the-counter
P2P	peer-to-peer
PBoC	People's Bank of China
PRA	Prudential Regulatory Authority
QDII	Qualified Domestic Institutional Investors
QE	quantitative easing
QFII	Qualified Foreign Institutional Investors
RBA	Reserve Bank of Australia
RMB	renminbi
RQFII	Renminbi Qualified Foreign Institutional Investors
SDR	Special Drawing Rights
SEC	Securities and Exchange Commission
SFTZ	Shanghai Free Trade Zone
SIFI	systemically important financial institution
SIFMU	systemically important financial market utility
SLS	Special Liquidity Scheme
SMF	Sterling Monetary Framework
SMP	Securities Markets Programme
SOE	state-owned enterprise
SPV	special purpose vehicle
SRB	Single Resolution Board
SRM	Single Resolution Mechanism
SSM	Single Supervisory Mechanism
TAF	Term Auction Facility
TALF	Term Asset-Backed Securities Lending Facility
TARP	Troubled Asset Relief Programme
TBTF	too-big-to-fail
TEU	Treaty on European Union
TFEU	Treaty on the Functioning of the European Union
UCC	Uniform Commercial Code
USD	US dollar
VaR	value at risk

List of Contributors

Anita Anand is a Professor of Law and the J.R. Kimber Chair in Investor Protection and Corporate Governance at the University of Toronto Faculty of Law. She served as Associate Dean (JD Program) from 2007–09. Since 2010, she has served as the Academic Director of the Centre for the Legal Profession at U of T, and in this role has led the development of its new Program on Ethics in Law and Business. She is a Senior Fellow, Massey College and is cross-appointed to the University of Toronto's School of Public Policy and Governance. In 2009–10, she was a visiting scholar at the Bank of Canada. She is the recipient of research grants from the Social Sciences and Humanities Research Council of Canada (three awards), the Foundation for Legal Research (three awards), the Connaught Foundation as well as the Canadian Association of Law Teachers' Scholarly Paper Award (2003). In Fall 2004, she received the Queen's Law Students' Society Award for Excellence in Teaching and in Fall 2006, she and co-authors Frank Milne and Lynnette Purda were awarded the Best Paper in Managerial Finance by the International Journal of Managerial Finance for their empirical research relating to corporate governance.

Dan Awrey is an Associate Professor of Law and Finance and Academic Director of the MSc in Law and Finance programme. Dan's teaching and research interests reside in the area of financial regulation and, more specifically, the regulation of banks, investment funds, derivatives markets, and financial market infrastructure. He has undertaken research and provided advice at the request of organizations including HM Treasury, the UK Financial Conduct Authority, the Commonwealth Secretariat, and the European Securities and Markets Authority. Before entering academia, Dan served as legal counsel to a global investment management firm and, prior to that, as an associate practising corporate finance and securities law with a major Canadian law firm. He holds degrees from Queen's University (BA, LLB), the University of Toronto (LLM), and Oxford University (DPhil).

Weitseng Chen is an Assistant Professor and Deputy Director of the Center for Asian Legal Studies at National University of Singapore (NUS) Faculty of Law. His research interests focus on comparative Asian legal studies with an emphasis on property, financial institutions, and law and economic development in the greater China area. Weitseng received his JSD from Yale Law School (2007) where he was a Fulbright scholar. Thereafter, he worked for Stanford University as a Hewlett Fellow of the Center on Democracy, Development and the Rule of Law. He previously received his LLB and LLM from National Taiwan University. Immediately before he joined NUS Faculty of Law, Weitseng Chen worked as a corporate lawyer at Davis Polk & Wardwell, specializing in cross-broader capital markets transactions. He is also the principal investigator of an international research project 'The

Beijing Consensus? How China has changed the Western ideas of law and economic development' (CUP forthcoming 2016).

Edward M Iacobucci is the Dean of the Faculty of Law, University of Toronto. He started at the Faculty of Law in 1998. He was Visiting Professor at New York University Law School in 2007, Visiting Professor at University of Chicago Law School in 2003, and a John M Olin Visiting Fellow at Columbia University Law School in 2002. Prior to joining the Faculty of Law, he was the John M Olin Visiting Lecturer at the University of Virginia in 1997–98 and served as Law Clerk at the Supreme Court of Canada for Mr Justice John Sopinka in 1996–97. He won a teaching prize at the Faculty of Law in 2000 and was a joint winner with his co-authors of the 2002–03 Doug Purvis Prize in Canadian Economics for *The Law and Economics of Canadian Competition Policy*. His areas of interest include corporate law, competition law, and law and economics more generally.

Rosa María Lastra is Professor of International Financial and Monetary Law at the Centre for Commercial Law Studies (CCLS), Queen Mary University of London. She is a member of Monetary Committee of the International Law Association (MOCOMILA), a founding member of the European Shadow Financial Regulatory Committee (ESFRC), an associate of the Financial Markets Group of the London School of Economics and Political Science, and an affiliated scholar of the Centre for the Study of Central Banks at New York University School of Law. She has served as a consultant to the International Monetary Fund, the European Central Bank, the World Bank, the Asian Development Bank, and the Federal Reserve Bank of New York. From November 2008 to June 2009 she acted as Specialist Adviser to the European Union Committee [Sub-Committee A] of the House of Lords regarding its Inquiry into EU Financial Regulation and responses to the financial crisis. She speaks regularly at international conferences. Professor Lastra lives in London with her husband and their four children.

Roberta Romano is Sterling Professor of Law at Yale Law School and Director of the Yale Law School Center for the Study of Corporate Law. Her research has focused on state competition for corporate charters, the political economy of takeover regulation, shareholder litigation, institutional investor activism in corporate governance, and the regulation of securities markets and financial instruments and institutions. Professor Romano is a fellow of the American Academy of Arts and Sciences and the European Corporate Governance Institute, a research associate of the National Bureau for Economic Research, a past President of the American Law and Economics Association and the Society for Empirical Legal Studies, and a past co-editor of the Journal of Law, Economics and Organization. She has received the Yale Law Women teaching award three times and is the author of *The Genius of American Corporate Law* (1993) and *The Advantage of Competitive Federalism for Securities Regulation* (2002), and series editor of the Foundations of Law reader series and editor of the volume in the series, Foundations of Corporate Law, 2nd edn (2010).

Michael Rosenstock has completed his JD at the University of Toronto, Faculty of Law. Before entering law school, he worked as a senior economist for the Government of Ontario and a policy advisor and strategist for a Canadian political party.

Steven L Schwarcz is the Stanley A Star Professor of Law & Business at Duke University, Founding Director of Duke's interdisciplinary Global Capital Markets Center (now renamed the Global Financial Markets Center), and Senior Fellow at the Centre for International Governance Innovation (CIGI). Prior to joining the Duke faculty, he was a partner at two leading international law firms where he represented top banks and other financial institutions in structuring innovative capital market financing transactions, both domestic and international. He also helped to pioneer the field of asset securitization, and his book, *Structured Finance, A Guide to the Principles of Asset Securitization*, is one of the most widely used texts in the field.

Professor Schwarcz has been an adviser to the United Nations and has given numerous endowed or distinguished public lectures, including at The University of Hong Kong, the University of Oxford, Georgetown University Law Center, National University of Singapore, and The National Assembly of the Republic of Korea. He has served as an expert at meetings of the World Economic Forum. He also has given numerous keynote speeches, including at annual conferences of the European Central Bank, the Corporate Law Teachers Association of Australia, New Zealand, and Asia-Pacific, Moody's Corporation, and the Asian Securitization Forum.

Michael J Trebilcock is the holder of the Chair in Law and Economics at the Faculty of Law, University of Toronto. He graduated from the University of Canterbury in New Zealand in 1962 with an LLB and completed his LLM at the University of Adelaide in 1965. He joined the Faculty of Law at the University of Toronto in 1972. He was selected as a University Professor in 1990. He was a Fellow in Law and Economics at the University of Chicago Law School in 1976, a Visiting Professor of Law at Yale Law School in 1985 and 2005, and a Global Law Professor at New York University Law School in 1997 and 1999. He was a Visiting Professor at Harvard Law School in 2011–12. In 1987 he was elected a Fellow of the Royal Society of Canada. In 1999, Professor Trebilcock received an Honorary Doctorate in Laws from McGill University and was awarded the Canada Council Molson Prize in the Humanities and Social Sciences. In the same year (1999) he was elected an Honorary Foreign Fellow of the American Academy of Arts and Sciences. In 2002 Professor Trebilcock was elected President of the American Law and Economics Association. In 2007 he was the recipient of the Ontario Attorney General's Mundell Medal for contributions to Law and Letters. In 2010, he was the recipient of the Ontario Premier's Discovery Award for the Social Sciences.

1

Institutional Design and the New Systemic Risk in Banking Crises

Anita Anand, Michael Trebilcock, and Michael Rosenstock

1. Introduction

Financial crises come in many shapes and forms. In a recent widely acclaimed survey of eight centuries of financial crises around the globe, Reinhart and Rogoff helpfully categorize them as follows: sovereign defaults, which occur when a government fails to meet payments on its external or domestic debt obligations; banking crises, such as those the world has experienced since 2008, where a significant part of a country's banking sector has become insolvent after heavy investment losses; exchange rate crises, where the value of a country's currency falls precipitously; and, finally, crises marked by bouts of very high inflation that constitute the de facto equivalent of outright default on public or private sector debt.[1]

Reinhart and Rogoff argue that historically speaking, the categories of financial crises share common causes and consequences such as a dramatic and unsustainable expansion of credit, often fuelled by external financial inflows reflecting global monetary imbalances.[2] Importantly, the authors show that what may begin as one category of crisis can quickly transform into a different class of crisis both within and across countries. As they note, 'A country experiencing an exchange rate crisis may soon find itself in banking and inflation crises, sometimes with domestic and external default to follow.'[3] Financial risks are transmitted internationally through two channels: shocks

[1] See Carmen Reinhart and Kenneth Rogoff, *This Time Is Different: Eight Centuries of Financial Folly* (Princeton University Press 2009). See also 'The Slumps that Shaped Modern Finance' *The Economist* (12 April 2014) 49–54.

[2] Reinhard and Rogoff (n 1) xxv–xxxvi. See also Charles Kindleberger and Robert Aliber, *Manias, Panics and Crashes: A History of Financial Crises* (6th edn, Palgrave McMillan 2011) 13–24.

[3] Reinhart and Rogoff (n 1) 248.

Institutional Design and the New Systemic Risk in Banking Crises. First Edition. Anita Anand, Michael Trebilcock, and Michael Rosenstock. Published 2016 by Oxford University Press.

that are common between countries, and contagion that spills over from one country to another through cross-linkages.[4] In the 2008 financial crisis, the authors note that risk was transmitted through both channels as financial institutions outside the US were exposed to the US subprime housing market (contagion) while many countries were exhibiting the same kind of unsustainable real estate prices and current account deficits as the US (common shocks).[5]

In this chapter, we focus on banking crises with regards to both commercial and other financial institutions. We focus on lessons to be learned from the global financial crisis that began in 2008, typified by the dramatic growth in the scale and complexity of financial instruments in wide use throughout the financial sector; the expansion of a 'shadow' banking sector implicating solvency and liquidity concerns for many financial institutions beyond the traditional focus on the solvency and liquidity of commercial banks; major contagion effects across national borders, reflecting the internationalization of financial institutions and financial transactions; and finally, the engagement of a broader range of regulatory institutions, both domestic and international, beyond the traditional regulatory focus on the solvency and liquidity of commercial banks.[6] While we acknowledge the growing importance of financial regulation in emerging markets, the regulatory design and coordination issues evaluated in this chapter are considered primarily from the perspective of developed economies.

We argue that the concept of 'systemic risk', which traditionally focused on the relative stability of financial institutions and the consequences of their failure, has evolved to include macroprudential risk and the possibility that an entire economy will be affected by a triggering event or exogenous shock. Systemic risk has also developed to extend well beyond the formal commercial banking sector to include shadow banking and the cross-border dimensions of the phenomenon. As a result of this evolution, regulators have an important role to play in monitoring and managing systemic risk. We explore key policy instruments and the complement of domestic and international institutions that most effectively enable financial market regulators to discharge their role in monitoring and managing this new conception of systemic risk, which we refer to as the 'new systemic risk' (NSR).

We begin with an acknowledgement that existing academic literature can be divided into two camps. On the one hand are traditional definitions of systemic risk; these definitions centre on counterparty contagion within the banking sector whereby one bank's default (on a loan, deposit, or payment) to

[4] ibid 240–42. [5] ibid.

[6] See Barry Eichengreen, *Hall of Mirrors* (OUP 2014).

another bank occasions a loss greater than the second bank's capital, forcing the second bank to default on obligations to a third bank, occasioning a loss greater than the third bank's capital and so on.[7] The concept of a domino or contagion effect that negatively impacts financial institutions is thus central to the traditional understanding of systemic risk.

On the other hand is the notion that such a 'domino effect' will often occasion negative consequences not only for financial institutions (predominantly banks) but also for the financial system as a whole.[8] Helwege explains that systemic risk is 'the risk that the financial system will fail to function properly because of widespread distress'.[9] Similarly, Billio et al. define systemic risk as 'any set of circumstances that threatens the stability of or public confidence in the financial system'.[10] Key policy-makers have now adopted a broader definition of 'systemic risk'. Mark Carney, past Governor of the Bank of Canada and current head of the Bank of England, as well as Ben Bernanke, former Federal Reserve Chairman, have defined systemic risk as some form of system-wide financial distress or disruption with significant consequences for the real economy.[11] During the recent financial crisis, systemic consequences stemming from the failure of individual banks have been amplified with the

[7] Andrew Crockett, 'Why Is Financial Stability a Goal of Public Policy?' in Federal Reserve Bank of Kansas City, *Maintaining Financial Stability in a Global Economy* (Federal Reserve Bank of Kansas City 1997) 7–36. There are notable 'outliers'—examples of economists who define 'systemic risk' differently. For instance, De Bandt and Hartmann note that although 'systemic risk' traditionally refers to vulnerability in the banking sector, 'at the heart of the concept is the notion of "contagion," a particularly strong propagation of failures from one institution to another': Olivier de Bandt and Philipp Hartmann, 'Systemic Risk: A Survey' (2000) European Central Bank Working Paper 35, 8. Taylor similarly defines systemic risk as 'macroeconomic risk that the entire economy will be affected', including money supply and asset price shocks as potential sources of systemic risk: John Taylor, 'Defining Systemic Risk Operationally' in George Shultz, Kenneth Scott, and John Taylor (eds), *Ending Government Bailouts As We Know Them* (Hoover Press 2003) 36–42.

[8] Hal S Scott, 'The Reduction of Systemic Risk in the United States Financial System' (2010) 33 Harvard Law & Policy Review 671, 675 ('Here the concern is that if institution X fails to settle its derivative position with institution Y, both X and Y will fail. If Y in turn cannot settle its positions, other institutions will also fail.').

[9] Jean Helwege, 'Financial Firm Bankruptcy and Systemic Risk' (2009) Regulation 24, 24.

[10] Monica Billio, Mila Getmansky, Andrew W Lo, and Loriana Pelizzon, 'Econometric Measures of Connectedness and Systemic Risk in the Finance and Insurance Sectors' (2012) 104 Journal of Financial Economics 535, 537.

[11] Carney describes systemic risk as 'the probability that the financial system is unable to support economic activity': Nikil Chande, Nicholas Labelle, and Eric Tuer, 'Central Counterparties and Systemic Risk' (December 2010) Bank of Canada Financial System Review 1. Ben Bernanke advocates for a broad definition that includes 'developments that threaten the stability of the financial system as a whole and consequently the broader economy': Corey Boles, 'Bernanke Offers Broad Definition of Systemic Risk' *Wall Street Journal* (18 November 2009) <http://blogs.wsj.com/economics/2009/11/18/bernanke-offers-broad-definition-of-systemic-risk> accessed 26 October 2013. We acknowledge that financial crises come in all kinds of forms: see Reinhart and Rogoff (n 1) (surveying eight centuries of financial crises in different countries).

banking sector's evolution from an 'originate-to-hold' to an 'originate-to-distribute' model. That is, banks have historically occupied the role of lender in issuing home mortgages or other credit instruments. Over time, they began not only to hold the risks but also to seek additional returns on loans by bundling mortgages and selling them to other (often non-bank) financial intermediaries.[12] But when banks offloaded exposure to risks associated with loans, they had weaker incentives to scrutinize the creditworthiness of their borrowers. Furthermore, in ceasing to hold the loans, banks dispensed with their incentive to monitor borrowers as the loans matured.[13]

Banks, especially in the US, devised innovative means of expanding the market for securitized loans. They began by securitizing more kinds of home loans, beyond those that Fannie Mae or Freddie Mac were allowed to acquire via relatively simple securitizations with only prepayment risk. As the demand for mortgage-backed securities increased, banks found yet more ways to securitize, culminating in highly complex subprime loan agreements underlying the securities.[14] Judge explains that '[o]f the roughly $1.2 trillion in sub-prime loans extended in 2005–2006, more than 80% were subsequently securitized.'[15] Beyond securitizing mortgages, banks were increasingly distributing all kinds of loans: in 2007, the syndicated loan market rose from $339 billion in 1988 to $2.2 trillion and loan securitization reached $180 billion.[16]

Understanding that the concept of the NSR is more ubiquitous or at least more elusive relative to the paradigm of systemic risk that prevailed under traditional conceptions of such risk, we seek to answer two questions.[17] First,

[12] Kathryn Judge, 'Fragmentation Nodes: A Study in Financial Innovation, Complexity, and Systemic Risk' (2012) 64 The Stanford Law Review 657, 671. See also Anita I Anand, 'Systemic Risk and Securities Regulation' (2010) 60 University of Toronto Law Journal 941, 942.

[13] The bank originally acted as originator, recipient of monthly payments, and re-negotiator of the loan's terms. With securitization, banks were replaced by 'servicers'. Various scholars have argued that banks were better suited to their previous role. See Douglas W Diamond, 'Financial Intermediation and Delegated Monitoring' (1984) 51 The Review of Economic Studies 393; Bengt Holmström and Jean Tirole, 'Market Liquidity and Performance Monitoring' (1993) 101 Journal of Political Economy 678; Ram TS Ramakrishnan and Anjan V Thakor, 'Information Reliability and a Theory of Financial Intermediation' (1984) 51 The Review of Economic Studies 415.

[14] For an account of their complexity and its attendant complication of the security, see Oren Bar-Gill, 'The Law, Economics, and Psychology of Subprime Mortgage Contracts' (2009) 94 Cornell Law Review 1073, 1078.

[15] Judge (n 12) 679.

[16] Vitaly M Bord and João AC Santos, 'The Rise of the Originate-to-Distribute Model and the Role of Banks in Financial Intermediation' (2012) 18 Federal Reserve Bank of New York Economic Policy Review 21, 21–22.

[17] There is also a threshold question related to how to measure the new systemic risk. Clearly measurement is critical to monitoring and responding to systemic risk. While this issue falls outside the scope of this chapter, a number of scholars have addressed this issue. Reinhart and Rogoff, for example, underscore the paucity of international financial data necessary for regulators to understand and monitor systemic risk: Reinhart and Rogoff (n 1) 279–81.

what are some more prominent examples of policy instruments that are (or might be) required to respond to the NSR? Second, assuming that a broader range of policy instruments is required either to pre-empt or mitigate systemic risk (to the extent possible)—in much more fluid and less institutionally and functionally defined financial systems—what form of institutional or regulatory architecture is best adapted to the effective deployment of these instruments?

We argue for more integration and coordination among institutions charged with systemic risk oversight and regulation, both domestically and internationally, recognizing that the existing set of institutions developed at a time when a more restricted conception of systemic risk prevailed. Specifically, we favour an approach to regulation under which financial markets are regulated according to certain regulatory objectives that are specified in the applicable legislation.[18] Indeed, this approach identifies three basic regulatory objectives that the regulatory architecture must address: macroeconomic stability typically associated with central banks in terms of implementing monetary policy and acting as lender of last resort in maintaining liquidity in the financial system; microprudential regulation which focuses on the financial stability of individual financial institutions; and conduct of business regulation designed to protect consumers of financial services and investors in financial institutions. We argue that this model benefits from coordination and cost advantages, while differentiating among objectives that are widely seen to require distinct regulatory strategies.[19]

Our argument builds on a growing body of literature that probes the concept of systemic risk. Anabtawi and Schwarcz, for example, argue that incentives to discount inter-firm and intra-firm risk-taking generate externalities on other market participants and increase systemic risk.[20] Along similar lines, Hanson, Kashyap, and Stein show how financial institutions respond to market downturns by reducing the size of their asset base; the failure by each affected financial institution to internalize the social costs of their response drives system-wide credit freezes and significant declines in asset prices (ie,

[18] Group of Thirty, 'The Structure of Financial Supervision' (2008) Group of Thirty 24. See also US Department of the Treasury, 'Blueprint for a Modernized Financial Regulatory Structure' (2008) 142. The lines between categories may blur and some commentators use different terminology. For example, Wymeersch terms regulation-by-objective as the functional approach and places the 'twin peaks' model within this category: Eddy Wymeersch, 'The Structure of Financial Supervision in Europe: About Single Financial Supervisors, Twin Peaks and Multiple Financial Supervisors' (2007) 8 The Review of Economic Studies 237, 258.

[19] Eric J Pan, 'Structural Reform of Financial Regulation' (2011) 19 Transnational Law & Contemporary Problems 796, 820.

[20] Iman Anabtawi and Steven L Schwarcz, 'Regulating Systemic Risk: Towards an Analytical Framework' (2011) 86 The Notre Dame Law Review 1349, 1360, and 1382–86.

'credit crunch' and 'fire sales').[21] Gorton and Metrick describe the relationship between the growth of the shadow banking sector (particularly money market mutual funds, securitizations, and repurchase agreements) and systemic risk: sudden uncertainty about the position of financial institutions triggered the belief that these instruments, which are used as collateral in short-term lending arrangements, would be sold to meet various obligations—triggering a fire sale.[22] Judge argues that the complexities stemming from financial innovations in securitization are a source of systemic risk that require a policy response beyond responses taken by the Dodd-Frank Wall Street Reform and Consumer Protection Act and other measures.[23] These scholars are among others who have also noted the importance of systemic risk for prudential regulators in regulating today's financial markets and have proposed some form of regulatory restructuring.[24]

Our chapter differs from this literature, however, in its recognition that the emergence of the NSR requires a serious rethinking of the institutional architecture for regulating systemic risk rather than simply focusing on prudential regulators alone. We do not argue for an overhaul of any one country's institutions but argue for greater emphasis on coordination among domestic financial regulators. Thus, the objectives-based approach, which focuses not on the creation or extinction of institutions themselves but on existing institutions' adherence to certain regulatory objectives, is fundamentally important. At the international level, we propose to address deficiencies in compliance with an increasing use of memoranda of understanding (MOU) among countries to bind them to a system of monitoring, management, and enforcement of regulatory oversight of the NSR.

Our approach is unique in that we recognize a certain level of path dependency in the evolution and persistence of domestic institutions—the bodies tasked with making, administering, and enforcing laws (governmental or non-governmental).[25] Path dependency helps to explain why institutions that govern financial markets are difficult to alter because of set-up or fixed costs in establishing a new institution and switching or transition costs to the new

[21] Samuel G Hanson, Anil K Kashyap, and Jeremy Stein, 'A Macroprudential Approach to Financial Regulation' (2011) 25 Journal of Economic Perspective 3, 6–7.

[22] Gary Gorton and Andrew Metrick, 'Regulating the Shadow Banking System' (2010) Brookings Papers on Economic Activity 261, 269–80.

[23] Judge (n 12) 691–717; Dodd-Frank Wall Street Reform and Consumer Protection Act, Pub L No 111-203, § 971, 124 Stat 1376 (2010) (Dodd-Frank) (codified as amended in scattered sections of 5, 7, 12, 15, 22, 26, 28, 31, and 42 of USC).

[24] See Wymeersch (n 18) 13; Pan, 'Structural Reform of Financial Regulation' (n 19) 14; Scott n (8) 726.

[25] Mariano Prado and Michael J Trebilcock, 'Path Dependence, Development and the Dynamics of Institutional Reform' (2009) 59 University of Toronto Law Journal 342, 346–49.

institution, among other things. We draw upon the argument of Prado and Trebilcock that while path dependency can clarify what has happened in the past, it can also be used to inform the feasibility of institutional reforms.[26] Rather than suggest the amalgamation of institutions, or the creation of new regulators, we focus on the importance of ensuring that managing and monitoring systemic risk as an objective should be integral to a country's regulatory scheme.

As a new and more expansive conception of systemic risk, the NSR implicates more financial entities and financial instruments than traditional notions of systemic risk that focused on the prudential regulation of commercial banks. Hence, it stands to reason that the NSR implicates a broader range of potential regulatory instruments than merely setting prudential standards for commercial banks. We examine some of these tools in Section 2, including mandating disclosure, regulating over-the-counter (OTC) derivatives and overseeing credit rating agencies (CRAs). In Section 3, we explore various institutional models to deploy these policy instruments, focusing on differing institutional arrangements in place in various jurisdictions and their respective strengths and weaknesses. In Section 4, we explore the role of international coordinating institutional mechanisms, including soft law initiatives, for addressing the effects of interjurisdictional systemic risks. Section 5 concludes the chapter and suggests directions for future research.

2. Mitigating Systemic Risk

Most countries have in place a regulator whose legislative purview is to focus on the financial soundness of individual financial institutions, such as banks and insurers. The regulator's typical role is to establish rules relating to risk management and capital adequacy and to intervene in cases of deficiency.[27] Prior to the recent financial crisis, the idea that this regulator would also regulate the stability of the entire financial system—and have carriage over 'systemic risk'—was not a matter of debate, perhaps because financial system stability was understood solely to be 'the sum of the safety and soundness of individual institutions'.[28] Following the crisis, however, it has become

[26] ibid 353.

[27] Nick Le Pan, 'Look Before you Leap: A Skeptical View of Proposals to Meld Macro- and Microprudential Regulation' (2009) 296 CD Howe Institute 1. Le Pan points to Canada's Office of the Superintendent of Financial Institutions (OSFI) as an example.

[28] ibid 1 (citing Claudio Borio, 'Towards a Macro-Prudential Framework for Financial Supervision and Regulation' (2003) Bank for International Settlements Working Paper 23; Bank for International Settlements, '78th Annual Report' (2008)).

clear that financial institutions and the markets in which they function are intricately connected quite apart from whether any individual institution has sound risk management practices in place.

The G20 countries and the International Organization of Securities Commissions (IOSCO) thus have called for additional regulation to address systemic risk, including greater coordination among all financial market regulators in an effort to address concerns of the NSR.[29] A host of policy instruments designed to address the NSR has emerged throughout common and civil law countries. As discussed below, some of these instruments have included increasing disclosure obligations, regulating OTC derivatives, monitoring CRAs, and developing a regulatory approach to shadow banking.

(a) Enhanced Disclosure

It is generally recognized that a shock to the US subprime mortgage market triggered major declines in higher-rated asset-backed securities and other markets as investors lacked sufficient information to evaluate adequately the riskiness of the financial products they held.[30] Comprehensive disclosure may have better enabled investors to ascertain asset quality, thus reducing the impact of panicked investor responses to a failure of financial products on the broader market.[31] As an immediate response to the financial crisis, therefore, scholars, regulators, and international organizations have proposed stronger disclosure requirements for financial products.[32]

Of course, disclosure obligations for public issuers of asset-backed and other securities long predate the financial crisis. Issuers are responsible for

[29] G20 Leaders Statement, 'Declaration of the Summit on Financial Markets and the World Economy' (Washington, 15 November 2008) <https://g20.org/wp-content/uploads/2014/12/Washington_Declaration_0.pdf> accessed 18 June 2015; G20 Leaders Statement, 'The Pittsburgh Summit' (Pittsburgh, 24–25 September 2009) <https://g20.org/wp-content/uploads/2014/12/Pittsburgh_Declaration_0.pdf> accessed 18 June 2015; International Organization of Securities Commissions, 'IOSCO Open Letter to G20 Summit' (Madrid, 12 November 2008) <https://www.iosco.org/library/pubdocs/pdf/IOSCOPD282.pdf> accessed 18 June 2015.

[30] Scott Hendry, Stéphane Lavoie, and Carolyn Wilkins, 'Securitized Products, Disclosure, and the Reduction of Systemic Risk' (December 2010) Bank of Canada Financial System Review 47, 49. See also Gorton and Metrick (n 22) 268.

[31] Hendry, Lavoie, and Wilkins (n 30) 48. But see Robert P Bartlett III, 'Inefficiencies in the Information Thicket: A Case Study of Derivative Disclosures During the Financial Crisis' (2010) 36 The Journal of Corporation Law 1, 57 ('the results of this study indicate that the traditional disclosure model aimed at simply disseminating information to the public domain is unlikely to have significant efficacy when it comes to disclosures pertaining to complex credit derivatives').

[32] Anand, 'Systemic Risk and Securities Regulation' (n 12) 963; Anabtawi and Schwarcz (n 20) 1383–84; Technical Committee of the International Organization of Securities Commissions, 'Mitigating Systemic Risk: A Role for Securities Regulators' (2011) International Organization of Securities Commissions 43.

meeting various prospectus and continuous disclosure requirements, including providing 'full, plain, and true disclosure of all material facts' and reporting material changes.[33] However, securities regulators historically allowed complex securities like short-term asset-backed commercial paper to be issued on the exempt (or private) market—that is, exempt from the disclosure obligations that apply to publicly issued asset-backed securities—provided that they were rated by a CRA.[34] This approach was based on the notion that investors in these financial products were large institutional investors with the capacity and incentives to conduct necessary due diligence.[35] Several authors persuasively argue that the financial crisis and freeze of the $30 billion asset-backed commercial paper market in Canada show that even sophisticated investors lack the incentives or capacity to invest in desirable levels of information.[36]

Regulators have responded by increasing disclosure requirements for asset-backed securities, broadening the definition of securitized products such that more products fall within the scope of regulation, consequently ending many of the exemptions for private issuers. Under the Dodd-Frank Act[37] and accompanying SEC regulations,[38] the US adopted ongoing disclosure requirements for asset-backed securities, standardized disclosure requirements to facilitate comparison of assets of similar classes, and required the release of specific asset-level data, including the degree of risk retention by the sponsor and compensation provided to the broker.[39] These measures were designed to provide necessary information for investors to conduct due diligence and reduce the likelihood of market contagion. Other countries

[33] Ontario Securities Act, RSO 1990 c S5, s 56(1) and National Instrument 52-101 (Canada). See also UK Financial Conduct Authority, 'Disclosure Rules and Transparency Rules' (2014) Financial Conduct Authority Handbook (Release 146) (UK), 2.1.3; Securities Act of 1933, 15 USC §77g and §77j (United States); Australia Corporations Act 2001 (Cth), Div 2 (Australia).

[34] Anand, 'Systemic Risk and Securities Regulation' (n 12) 944; Hendry et al. (n 30) 49.

[35] Hendry et al. (n 30) 49.

[36] John Chant, 'The ABCP Crisis in Canada: The Implications for the Regulation of Financial Markets' (2008) Research Study Prepared for the Expert Panel on Securities Regulation <http://www.expertpanel.ca/documents/research-studies/The%20ABCP%20Crisis%20in%20Canada%20-%20Chant.English.pdf> 22 accessed 20 July 2016. For a discussion and analysis of the commercial paper crisis outside of Canada, see Marcin Kacperczyk and Philipp Schnabl, 'When Safe Proved Risky: Commercial Paper during the Financial Crisis of 2007–2009' (2010) 24 Journal of Economic Perspective 29.

[37] Dodd-Frank Act §§ 942 and 944 (codified at § 15 USC 78o(d) and § 15 USC 77d).

[38] Securities and Exchange Commission, 'Disclosure for Asset-Backed Securities Required by Section 943 of the Dodd-Frank Wall Street Reform and Consumer Protection Act' (28 March 2011) 17 CFR Parts 229, 232, 240 and 249.

[39] See Technical Committee of the International Organization of Securities Commissions, 'Principles for Ongoing Disclosure for Asset-Backed Securities—Consultation Report' (2012) International Organization of Securities Commissions 34–35.

explored similar measures, including the form that disclosure should take in order to be understandable to investors.[40]

Poor disclosure of complex securities was only one aspect of the market failure that warranted additional regulatory intervention. As several commentators explain, the complexity of financial instruments limits the effectiveness of disclosure, as even sophisticated investors may be unable to conduct a proper valuation.[41] At the heart of the crisis were complex derivatives, such as credit default swaps (CDSs), whose distribution was facilitated by market players, including CRAs and dealers. Financial market regulators needed to develop mechanisms to address both complex derivatives and those who facilitated their trading. We turn now to examine these mechanisms.

(b) Clearing Trades: OTC Derivatives

Beginning in the 1980s, the market for OTC derivatives in the US grew rapidly; the gross market value of financial derivatives rose from $3.2 trillion in 2000 to $20 trillion in 2008,[42] in part a result of the effective deregulation of financial derivatives by the US in 2000.[43] Businesses and financial institutions used these securities to manage risk.[44] CDSs, for example, were used as an insurance-like instrument in which one party assumed credit risks associated with a particular debt instrument (eg, mortgage-backed securities) in exchange for payments over the lifecycle of that debt.[45] High leverage, limited collateral, and the interconnectedness of parties meant that if one participant was unable to settle its position with its counterparty, the ability

[40] In Canada, see, for example, (2011) 34 OSCB 3835 (Form 41-103F1—Supplementary Information Required in a Securitized Products Prospectus). Like Canada, the Bank of England and European Central Bank have raised disclosure standards by demanding that asset-backed securities used as collateral include specific data on the underlying asset, meet prospectus requirements, and cash flow projections: IOSCO ABS Consultation Report 2012 (n 39) 33–34.

[41] For a pre-financial crisis view of the limitations of disclosure, see Steven L Schwarcz, 'Rethinking the Disclosure Paradigm in a World of Complexity' (2004) University of Illinois Law Review 1, 11–17; Judge makes a similar point about mortgage-backed securities in the post financial crisis context: Judge (n 12) 713.

[42] Financial Crisis Inquiry Commission, 'Financial Crisis Inquiry Commission Report' (US Government Printing Office 2011) at 29.

[43] ibid 48. See also Lynn A Stout, 'Why re-regulating derivatives can prevent another disaster' (Harvard Law School Forum on Corporate Governance and Financial Regulation, 21 July 2009) <http://corpgov.law.harvard.edu/2009/07/21/how-deregulating-derivatives-led-to-disaster/> accessed 21 October 2013.

[44] Adam R Waldman, 'OTC Derivatives & Systemic Risk: Innovative Finance or Dance into the Abyss?' (1994) 43 American University Law Review 1023, 1038.

[45] Anabtawi and Schwarcz (n 20) 1372 ('Derivatives, most notably credit-default swaps … allow firms to trade credit risks on a variety of exposures.'); Financial Crisis Inquiry Commission (n 42) 50.

of the counterparty to settle other derivative positions was put into question, and so forth.[46]

The G20 responded to systemic risk associated with OTC derivatives through two policy measures. First, the G20 agreed to require participants to report derivatives transactions to trade depositories.[47] This move was part of broader international efforts to close gaps in data necessary to assess and respond to systemic risk, which now includes monitoring of financial linkages between global systemically important financial institutions and the soundness of financial institutions.[48] Ultimately, transparency in transactions helps keep markets fair and efficient and maintains public confidence in markets and products during periods of stress, while helping regulators to assess concentrations of risk and counterparty exposures and protect the market against abusive practices.[49]

Second, the G20 mandated central counterparty (CCP) clearing and settlement of standardized OTC derivatives.[50] Under CCP clearing, the clearinghouse acts as the counterparty to a transaction between financial participants, providing an effective guarantee that transactions will settle.[51] The risk absorbed by the clearinghouse is funded through margin and capital requirements, essentially pooling the risk of derivatives contracts across all transactions.[52] While the shift to CCP clearing raises costs for participants by requiring them to meet margin and collateral requirements, the objective is to reduce counterparty and contagion risk in the event of a default by serving as the buyer to every seller and the seller to every buyer,[53] although not all commentators are persuaded of the efficacy of such measures in reducing systemic risk.[54]

[46] Scott (n 8) 675; Anabtawi and Schwarcz (n 20) 1372.

[47] OTC Derivatives Regulators Group, 'Report on Agreed Understandings to Resolving Cross-Border Conflicts, Inconsistencies, Gaps and Duplicative Requirements' (US Commodity Future Trading Commission 2013) 3.

[48] Staff of the IMF and the FSB Secretariat, 'The Financial Crisis and Information Gaps: Report to the G-20 Finance Ministers and Central Bank Governors' (Financial Stability Board and International Monetary Fund 2009) 5; Staff of the IMF and the FSB Secretariat, 'Fourth Progress Report on the Implementation of the G-20 Data Gaps Initiative' (Financial Stability Board and International Monetary Fund 2013) 7.

[49] E-mail from Department of Finance Canada to author (3 June 2014).

[50] Basel Committee on Banking Supervision and Board of International Organization of Securities Commissions, 'Margin Requirements for Non-centrally Cleared Derivatives' (Bank for International Settlements 2013) 1.

[51] Anabtawi and Schwarcz (n 20) 1394.

[52] Scott (n 8) 688.

[53] ibid 687–88; Bank for International Settlements 2013 (n 50) 3–4.

[54] See generally Craig Pirrong, 'A Bill of Goods: Central Counterparties and Systemic Risk' (2014) 2 Journal of Financial Market Infrastructures 55.

Non-standardized OTC derivatives represent a substantial proportion of the derivatives market.[55] Because they are customized, they are difficult to price and also face liquidity constraints. They are therefore less suited to CCP clearing mechanisms.[56] To help meet the policy objective of central clearing and disincentivize a shift towards non-standardized OTC derivatives, the G20 agreed to substitute CCP clearing requirements with minimum margin and capital requirements for these transactions.[57] The aim was to create a disincentive for participants to migrate away from the CCP clearing system to a less costly model, in addition to lowering individual and systemic risk.[58]

As will be discussed in Section 4, effective implementation of international standards, including G20 recommendations, depends on the individual country and its financial regulators. Unsurprisingly, jurisdictions have adopted differing approaches to implementing these requirements[59] with regulators' roles dramatically shifting from virtually no oversight of derivatives contracts[60] to, in most jurisdictions, managing the registration of dealers, advisers, and participants; acting as a repository for derivatives trades; overseeing CCPs; and, given the international nature of the derivatives market, coordinating the regulation of derivatives with regulators in other jurisdictions.

But these varying approaches do not necessarily facilitate seamless trading and oversight of OTC derivatives using CCPs across borders. In the US, for example, the Dodd-Frank Act and related guidelines require registration and central clearing of most swaps by US persons (broadly defined) and counterparties,[61] and assign regulation of securities-based swaps markets to the SEC and other swaps to the Commodity Futures Trading Commission (CFTC).[62] Canada, on the other hand, authorized federally regulated Canadian

[55] Bank for International Settlements (n 50) 2. [56] Scott (n 8) 688–90.

[57] See Bank for International Settlements (n 50) 25. [58] ibid 3.

[59] There is, however, general uniformity in terms of implementing trade repository requirements. Europe requires that all derivative contracts—OTC and non-standardized—must be reported. See Benoit Coeuré, 'Four Years After Pittsburgh: What has the OTC Derivatives Reform Achieved So Far' (joint Banque de France, Bank of England, and ECB Conference on OTC Derivatives Reform, Paris, 11 September 2013) <https://www.ecb.europa.eu/press/key/date/2013/html/sp130911.en.html> accessed 18 June 2015.

[60] In Canada, for example, many provincial securities regulators did not initially have legislative authority to regulate the OTC derivatives market. See Mary Condon, 'Canada's Role in Expanded IOSCO Principles' (Toronto Securities Leadership Seminar, 9 July 2012) 13.

[61] Dodd-Frank Act §§ 721–74 (codified as amended in scattered sections of 7, 12, and 15 USC); Interpretive Guidance and Policy Statement Regarding Compliance With Certain Swap Regulations, 78 Federal Register 45292 (26 July 2013) 45317 ('the Commission would expect that a non-U.S. person whose swap dealing transactions with U.S. persons exceed the *de minimis* threshold would register as a swap dealer. Likewise, under the Proposed Guidance, the Commission would expect that a non-U.S. person who holds swaps positions where one or more U.S. persons are counterparties above the specified MSP thresholds would register as an MSP.').

[62] Dodd-Frank Act §§ 721 and 761 (codified as amended in scattered sections of 7 and 12 USC).

derivatives market participants to meet regulatory requirements through regulated CCP clearing mechanisms outside of Canada.[63] UK regulators oversee Clearnet—a UK-based clearinghouse that clears most of the interest rate swaps used by Canadian banks.[64]

How to address the regulation of OTC derivatives, including the clearing of trades, has been an issue that has persisted in the years following the crisis. There is little agreement among countries regarding harmonizing the regulation of cross-border OTC derivative transactions: how should countries implement G20 commitments in a manner that is appropriate for their own markets?[65] The need to ensure that information is shared among international regulators as well as cooperation agreements with these regulators, foreign trade repositories, and CCPs remain outstanding issues.[66] In concept, mandating central clearing and establishing trade repositories means little if domestic regulators cannot coordinate the implementation of these requirements.

(c) Rating Complex Securities

One of the reasons that certain tranches of asset-backed securities and collateralized debt obligations (CDOs) were attractive to investors was that they carried Triple-A ratings from what appeared to be reputable credit-rating agencies ('CRAs'). In hindsight, it seems surprising that CRAs historically operated with no regulatory oversight since these were the institutions that rated the complex derivative securities that ultimately triggered the collapse or near collapse of financial institutions including Lehman Brothers and AIG.[67] Canada, US, Australia and the UK have adopted a number of rules designed to mitigate conflicts endemic to CRAs, including mandatory registration and oversight.[68]

[63] Bank of Canada, 'Statement by Canadian authorities on clearing of standardized OTC derivatives contracts' (1 October 2012) Bank of Canada News Release; Nikil Chande et al., 'The Canadian Approach to Central Clearing for Over-the-Counter Derivatives' (2012) Bank of Canada Financial System Review 43, 44.

[64] Chande et al., 'The Canadian Approach to Central Clearing for Over-the-Counter Derivatives' (n 63) 49.

[65] Canadian Securities Administrators Derivatives Committee, 'Consultation Paper 91-401 on Over-the-Counter Derivatives Regulation in Canada' (2 November 2010) 1.

[66] ibid. [67] Anand, 'Systemic Risk and Securities Regulation' (n 12) 973.

[68] NI 25-101 35 OSCB 913 (2012) (Designated Rating Organizations) (Canada); Council Regulation (EC) 1060/2009 of 16 September 2009 on credit rating agencies (16 September 2009) Official Journal of the European Union [2009] OJ L302/1 (Europe); 09-224MR (November 2009) Australian Securities and Investments Commission (Australia); Dodd-Frank Act §§ 931–931H (codified as amended in scattered sections of 15 USC) (United States).

The key issue for each of these countries in regulating CRAs involves conflicts of interest inherent in the rating process. A company will hire a CRA to rate its debt in return for a fee. The CRA provides the rating but perhaps also seeks to maintain a longer-term relationship with the company. CRAs have an incentive to provide a rating with which the issuer is satisfied. This incentive can undermine CRAs' neutrality as arm's length agencies that offer objective assessments of the creditworthiness of the securities. Furthermore, the monetary incentives for providing favourable ratings have grown with the market for structured finance products, because expected revenue from these ratings would also correspondingly increase.

Legislation enacted after the crisis to regulate CRAs required CRAs to register with securities regulators, to manage conflicts of interest and the inappropriate use of information, appoint a compliance officer, and annually file a report relating to these activities. Once designated, rating agencies would become subject to potential enforcement actions and compliance reviews.[69] But legislation throughout common law jurisdictions generally does not address the core conflict of interest—ie, the issuer that pays for the rating is the issuer that also receives the rating. CRAs are required to 'register' with securities regulators, but such registration does not mean that conflicts have been eradicated: if CRAs are unable to eliminate a conflict, they are required only to 'manage and disclose' it.[70]

Conflicts affect ratings, and objective ratings in particular. Further, the new legislation does not speak to the role that CRAs could and should play in alerting investors to potential systemic risk concerns that can arise from a particular instrument that they are rating. It does not oversee the content or methodology of ratings; even with a compliance officer in place and an annual report filed with securities regulators, investors could continue to lack full and accurate information regarding the securities they are purchasing. Finally, across jurisdictions, it is not clear what, if any, sanctions are in place for those who fail to comply with the new rules. While the regulation of CRAs implemented post crisis fills a gap in the securities regulatory framework, securities regulators have an unfinished agenda in this area.[71]

[69] NI 25-101 35 OSCB 913 (2012) (Designated Rating Organizations) (Canada).

[70] Technical Committee of the International Organization of Securities Commissions, 'Code of Conduct Fundamentals for Credit Rating Agencies' (International Organization of Securities Commissions 2008) 7 ('A CRA should adopt written internal procedures and mechanisms to (1) identify, and (2) eliminate, or manage and disclose, as appropriate, any actual or potential conflicts of interest').

[71] See Technical Committee of the International Organization of Securities Commissions, 'Credit Rating Agencies: Internal Controls Designed to Ensure the Integrity of the Credit Rating Process and Procedures to Manage Conflicts of Interest' (International Organization of Securities Commissions 2012).

(d) Shadow Banking

The migration of financial institution activity from the formal regulated banking sector to the shadow banking system—a term that describes non-bank lending such as corporate and private debt—has been extensive.[72] In the US, the ratio of assets held off bank balance sheets rose to 60 per cent in 2007 from nil in 1980.[73] Globally, shadow lending now constitutes at least one-quarter of all financial assets.[74] Shadow banking has grown even more significantly after the financial crisis. Banks have responded to higher capital requirements and regulatory efforts that limit their capacity to engage in off-balance sheet transactions (see below) by reducing lending to individuals and businesses, creating incentives for non-bank intermediaries to assume that role.[75]

Despite its name, shadow banking is not inherently problematic: there are obvious economic benefits in expanded access to credit, especially when such non-bank lending is not implicitly the subject of government guarantees.[76] Further, a wider spectrum of lenders can reduce systemic risk by 'disseminating risks beyond the banks'.[77] However, several aspects of the shadow banking system—many of which involved efforts by banks to migrate away from the formal banking sector—were brought to light in the financial crisis and have since attracted the scrutiny of regulators. Regulators began to be concerned about the liquidity of institutions in the shadow banking sector, particularly money market funds.

Securitizations and subsequent trading in mortgages (and other forms of debt) gave rise to these concerns. Loans were classified by their apparent riskiness ('tranches') and sold to investors; Triple A tranches are particularly suited to international demand for safe assets and yield.[78] In the event of default

[72] Gorton and Metrick define the shadow banking sector as including, for example, money market mutual funds, investment banks, mortgage brokers, and instruments such as securitizations and repurchase agreements: Gorton and Metrick (n 22) 261–62. See also Edward McBride, 'Shadow and Substance' *The Economist* (10 May 2014) 4–6. For other definitions of shadow banking, see: Zoltan Pozsar, Tobias Adrian, Adam Ashcraft, and Hayley Boesky, 'Shadow Banking' (2012) Federal Reserve Bank of New York; Perry Mehrling, Zoltan Pozsar, James Sweeney, and Dan Neilson, 'Bagehot was a Shadow Banker: Shadow Banking, Central Banking, and the Future of Global Finance' (2013) Institute for New Economic Thinking Working Paper <http://papers.ssrn.com/sol3/papers.cfm?abstract_id=2232016> accessed 19 June 2015.

[73] Gorton and Metrick (n 22) 265.

[74] McBride (n 72) 5. See also Financial Stability Board, 'Global Shadow Banking Monitoring Report 2013' (2013) 8.

[75] McBride (n 72) 4–5.

[76] ibid 5.

[77] 'Do it Right' *The Economist* (10 May 2014) 16.

[78] See Douglas W Diamond and Raghuram G Rajan, 'The Credit Crisis: Conjectures about Causes and Remedies' (2009) 99 American Economic Review 606, 606–07.

(or other credit event) among individual loans, investors holding the safest tranche received priority to associated cash flows.[79] The aggregation of securities into Triple A tranches diminished the incentive for market participants to invest in information about the quality of individual assets.[80] More generally, securitization has given rise to perverse incentives among market participants (eg, dealers, brokers, credit rating agencies, sponsors), inadequate risk management practices, and lack of disclosure.[81]

In response, IOSCO has proposed a set of broad principles governing the regulation of securitization practices, including requiring originators of securitizations to retain credit risk in the security, better disclosure (transparency and standardization), and independent evaluation of the performance of the underlying assets.[82] The Dodd-Frank Act requires securitizers (sponsors) to retain a percentage of the credit risk associated with the security,[83] unless the security is a high quality loan, in which case only underwriting standards apply.[84] European regulators have instituted similar credit retention requirements, but without the exempting provisions.[85] Canadian securities regulators have proposed disclosure requirements on securitizations but have not adopted similar provisions on credit risk retention.[86]

These transactions have been a concern for regulators not least because of the fact that the complexity created by securitization is *itself* a new source of the NSR.[87] This complexity arises from the increased chain between the investor and the economic return; the competition between investors arising out of 'waterfall' or distribution provisions; the limited consequences of the failure of the underlying asset for investors with priority claims; and the process of multiple securitizations that further stretches the connection between investor and underlying asset.[88] While international regulators note the benefits of the securitization process in terms of diversifying and apportioning

[79] Financial Crisis Inquiry Commission (n 42) 43.

[80] Hanson, Kashyap, and Stein (n 21) 16.

[81] Technical Committee of the International Organization of Securities Commissions, 'Unregulated Financial Markets and Products' (International Organization of Securities Commissions 2009) 15.

[82] ibid 21.

[83] Dodd-Frank Act § 941 (codified as amended in 15 USC 78a et seq).

[84] 'High quality' includes home, auto, and commercial real estate loans: Board of the International Organization of Securities Commissions, 'Global Developments in Securitization Regulation' (International Organization of Securities Commissions 2012) 12.

[85] Board of the International Organization of Securities Commissions, 'Global Developments in Securitization Regulation' (International Organization of Securities Commissions 2012) 14.

[86] See Canadian Securities Administrators, 'Proposed Securitized Product Rules' (Ontario Securities Commission 2011) <https://www.osc.gov.on.ca/en/SecuritiesLaw_ni_20110401_51-106_req-securitized-products.htm> accessed 19 June 2015.

[87] Judge (n 12) 691–92, 701–02.

[88] ibid 685.

risks,[89] the failure of the mortgage-backed security market during the financial crisis and dramatic consequences in terms of systemic risk have led regulators to reconsider securitization's historically unregulated status.[90]

(e) Summary

The above is not an exhaustive list of policy instruments to address the NSR that have been introduced since the financial crisis. We note first that financial institutions beyond commercial banks may create systemic risk and second, that a greater number of regulatory instruments than those implemented by prudential regulators are engaged. We turn now to examine a third issue: that monitoring and regulating the NSR involves regulatory institutions other than prudential regulators, both domestically and internationally, and these regimes pose novel challenges of regulatory integration/coordination within and across geographical borders.

3. Institutional Design and Coordination

In the previous section, we outlined various substantive areas of financial market activity that have warranted regulation or oversight on the part of financial regulators in order to address the NSR. These areas range from ensuring greater disclosure to maintaining a clearing facility for OTC derivatives to regulating CRAs. In this section, we move to a discussion of institutional design: which approach to regulating financial markets offers the most promise for regulating the NSR?[91] As we see in the analysis of the approaches, much of the potential for regulating systemic risk depends on the coordination

[89] Technical Committee of the International Organization of Securities Commissions, 'Unregulated Financial Markets and Products' (International Organization of Securities Commissions September 2009) 15.

[90] See ibid 13.

[91] The debate surrounding the merits of objectives-based or integrated regulatory structures appears to have emerged in the early 1990s in debates over the future of UK financial regulation. The debate centred around, inter alia, (a) perceived conflicts in the Bank of England's role in managing systemic risk and protecting depositors; and (b) the belief that the institutional approach was inadequate given the rise of major non-bank financial institutions. To address concerns, some had proposed a single agency. Others, such as Michael Taylor, proposed the creation of one commission to monitor prudential regulation (and systemic risk), and a second commission to undertake business conduct regulation. The Bank of England would remain independent and carry out monetary policy: Michael Taylor, 'Twin Peaks: A Regulatory Structure for the New Century' (1995) Centre for the Study of Financial Innovation <http://static1.squarespace.com/static/54d620fce4b049bf-4cd5be9b/t/55241159e4b0c8f3afe1d11e/1428427097907/Twin+Peaks+A+regulatory+structure+for+the+new+century.pdf> accessed 3 August 2016.

capacity of regulators within a country, except where a single entity is charged with the responsibility for regulating all facets of financial markets.

Before we begin, we note the importance of path dependency to our analysis. In the development context, Prado and Trebilcock argue that despite strong empirical evidence showing that institutions are key determinants of economic and social development, and international support for reforms, institutional reform in developing countries has proven extremely difficult.[92] The authors explain these disappointing outcomes in terms of path dependency, a term that 'describes how the reinforcement of a given set of arrangements over time raises the cost of changing them'.[93] Institutions may be self-reinforcing and persist when there are: significant fixed costs associated with change; 'learning effects' which reward knowledge of a particular practice; and finally, expectations or preferences that solidify around the status quo.[94] The self-reinforcing characteristic implies increasing returns to institutional structures, practices, or norms while switching costs associated with institution reform can be expected to rise over time. Pierson explains that increasing returns implies that small events can have significant long-term consequences ('critical junctures');[95] timing and political 'inertia' are central, but change will usually be incremental.[96]

We apply this argument to the issue of financial system design. While the financial crisis (including the collapse of major investment banks) may have indicated that some form of reform is necessary to the complement of regulators governing our financial system, arguments from path dependency suggest that grand transformative changes are unlikely—or at least uncertain—and not necessarily a function of the severity of the crisis or the country at issue. But we can, and should, highlight the possibility of incremental reforms, including the legal objectives which existing regulatory institutions are charged with pursuing.

(a) Integrated Approach

The integrated approach tasks a single entity with the regulation of financial markets, including banking and insurance, microprudential regulation,[97] and

[92] Prado and Trebilcock (n 25) 346–49. [93] ibid 350.

[94] ibid 351. See also Paul Pierson, 'Increasing Returns, Path Dependence, and the Study of Politics' (2000) 94 American Political Science Review 251, 254.

[95] See Prado and Trebilcock (n 25) 357.

[96] Paul Pierson, *Politics in Time* (Princeton University Press 2004) 44, 153.

[97] See Richard J Herring and Jacopo Carmassi, 'The Structure of Cross-Sector Financial Supervision' (2008) 17 Financial Markets, Institutions & Instruments 51, 52–53, 63.

business conduct.[98] In addition to the benefits related to administrative simplicity and cost-minimization, its main strengths rest in eliminating regulatory gaps, ensuring regulatory consistency, and limiting the opportunities for regulatory arbitrage.[99] Integration in theory creates comprehensive financial regulation since one body is charged with administering all of the rules and procedures.

Integration is a regulatory response to financial innovation that blurred the lines between historically divided financial activities.[100] For example, the securitization by banks of home or auto loans and the development of so-called 'bancassurance'—the merger of banking and insurance services—seemed to demand a combined regulatory approach.[101] The appeal was that integration would reduce inter-agency coordination problems by providing the regulator with a broader view of a firm's financial activity from an individual investor, firm-level, and systemic perspective.[102]

Currently only one country in the G20, Ireland, operates under an integrated structure.[103] All aspects of Ireland's financial sector are regulated through the Irish Central Bank. Singapore, a non-G20 common law jurisdiction, has an integrated model and until recently, the UK did so also. Until extensive market reform in 2012, the UK's Financial Services Authority (FSA) supervised financial markets, securities regulation, and the prudential oversight of banks, investment firms, and insurers. The Bank of England carried out market stability functions for those markets not subject to securities laws.

While there are obvious coordination benefits in this model, the model also exhibits weaknesses. Some have argued that integration may send negative signals to the market. For example, regulating financial supervision and deposit guarantees together might signal to market participants that all regulated institutions are government-backed, creating a lower disciplining effect (ie, more moral hazard).[104] Other concerns, more prevalent in large jurisdictions, relate to the possible creation of a megaregulator that is of 'unmanageable' magnitude[105]—a key concern identified in the US context.[106]

[98] Group of Thirty (n 18) 24. See also Wymeersch (n 18) 251–68. Some authors refer to the integrated approach as the 'single (or unified)' approach. See Herring and Carmassi (n 97) 57.

[99] Pan, 'Structural Reform of Financial Regulation' (n 19) 819; Herring and Carmassi (n 97) 65.

[100] Wymeersch (n 18) 278.

[101] Group of Thirty (n 18) 21; Wymeersch (n 18) 263.

[102] Group of Thirty (n 18) 36.

[103] Central Bank Reform Act 2010 (Ireland); Wymeersch (n 13) 295. The Group of Thirty refers to Canada as an integrated model, which may be incorrect given the structure of securities regulation: see Group of Thirty (n 18) 14.

[104] US Department of the Treasury (n 18) 141; Wymeersch (n 18) 278.

[105] Wymeersch (n 18) 268.

[106] US Department of the Treasury (n 18) 141.

But the biggest risk to having an integrated or single regulator is the potential for conflict between and among objectives, all of which may be critical for the functioning of a country's financial system.[107] For example, while securities regulation has investor protection as one of its primary mandates, prudential regulation focuses on the stability of financial institutions; the two objectives may not always lead to consistent policy choices. Indeed, timely disclosure is central to the former, but may compromise the achievement of the latter.

This issue was the main reason that the UK reformed its integrated structure[108] as indicated in comments made by George Osborne, Chancellor of the Exchequer, who stated, 'The Bank of England was mandated to focus on consumer price inflation to the exclusion of other things. The Treasury saw its financial policy division drift into a backwater. The FSA became a narrow regulator, almost entirely focused on rules based regulation.'[109] Thus, criticizing the structure as inadequately regulating the practices that gave rise to bank collapses and severe systemic risk, Parliament enacted the Financial Services Act 2012,[110] which replaced the FSA with a 'twin peaks' regulatory structure, described below.[111]

In short, the objectives of financial regulation can be inconsistent, complex, and numerous and it will be difficult if not impossible for a single regulatory authority to prioritize the objectives even with legislative guidance.[112] Furthermore, in the event that the integrated regulator determines that it does not have a role to play in any given financial market event, or simply overlooks a market event that warrants regulatory attention, there are

[107] Pan, 'Structural Reform of Financial Regulation' (n 19) 819; See also Financial Services Authority, 'The Turner Review: A Regulatory Response to the Global Banking Crisis' (2009) 92 (Turner Review); Taylor (n 91) 81.

[108] See 'Memorandum of Understanding between HM Treasury, the Bank of England and the Financial Services Authority' (Financial Services Authority 22 March 2006) <http://www.bankofengland.co.uk/financialstability/Documents/mou.pdf> accessed 20 June 2015. See also Group of Thirty (n 18) 24, 28.

[109] Rt Hon George Osborne, Chancellor of the Exchequer, 'Speech at Lord Mayor's Dinner for Bankers and Merchants of the City of London' (London, 16 June 2010) <https://www.gov.uk/government/speeches/speech-by-the-chancellor-of-the-exchequer-rt-hon-george-osborne-mp-at-mansion-house> accessed 19 June 2015. See also 'UK Financial Regulation Overhauled', BBC News (1 April 2013), <http://www.bbc.com/news/business-21987829> accessed 20 October 2013; Turner Review (n 107) 87 ('A balance between conduct of business regulation and prudential regulation which, with the benefit of hindsight, now appears biased towards the former.... This failure to spot emerging issues was rooted in the paucity of macro-prudential, systemic- and system-wide analysis.').

[110] Financial Services Act 2012 (UK).

[111] Bank of England, 'Prudential Regulation Authority' <http://www.bankofengland.co.uk/pra/Pages/about/default.aspx> accessed 20 October 2013.

[112] Wymeersch (n 18) 250.

no other regulatory bodies to fill regulatory gaps. In other words, there is a paucity of regulatory checks and balances in a system with only one financial market regulator in place. These factors lend support for alternative regulatory structures with separate institutions charged with differing tasks, all of which are important to the functioning of a financial system and the regulation of the NSR. We turn now to examine such approaches.

(b) Institutional Approach

The institutional approach assigns a firm to a regulator based on the firm's legal status and the regulator's legal authority.[113] A bank falls within the purview of a prudential regulator, for example, while securities dealers fall within the responsibility of securities commissions and/or self-regulatory organizations. The functions of the respective regulator are established by statute, which creates legal divisions among regulators and their regulatory mandates.[114] Many European countries, including France, Italy, Spain, Portugal, and Greece, adopt an institutional approach. There are separate supervisory bodies for banks or credit institutions, investment firms and insurance companies as well as securities trading.

One could argue that the institutional approach applies to a certain extent in Canada. Along with having separate securities regulators at the sub-national level and prudential regulators at the federal and sub-national levels, five provinces (British Columbia, Saskatchewan, Ontario, New Brunswick, and Prince Edward Island) and the federal government are proposing the creation of a Cooperative Capital Markets Regulator (CCMR). Under the framework, participating provinces and territories have agreed to enact uniform provincial and territorial capital markets legislation addressing matters within their jurisdictions. The federal government will enact complementary legislation pertaining to national data collection, systemic risk related to capital markets, and criminal law matters.[115] Drafts of both the uniform

[113] Herring and Carmassi (n 97) 57. [114] Wymeersch (n 18) 265.

[115] Government of Canada, Province of Ontario, and Province of British Columbia, 'Agreement in Principle to Move Towards a Cooperative Capital Markets Regulatory System' (19 September 2013) <www.fin.gc.ca/pub/ccmrs-scrmc/agreement-principle-entente-principe-eng.asp> accessed 18 June 2015; 'Saskatchewan and New Brunswick agree to join the Cooperative Capital Markets Regulatory System' (Department of Finance Canada 9 July 2014) <http://www.fin.gc.ca/n14/14-090-eng.asp> accessed 18 June 2015; 'Prince Edward Island Agrees to Join the Cooperative Capital Markets Regulatory System' (Government of Canada 9 October 2014) <www.fin.gc.ca/n14/14-135-eng.asp> accessed 18 June 2015. 'Amended Agreement in Principle to Move Towards a Cooperative Capital Markets Regulatory System' (Government of Canada 9 July 2009) <http://www.fin.gc.ca/n14/docs/ccmr-rmc-eng.pdf> accessed 18 June 2015.

provincial capital markets legislation and complementary federal legislation have been posted for comment.[116] A single regulator, governed by an expert board of directors, would administer both the federal and provincial legislation. The regulator would be tasked with identifying and managing capital markets-related systemic risk, and would possess delegated authority to enact regulations, make orders, exercise emergency powers, and gather necessary information on systemic risk related to capital markets. A council of ministers from participating jurisdictions would oversee the CCMR and provide accountability to their respective legislatures. The advantage of this regulatory structure is that there is one institution within a country that is charged with managing systemic risk in national capital markets. With such an explicit mandate, there can be no doubt in times of financial crisis which body bears the authority to respond.

However, a 'sector by sector' approach does not readily apply to today's capital markets. Firms regularly operate across formal legal lines and may also be subject to the rules of more than one regulator.[117] For example, banks are often subject to the rules of the prudential regulator while also subject to disclosure rules established and enforced by securities regulators. A further potential problem is that when statutes create multiple regulators to oversee markets, they can give rise to a 'regulatory silo' issue whereby regulators do not communicate on issues of mutual concern to them, including systemic risk issues. This was obviously an issue during the financial crisis when no one regulator believed that it bore responsibility for addressing the massive market failures that occurred.[118]

The persistence of regulatory silos may give rise to failures in institutional coordination. Regulators may develop differing rules that apply to the same activity[119] or they may fail to take into account all relevant issues given that their area of expertise is statutorily limited. These issues in turn may give rise to regulatory arbitrage opportunities whereby firms seek permission from one regulator to complete a transaction if there is a strong likelihood that another regulator would not permit the activity.

[116] 'British Columbia, Ontario, Saskatchewan, New Brunswick and Canada Strengthen their Commitment to the Cooperative Capital Markets Regulatory System' (Department of Finance Canada 8 September 2014) <http://www.fin.gc.ca/n14/14-119-eng.asp> accessed 18 June 2015.

[117] Wymeersch (n 18) 260–61, 265.

[118] See Anita Anand, 'After the Reference: Regulating Systemic Risk in Canadian Financial Markets' in Anita Anand (ed), *What's Next for Canada: Securities Regulation After the Reference* (Irwin Law 2011) 207 (referring to Canada's asset-backed commercial paper crisis).

[119] Group of Thirty (n 18) 34.

(c) Functional Approach

The functional approach focuses not on a regulator's legal authority or a firm's legal status but on the economic activity in which a firm engages.[120] Unlike the institutional approach, the functional approach envisions that regulatory responsibility will be assigned based on the nature of market activity. For example, the US Commodity Futures and Trade Commission regulates futures while the Securities and Exchange Commission regulates securities.[121] Regardless of the nature of the firm, the regulator's jurisdiction is engaged depending on the type of economic activity.

Overlaps can arise between the institutional and functional approaches. The US, for example, combines both functional and institutional approaches, further complicated by overlapping state and federal powers.[122] Four federal agencies oversee deposit-taking institutions.[123] Moreover, state chartered banks fall under the supervision of federal and state regulators.[124] States also separately regulate securities, although federal regulations pre-empt most state regulation.[125] Finally, states oversee insurance activities.[126]

Thus, one of the main difficulties with the functional approach relates to 'line-drawing' between financial activities, particularly given the complexities that arise from financial innovation.[127] Some would argue, for example, that futures as a type of derivatives contract are essentially securities and should be regulated as such.[128] Further, as is the case with the institutional approach, multiple regulators under functional supervision may not have the information, jurisdiction, or coordinative capacity to address the NSR.[129] Both the

[120] ibid 24. The lines between categories may blur and some commentators use different terminology. For example, Wymeersch terms regulation-by-objective as the functional approach and places the 'twin peaks' model within this category. See Wymeersch (n 18) 258. See also Jeroen JM Kremers, Dirk Schoenmaker, and Peter J Wierts, 'Cross-Sector Supervision: Which Model?' (2003) Brookings-Wharton Papers on Financial Services 225, 233.

[121] US Department of the Treasury (n 18) 48.

[122] Group of Thirty (n 18) 32.

[123] These agencies are the Office of the Comptroller of the Currency (OCC), the Federal Reserve (FRB), the Federal Deposit Insurance Corporation (FDIC), and the National Credit Union Administration: US Department of the Treasury (n 18) 32. The Office of Thrift Supervision was disbanded as part of the Dodd-Frank Act reforms; its functions were merged into the OCC, FRB, and FDIC: US Offices of Inspector General, 'Transfer of Office of Thrift Supervision Functions Is Completed' (24 March 2014) OIG-14-030, 2.

[124] Pan, 'Structural Reform of Financial Regulation' (n 19) 866.

[125] US Department of the Treasury (n 18) 55.

[126] ibid 63–64. However, the Dodd-Frank Act established a Federal Insurance Office (within the Department of the Treasury) with the goal of identifying systemic risk arising out of 'issues or gaps in the regulation of insurers': Dodd-Frank Act § 502 (codified as amended in 31 USC § 313).

[127] Group of Thirty (n 18) 35.

[128] See Expert Panel on Securities Regulation, 'Final Report and Recommendations' (Government of Canada 2009) 56.

[129] US Department of the Treasury (n 18) 27; Group of Thirty (n 18) 35.

functional and institutional models likely involve interaction with multiple regulators, raising compliance cost concerns. Absent coordination among regulators, the functional approach may not be effective in addressing concerns that arise from the NSR.

The US sought to address the coordination and information problems evident in the 2008 financial crisis through the creation of the Financial Stability Oversight Council (FSOC), one of the reforms enacted by the Dodd-Frank Act.[130] FSOC is tasked with identifying and responding to systemic risks arising from bank and non-bank financial institutions, as well as promoting market discipline.[131] The chair of FSOC, the heads of each of the eight federal institutions that regulate financial markets—including the Secretary of the Treasury, the Federal Reserve, the SEC, and the CFTC—and an appointee of the President, comprise the voting members of the council.[132] Non-voting members include state banking, securities, and insurance regulators.[133] Statutory duties include the collection and sharing of information between federal and state regulators, monitoring domestic and international regulatory developments and proposing new regulatory measures, and identifying systemically important (non-bank) financial institutions (SIFIs) to come under the authority (and prudential regulation) of the Federal Reserve.[134] The regulatory authority of the Federal Reserve is thus expanded.[135] The FSOC itself does not have regulation-making powers. At this stage, the performance of the relatively new organization is difficult to assess. By late 2013, FSOC designated three SIFIs: Prudential Financial, AIG, and General Electric Capital.[136]

(d) Objectives-based Approach

The objectives-based approach, sometimes known as 'twin peaks' regulation,[137] divides responsibility according to regulatory objective.[138] 'Twin peaks' is

[130] Dodd-Frank Act § 111 (codified as amended in 12 USC § 5321).

[131] 12 USC § 5322. [132] 12 USC § 5321. [133] ibid.

[134] 12 USC § 5322.

[135] Nellie Lang, 'Systemic Risk Monitoring and Financial Stability' (2013) 45 Journal of Money, Credit and Banking 129, 129–30.

[136] US Department of the Treasury, 'Financial Stability Oversight Council' (25 April 2013) <http://www.treasury.gov/initiatives/fsoc/Pages/home.aspx> accessed 14 March 2014. See also Financial Stability Oversight Council, '2013 Annual Report' (2013) 3.

[137] The term 'Twin Peaks', drawn from the television programme, is rooted in the distinction between prudential and conduct of business regulation: Taylor (n 91) 16. Others have proposed objectives-based regulatory models with multiple objectives: See Charles Goodhart, Philipp Hartmann, and David T Llewellyn, *Financial Regulation: Why, How and Where Now?* (Routledge 1998).

[138] Group of Thirty (n 18) 24. See also US Department of the Treasury (n 18) at 142. The lines between categories may blur and some commentators use different terminology. For example,

something of a misnomer, as the model identifies *three* basic regulatory objectives that the regulatory architecture must address: macroeconomic stability of the kind typically associated with central banks in terms of managing the money supply, overseeing payment systems, and acting as lender of last resort in maintaining liquidity in the financial system;[139] microprudential regulation focused on the financial stability of particular financial institutions; and business conduct regulation designed to protect investors and consumers of financial services, as well as arguably precluding or constraining excessively risky financial activities by financial institutions.

This model benefits from many of the coordination and cost advantages of the integrated approach, while differentiating between objectives that are widely seen to require distinct regulatory strategies.[140] Business conduct regulation of market participants can be adversarial, while prudential regulation is often cooperative, solutions-oriented, and based on repeated interactions between regulators and market participants.[141] Unlike the integrated approach, an objectives-based model is likely less prone to one priority giving way to another (eg, consumer protection prioritized over the soundness of financial institutions, or the converse).[142] The US Department of the Treasury has argued that the effect of centralizing prudential regulation would be to strengthen the 'focus on areas and institutions with the greatest potential for market failures in terms of limited market discipline'.[143] However, as several regulators would oversee different aspects of the same financial actor, one regulator's actions could have significant consequences for the regulatory capacity of others—making coordination all the more critical.[144]

Australia's regulatory structure is defined as a 'twin peaks' model: the Australian Prudential Regulatory Authority (APRA) is tasked with prudential regulation, the Australian Securities and Investment Commission (ASIC) with business conduct regulation, and the Reserve Bank of Australia (RBA) provides the macroeconomic stability function.[145] The implementation of

Wymeersch terms regulation-by-objective as the functional approach and places the 'twin peaks' model within this category: Wymeersch (n 18) 258.

[139] Wymeersch (n 18) 243.

[140] Pan, 'Structural Reform of Financial Regulation' (n 19) 820.

[141] ibid 820. A similar relationship is described by Anand and Green regarding prudential regulation of Canada's banking system: Anita Anand and Andrew Green, 'Regulating Financial Institutions: The Value of Opacity' (2011) 7 McGill Law Journal 399, 406 and 424–25.

[142] Group of Thirty (n 18) 38.

[143] US Department of the Treasury (n 18) 142.

[144] Pan, 'Structural Reform of Financial Regulation' (n 18) 821; US Department of the Treasury (n 18) 142.

[145] Australian Prudential Authority and the Reserve Bank of Australia, 'Macroprudential Analysis and Policy in the Australian Financial Stability Framework' (Australian Prudential Authority and the Reserve Bank of Australia 2012) 2. See also Group of Thirty (n 18) 31.

IOSCO principles including reforms of the OTC derivative markets, make the ASIC responsible for addressing certain systemic risks.[146] Coordination is carried out through the Council of Financial Regulators, a non-statutory body comprised of the four bodies (Chaired by the RBA), but has no independent regulatory functions.[147]

(e) Analysis

We note overlap among the four approaches. In Canada, for example, financial supervision has both institutional and objectives-based components: separate agencies regulate banking, insurance, and securities activities, suggesting a functional approach.[148] But *within* banking and insurance activities, a more objectives-based form of regulation is observed. The Office of the Superintendent of Financial Institutions (OSFI) is the prudential regulator of banks (an exclusive federal responsibility) and federally incorporated insurance companies.[149] The Financial Consumer Agency of Canada (FCAC) is responsible for administering the consumer provisions in the federal financial institution statutes.[150] While the FCAC administers some consumer protection measures in respect of federally incorporated insurance companies, the constitutional division of powers has led to the bulk of consumer protection regulation of both provincially and federally incorporated insurers being carried out by individual provincial insurance regulators.[151]

We also note certain difficulties with each model. The integrated approach is impractical for many states given their political structure and risks subordinating important objectives to others that may at any given time be deemed to take precedence. The institutional model has become obsolete, as many financial institutions operate across traditional financial boundaries. While the functional approach may have some advantages over the institutional approach, it entails multiple regulators regulating various classes of activities of given financial institutions, without any holistic or integrated perspective on the financial health of an institution. The objectives-based approach is perhaps the most likely to facilitate coordination across regulatory lines in a way that allows the NSR to be monitored and regulated.

146 Australian Prudential Authority and the Reserve Bank of Australia (n 145) 3.

147 ibid.

148 Pan, 'Structural Reform of Financial Regulation' (n 19) 822.

149 Office of the Superintendent of Financial Institutions Act, RSC 1985 c 18 (3rd Supp), s 4.

150 Financial Consumer Agency of Canada Act, SC 2001 c9, s 3(2); Christopher C Nicholls, *Financial Institutions: The Regulatory Framework* (LexisNexis Canada 2008) 27–28; Pan, 'Structural Reform of Financial Regulation' (n 19) 822–33.

151 Nicholls (n 150) 109.

The objectives-based approach, however, leaves important questions to be resolved, especially in terms of the regulation of the NSR. For example, should the central bank also be the microprudential regulator? If macroeconomic policy formulation and implementation is to be separated from microprudential regulation, how are capital adequacy and liquidity requirements for various kinds of financial institutions to be established, and by whom? Moreover, given that these two functions are very closely related and highly inter-dependent, how should two separate agencies coordinate their activities? That is, it is obviously highly salient for central banks to be aware that a major financial institution is at risk of failing, and may require liquidity support or even a bail-out, which information is likely to be more centrally within the mandate of the microprudential regulator.

This analysis of the four approaches to financial market regulation suggests that while numerous regulators have a role to play in the regulation of the NSR, that role necessarily varies depending on the institutional and legal structure in place in a given country. In our view, the most promising approach is to establish the objectives to be achieved and determine which institutions will be charged with pursuing these objectives, understanding that the three main objectives on which financial systems must focus relate to macroeconomic factors, microprudential policy, and business/market regulation (ie, consumer or investor protection). We argue in favour of coordination and especially information sharing among the domestic regulators charged with administering these objectives. Thus, the regulatory design that a country adopts, and the extent to which the relevant legislation facilitates coordination among all regulators in the system, is crucial.

4. International Mechanisms

As a concept, NSR encompasses more financial institutions than commercial banks and more instruments of intervention than simply prudential requirements. It also recognizes the cross-border contagion effects of domestic actors including banks, investment funds, hedge funds, and public corporations. Though we may easily agree that the concept of systemic risk has evolved and broadened in this way, the challenge of achieving better domestic and international coordination of multiple regulators persists. In this section, we examine international mechanisms of coordination and integration of financial sector regulation, with a view to better regulating the NSR that increasingly spills over national borders as financial institutions become global and financial transactions are often international in scope. We examine the institutional architecture for mitigating NSR, discussing oversight or coordinating mechanisms at the international level. We conclude by arguing that international coordination needs to be improved and propose ways in which this might evolve.

(a) International Institutions

Historically, international institutions tended to follow an institutional segmentation model which included: the Basel Committee on Banking Supervision for commercial banks, an international association of insurance regulators, and IOSCO in the area of securities regulation. International coordination efforts accelerated in response to the financial crisis, which demonstrated that systemic risk in one country, and even in one segment of the market, has potentially devastating international consequences.[152] Coordinated international regulation of NSR is thus of critical importance and even more so in the face of possible regulatory arbitrage among domestic supervisory structures.[153] That is, not only does global interconnectedness mean that a financial crisis has implications for the economies of other countries, a regulatory gap or failure in one jurisdiction can impose negative externalities on other jurisdictions' economies.

During the financial crisis, the G20 assumed a more prominent 'agenda setting' role in international financial regulation.[154] It acts as a political forum for framework agreements on macroeconomic policy (eg, stimulus, deleveraging, exchange rate flexibility),[155] and provides policy direction to the Financial Stability Board (FSB). Established by the G20, the FSB coordinates national financial regulators and international standard-setting bodies,[156] and effectively translates G20 policies into more technical directives to standard-setting bodies (for example, with regards to OTC derivatives[157] and

[152] Robert Lavigne and Surata Sarker, 'The G20 Framework for Strong, Sustainable and Balanced Growth: Macroeconomic Coordination Since the Crisis' (Winter 2012–2013) Bank of Canada Review 2. See also Lorenzo Bini Smaghi, 'What has the Financial Crisis Taught Us? The Global Dimension and International Policy Cooperation' (21st Century Forum, Beijing, 8 September 2010) <https://www.ecb.europa.eu/press/key/date/2010/html/sp100907.en.html> accessed 20 June 2015.

[153] Barry Eichengreen, 'International Financial Regulation After the Crisis' (2010) Daedalus 107, 107–08.

[154] Chris Brummer, *Soft Law and the Global Financial System* (CUP 2012) 68.

[155] Lavigne and Sarker (n 152) 3–4.

[156] Financial Stability Board, 'Charter of the Financial Stability Board' (Financial Stability Board 2012) Art 1 and Art 2.

[157] Financial Stability Board, 'OTC Derivatives Reforms Progress' (Financial Stability Board 2013).

regulation of the shadow banking system[158]). The FSB's state membership is somewhat broader than the G20, and includes international organizations such as the Bank of International Settlements (BIS), the World Bank, and the IMF.[159] International standards for banking, securities, insurance regulation, and payment and clearing arrangements are coordinated through the Basel Committee on Banking Supervision, IOSCO, the International Association of Insurance Supervisors, and the Committee on Payment and Settlement Systems, respectively.[160]

While setting standards is unquestionably important, ensuring compliance with international standards presents further challenges. The World Bank and IMF have been tasked with reporting on domestic compliance with international standards and principles, with individual states playing a role through a peer review process.[161] All monitoring is conducted through the Financial Assessment Sector Assessment Program, a voluntary process for all states.[162] Because of concerns with non-compliance, countries have decided that the twenty-five most systemically critical states undergo a stability assessment every five years.[163] This peer review process is one that we favour, as discussed below.

Quite apart from stability assessments, enforcement has historically been problematic in the international financial arena. The Basel frameworks, for example, have been called a failure for their inability to regulate bank capital and for allowing extreme rates of leverage while ignoring a burgeoning shadow banking system.[164] One European Central Bank member has noted that while finance was global, regulation was based on self-contained national regulation; the lack of common international rules encouraged regulatory arbitrage; and weak risk monitoring was prevalent.[165] But it is difficult to conclude definitively that more effective global coordination would have been effective in mitigating issues that led to the crisis. Citing the original Basel framework,

[158] Financial Stability Board, 'Strengthening Oversight and Regulation of Shadow Banking' (Financial Stability Board 2013).

[159] Financial Stability Board, 'FSB Members' (Financial Stability Board 2015) <http://www.financialstabilityboard.org/about/fsb-members> accessed 20 June 2015. See also Stavros Gadinis, 'The Financial Stability Board: The New Politics of International Financial Regulation' (2013) Texas International Law Journal 157, 158.

[160] Herring and Carmassi (n 97) 71.

[161] Brummer (n 154) 68–69.

[162] International Monetary Fund, 'Financial Sector Assessment Program: Frequently Asked Questions' (International Monetary Fund 2013) <http://www.imf.org/external/np/fsap/faq/#q16> accessed 20 January 2014.

[163] International Monetary Fund, Factsheet: 'The Financial Sector Assessment Program' (International Monetary Fund 2013) <http://www.imf.org/external/np/exr/facts/fsap.htm> accessed 20 January 2014.

[164] Eichengreen, 'International Financial Regulation After the Crisis' (n 153) 107, 111–12.

[165] Smaghi (n 152) 150.

some have expressed concern that these international efforts, which are by necessity driven by consensus, lead to 'lowest common-denominator regulation'.[166] Nevertheless, we believe that reform proposals (domestic and international) surrounding the NSR are unlikely to be effective in the long term without some structure in place for international coordination.

(b) Proposals for International Coordination and Enforcement

Most critics of the existing international framework argue that the bulk of the problems lie in weak prudential supervision, rather than in the organization or effectiveness of standard-setting bodies.[167] But many of the suggestions for an institutional order do not address the fact that a differing conception of systemic risk—what we have termed the 'NSR'—is in play. They thus focus on the reform of financial institution governance alone, rather than the entire financial system under which coordination among separate regulators charged with separate tasks is central (at the very least) for information-sharing purposes. Rolf Weber and others, for example, encourage greater use of 'college of supervisors' to supervise cross-border financial institutions.[168] Supervisory colleges are multilateral working groups comprised of domestic supervisors of international financial institutions, and have become a prominent feature of European financial regulation.[169] Supervisory colleges conduct prudential monitoring of institutions and would be considered an additional layer of governance rather than being in a subordinate or hierarchical relationship to state supervisors. [170] Similarly, Eric Pan proposes the creation of a new international prudential regulator, whose power would be delegated from the collective supervisory authority of national regulators.[171] The new

[166] Eichengreen, 'International Financial Regulation After the Crisis' (n 153) 110.

[167] The literature distinguishes between regulation (standard-setting) and supervision (monitoring and compliance): see Luis Garicano and Rosa M Lastra, 'Towards a New Architecture for Financial Stability: Seven Principles' in Thomas Cottier, John H Jackson, and Rosa M Lastra (eds), *International Law in Financial Regulation and Monetary Affairs* (OUP 2012) 73.

[168] Rolf H Weber, 'Multilayered Governance in International Financial Regulation and Supervision' in Cottier, Jackson, and Lastra (eds) (n 167) 168. See also Basel Committee on Banking Supervision, 'Good Practice Principles on Supervisory Colleges' (Bank for International Settlements 2010) 7.

[169] See European Banking Authority, 'Supervisory Colleges' (European Banking Authority 2014) <www.eba.europa.eu/supervisory-convergence/supervisory-colleges> accessed 20 January 2014.

[170] Weber (n 168) 169.

[171] Eric J Pan, 'Challenge of International Cooperation and Institutional Design in Financial Supervision: Beyond Transgovernmental Networks' (2011) 11 Chicago Journal of International Law 243, 273.

regulator would focus only on cross-border financial institutions, and would be operationally independent from states, comprised as an expert body with enforcement powers.[172] One such example is the agreement by EU states on the European Banking Union and Single Supervisory Mechanism, which has tasked the European Central Bank with supervising all banks in the euro area.[173]

Our analysis of the NSR suggests that prudential regulation alone, whether administered on a national or international basis, will be insufficient to monitor and regulate such risk; systemic risk is no longer an issue of prudential regulation alone. Rather, a regulatory approach that attempts to coordinate multiple domestic regulators across multiple countries is likely required. We favour using MOUs to regulate the NSR. A loose network of international institutions is responsible for various aspects of financial oversight. The G20 and Financial Stability Board determine policy direction, for example, but neither can coordinate the implementation of these standards across countries. We argue that countries should voluntarily enter into MOUs with each other to bind themselves to both monitoring and coordinating on systemic risk issues. Regarding OTC derivatives, for example, countries would seek a commitment at the national level from each member country to reach agreement about trade repositories and/or central counterparty clearing (with assistance no doubt from domestic regulators where needed). At present, countries are pursuing individual initiatives in this area that are not necessarily harmonized with each other.

The question that would then arise is which body, if any, would play an enforcement role if countries violate their obligations under an MOU? Three options present themselves. The first alternative is for individual countries to decide whether there will be domestic enforcement in case of violations of global standards. This option is a 'path of least resistance' of sorts and would not likely result in effective coordination among countries in the long term, given countries' willingness to defect in cases where it is in their own self-interest to do so. Countries may walk a grey line by choosing to 'cherry pick' from the international rules or under-enforce them.[174]

[172] ibid.

[173] European Commission, 'Banking union: restoring financial stability in the Eurozone' (Memo, Brussels, 15 April 2014) <http://europa.eu/rapid/press-release_MEMO-14-294_en.htm> accessed 20 June 2015.

[174] Brummer (n 154) 135–36 (referring to the ways in which states may defect from enforcing international standards domestically, including 'cherry picking' or under-enforcing standards); Joel P Trachtman, 'The International Law of Financial Crisis: Spillovers, Subsidiarity, Fragmentation and Cooperation' in Cottier, Jackson, and Lastra (eds) (n 167) 201 (on weighing the incentives to defect from enforcing international standards).

A second alternative would be to create a new governing body to play a coordinating and enforcement role not simply in the area of prudential supervision and enforcement but in all areas of financial regulation as specified in the MOU or treaty. Along these lines, Eisengreen calls for the creation of an international financial regulator—structured in the same general manner as the World Trade Organization—to establish and enforce principles upon member states.[175] Kern and Dhumale propose a global financial governance council to be established under a multinational treaty.[176] Treaty signatories would agree to meet standards developed by delegated standard-setting institutions such as Basel, IOSCO, etc.—which would largely be left unchanged.[177] The signatories could opt out of standards in certain cases, such as when they would undermine domestic financial stability. [178] The council would be comprised of any willing state, thus moving out of the G20 'agenda setting' model. Supervision (ie, monitoring and compliance) would remain with domestic authorities.[179] This proposal does not include enforcement as one of the roles of the international body. But we believe that some type of enforcement, including mandatory peer reviews that compel or incentivize countries and their financial institutions to follow international standards, is necessary in the international arena.

Whether or not it is charged with enforcement powers, the creation of a new international body would entail significant costs that may not be outweighed by the benefits of the new organization. While countries gain some status in taking membership in such organizations, they are likely to be reticent in implementing the policy recommendations of these organizations holus-bolus. They may not, therefore, yield to attempts by the organization to enforce its rules and standards by applying sanctions and settling disputes through adjudication. IOSCO is a clear example of an international organization that has numerous members and sets standards that members aim to follow.[180] Yet IOSCO has no remit to undertake enforcement actions against its members for failing to implement its recommendations. Its membership may decline if it attempted to do so.

A final alternative is to utilize existing international organizations, such as the IMF, the FSB, or IOSCO, to manage NSR. Under this alternative, countries would comply with obligations under an MOU or treaty into which they enter voluntarily. The costs of setting up an oversight programme would

[175] Eichengreen, 'International Financial Regulation After the Crisis' (n 153) 113–14.

[176] Alexander Kern and Rahul Dhumale, *Global Governance of Financial Systems* (OUP 2006) 172.

[177] ibid 164. [178] ibid 162. [179] ibid 169–70.

[180] IOSCO has members from over 100 different countries. These members regulate more than 90 per cent of the world's securities markets.

be less than under the second alternative because countries would be using a current organization in which they are members, including its infrastructure and bureaucracy. Countries would agree to coordinate their oversight efforts and share information regarding relevant NSR issues that come to their respective attention. Essentially, they would agree to alter the mandate of the existing organization and to abide by its standards and *ex post* reviews, including peer review assessments by other countries.

Along these lines, Garciano and Lastra seek to make the IMF a global sheriff.[181] They argue for a shift towards a hierarchical structure modelled after the WTO, with similar dispute settlement and enforcement powers. This proposal is potentially effective as it builds on the backbone of a relatively successful global organization that provides a framework for countries' conduct in negotiating and formalizing trade agreements as well as a formal dispute resolution process. Indeed, the WTO Financial Services Agreement may be appealing as a model to follow in the international realm of financial institution regulation. The main difficulty with this model, however, is that the dispute resolution process can take years to complete and may be impractical in financial markets that can move significantly and quickly on the basis of just one piece of information. It is impractical to expect that a WTO-type process can be transplanted to regulating systemic risk in the financial services sector.

We note that the objectives-based approach favoured above is agnostic on increased enforcement of NSR in the international sphere. Even with institutions charged with pursuing specific objectives in place on a national level, a global enforcement regime for NSR remains a missing piece of the puzzle and may raise legitimate concerns. Some states, for example, may not wish to cede control for financial supervision on sovereignty grounds, engaging similar debates as free trade and WTO reforms. They may also be critical of the regulatory convergence sought in enforcement mechanisms. They may, for example, see financial stability goals and a new form of global regulation as inconsistent with their own priorities, domestic or international.[182] Yet, there is a middle ground between hard sanctions at the international level and no enforcement at all.

Occupying this middle ground is 'soft law', a legitimate basis for institutional reform in the international sphere. 'Soft law' refers to the plethora of non-binding international agreements, guiding principles, and best practices that seek to strengthen oversight and regulatory coordination of financial

[181] Garicano and Lastra (n 167) 92.

[182] See generally Dani Rodrik, *The Globalization Paradox: Why Global Markets, States, and Democracy Can't Coexist* (OUP 2012).

markets.[183] Soft law is proving to be modestly effective in achieving harmonization in countries' financial market regulation. For example, the FSB's peer review process, wherein a team of experts reviews and reports on a state's compliance with international guidelines, has been successful in seeking to promote consistent implementation of post-crisis G20/FSB financial reforms.[184] Another example is IOSCO's Multilateral Memorandum of Understanding (MMOU), which requires signatories to share information with other securities regulators necessary in facilitating the investigation or prosecution of securities infractions. With some success, IOSCO has used various tactics to implement the MMOU, including offering technical assistance and 'naming and shaming' non-compliant jurisdictions.[185] Further, as Reinhart and Rogoff suggest, international coordination agreements on the standardization, collection, transparency, and sharing of financial indicator data would be significant in enabling regulators to assess, warn, and respond to global systemic risk.[186] In short, because soft law responds to countries' incentives to remain compliant with international standards relating to financial market regulation, it can be effective. The incentive is powerful because countries and their institutions do not wish to experience the flight of capital and credit or increased cost of capital that may persist if investors and depositors lose faith in financial markets.

Ferran and Alexander highlight the benefits of soft law, which include lower financing costs for a country's sovereign debt as well as more favourable financing terms for its financial institutions. By conforming to soft law such as FSB principles or Basel criteria, financial institutions signal their financial stability to global markets.[187] Soft law also allows for flexibility in implementation; unlike hard law, it is not 'directly enforceable [and] can be more open-textured'.[188] While soft law has its drawbacks, including an inability to constrain those countries and financial institutions that violate international

[183] See generally Eilis Ferran and Kern Alexander, 'Can Soft Law Bodies be Effective? Soft Systemic Risk Oversight Bodies and the Special Case of the European Systemic Risk Board' (2011) University of Cambridge Faculty of Law Working Paper 36; Brummer (n 154) 152.

[184] Financial Stability Board, 'Peer Review of the United Kingdom' (Financial Stability Board 2013).

[185] International Organization of Securities Commissions, 'Multilateral Memorandum of Understanding Concerning Consultation, Cooperation and the Exchange of Information' (International Organization of Securities Commissions 2012) <http://www.iosco.org/library/pubdocs/pdf/IOSCOPD386.pdf> accessed 20 June 2015; Janet Austin, 'IOSCO's Multilateral Memorandum of Understanding Concerning Consultation, Cooperation and the Exchange of Information' (2012) 23 Criminal Law Forum 393, 405; International Organization of Securities Commissions, 'Annual Report' (2012) 29.

[186] Reinhart and Rogoff (n 1) 279–81.

[187] Ferran and Alexander (n 183) 6.

[188] ibid.

standards, it also has benefits. It can lead to significant policy changes in the short term while countries may take years to agree to implement a hard-law-based regime, let alone the substantive components of that regime.[189]

We agree that global financial reform is extraordinarily difficult to effect for various political, legal, and economic reasons. That is, there is a certain path dependence that restricts major shifts in the institutional landscape from both a standard-setting and an enforcement perspective. As noted above, path dependence is driven by a series of self-reinforcing mechanisms that inhibit the adoption of different institutional arrangements. As an example, setting the constitutional debate aside, the persistence of a decentralized regime of Canadian securities regulation (ie, ten separate provincial securities regulators) could be seen in many respects as a product of switching costs. Several provincial governments (including Quebec and Alberta), with the support of their business sectors, opposed changes on the grounds that it would hinder local economic development and employment, and limit the growth of local firms in the legal, accounting, and banking sectors.[190] Thus, switching costs could be rooted in a combination of political economy considerations, learning costs (knowledge that has been built up in local securities commission), and network effects (impact on groups that rely upon a local commission).[191]

But major economic shocks may provide a window for such overhauls. The 2008 financial crisis, for example, led the UK government to shift from an integrated structure to an objectives-based form of regulation. The US eliminated a federal agency (the Office of Thrift Supervision) and established the Financial Stability Oversight Council and the Consumer Financial Protection Bureau as part of their Dodd-Frank Act reforms. Canada and participating provinces are in the midst of establishing a regulator with authority for managing systemic risk in national capital markets. At the international level, facing an international economic downturn, the G20 repositioned the FSB and accelerated policy reforms, effectively directing changes to regulatory standards through organizations such as Basel Committee on Banking Supervision and IOSCO.[192] Thus, the 2008 financial crisis could be seen as a

[189] See also Kenneth W Abbott and Duncan Snidal, 'Hard and Soft Law in International Governance' (2000) 54 International Organization 421, 444–46.

[190] Nicolas Van Praet, 'Quebec Business Community Ramps Up Calls to Cancel National Securities Regulator Plans' *Financial Post* (Toronto, 21 November 2013) <http://business.financialpost.com/news/fp-street/quebec-business-community-ramps-up-calls-to-plans-for-cancel-national-securities-regulator> accessed 20 June 2015; Karen Howlett and Janet McFarland, 'Fight Brewing Over Securities Watchdog Plan' *Globe and Mail* (Toronto, 15 June 2010) B4.

[191] Prado and Trebilcock (n 25) 370.

[192] Sungjoon Cho and Claire R Kelly, 'Promises and Perils of New Global Governance' (2012) 12 Chicago Journal of International Law 491, 552.

critical juncture, the 'brief moment' that can alter the course of institutional development.[193] Of course, the changes adopted during such a moment, as Prado and Trebilcock note, '[are] not a guarantee that *good* ideas will be adopted'.[194] The reforms in the US, for example, fall significantly short of earlier US Department of Treasury recommendations to adopt an objectives-based structure of financial supervision, and it is not clear whether reforms are capable of preventing future systemic shocks. International regulatory efforts remain constrained by non-compliance. Nevertheless, these examples of institutional restructuring imply that scholars and regulators should not discount reform simply because of institutional 'stickiness'.

5. Conclusion

The 2008 financial crisis sparked a series of policy responses by financial regulators aimed at, inter alia, increasing disclosure, reducing the adverse incentives of credit rating agencies, ensuring a clearing facility for the OTC derivatives market, and making securitizations more transparent. But beyond triggering policy efforts, the crisis further exposed the extent to which financial institutions are interconnected, cross formerly strict business lines, and are increasingly international in the scope of their activities and impacts. Rather than focusing simply on the relative financial positions of individual financial institutions (classically banks), financial regulators must address NSR—macroprudential risks resulting from financial contagion emanating from a triggering event or exogenous shock.

Containing and managing this new form of systemic risk presents coordination challenges both domestically and internationally. In many states, NSR implicates multiple domestic regulators. In Canada, for example, addressing systemic risk requires coordination between the federal prudential regulator (OSFI), ten provincial securities regulators, and the Bank of Canada. The US has an even more complicated regulatory structure. Similarly, at the international level, cross-border contagion requires a coordinated response among international standard-setters. The voluntary and informal nature of these international arrangements presents an additional problem in monitoring and enforcement of these standards.

These regulatory challenges are further compounded by the fact that as we noted in the introduction, financial crises that begin as one category of crisis can quickly translate into other classes of crises both within countries and

[193] Prado and Trebilcock (n 25) 358. [194] ibid 369 (emphasis in original).

across countries. For example, a financial crisis that begins in one country's banking sector but triggers a sovereign debt crisis domestically or internationally (through financial linkages or common shocks) would test multiple regulators across jurisdictions and further complicate coordination efforts.

Ultimately, we argue that the coordination challenges presented by NSR suggest a need for institutional reform in the structure of financial supervision but that any reform is likely to be incremental. At the domestic level, we argue that the objectives-based approach is the most likely to facilitate the coordination necessary to mitigate NSR while allowing uncompromised prudential and business conduct regulation. This approach has been adopted in Australia and more recently the UK. We also argue for greater emphasis on coordination among domestic financial regulators, rather than simply focusing on prudential regulators alone and expecting these regulators to be solely responsible for the NSR. At the international level, we propose an expanded use of soft law including MOUs among countries to bind them to a system of monitoring and managing the NSR.

Much of this chapter has focused on the experience in developed countries. Section 3 in particular examines, contrasts, and comments on the structure of financial regulation in Canada, the US, the UK, and Australia. Similar questions regarding institutional design and systemic risk ought to be asked about developing countries, especially the larger developing countries such as Brazil, Russia, India, and China (the BRIC economies). However, such an analysis must account for differences in the structure of the financial sector, which in many developing countries are characterized by significant involvement of state-owned financial institutions; the limited independence of financial institutions and regulators from the political branch of government; the limited institutional capacity of financial regulators to become sources of technical expertise; and major differences in political and legal arrangements. These differences may compound the difficulties around global coordination of policies to mitigate systemic risk. Such questions are beyond the scope of this chapter but define a path for future research. Given rapid expansions in the financial market activity in countries such as China and India—raising growing concerns about systemic risk[195]—we believe that questions revolving around institutional design and systemic risk in developing economies will represent a key issue for future scholarship.

[195] Wayne Arnold, 'China's Banks Pose World's Largest Systemic Risk' *Wall Street Journal* (29 July 2014) <http://blogs.wsj.com/economics/2014/07/29/chinas-banks-pose-worlds-largest-systemic-risk> accessed 20 June 2015.

2

Perspectives on Regulating Systemic Risk

Steven L Schwarcz[*]

1. Introduction

This chapter attempts to provide useful perspectives on regulating systemic risk. First, it argues that systemic shocks are inevitable. Accordingly, regulation should be designed not only to try to reduce those shocks but also to protect the financial system against their unavoidable impact. This could be done, the chapter explains, by applying chaos theory to help stabilize the financial system.

The chapter then focuses on trying to prevent excessive corporate risk-taking, which is one of the leading triggers of systemic shocks and widely regarded to have been a principal cause of the financial crisis.[1] It begins by inquiring why so few managers have been prosecuted for the excessive corporate risk-taking that led to the financial crisis.[2] Targeting managers in their personal capacity would be a greater deterrent to excessive risk-taking than

[*] I thank Theodore D Edwards and Tashi Sun for valuable research assistance. Support is provided in part by a Fuller-Purdue grant. Portions of this chapter are based on Professor Schwarcz's articles, including 'Regulating Financial Change: A Functional Approach' (2016) 100 Minnesota Law Review <http://ssrn.com/abstract=2469467> (forthcoming) accessed 24 September 2015; Steven L Schwarcz, 'Excessive Corporate Risk-Taking and the Decline of Personal Blame' (2015) 65 Emory Law Journal <http://ssrn.com/abstract=2553511> (forthcoming) accessed 24 September 2015.

[1] See, eg, Financial Crisis Inquiry Commission, 'The Financial Crisis Inquiry Report: Final Report of the National Commission on the Causes of the Financial and Economic Crisis in the United States' (2011) <http://fcic-static.law.stanford.edu/cdn_media/fcic-reports/fcic_final_report_full.pdf> accessed 24 September 2015 (identifying excessive risk-taking as a primary cause of the financial crisis); 'The Origins of the Financial Crisis: Crash Course' *The Economist* (7 September 2013) <http://www.economist.com/news/schoolsbrief/21584534-effects-financial-crisis-are-still-being-felt-five-years-article> accessed 24 September 2015 (identifying excessive risk-taking as one of three causes of the financial crisis, the other causes being irresponsible lending and regulators being asleep at the wheel); Jacob Lew, 'Let's Leave Wall Street's Risky Practices in the Past' *Washington Post* (9 January 2015) (in which US Treasury Secretary Lew repeatedly attributes the financial crisis to 'excessive risks taken by financial' firms).

[2] See Section 3(a).

fallbacks such as imposing firm-level liability.[3] The chapter finds, however, a host of reasons why managerial prosecution is not—and is unlikely to become—a credible deterrent. Finally, the chapter examines how else excessive risk-taking could, and should, be regulated.[4]

2. General Perspectives on Regulating Systemic Risk

Perfect markets would never, in theory, need external regulation. But markets, including financial markets, are imperfect, so government intervention is sometimes necessary. Traditional financial regulation focuses on maximizing economic efficiency within the financial system of the system's underlying economic functions—the provision, allocation, and deployment of capital. However, these functions can be carried out efficiently only when the financial system itself operates efficiently as a network. Systemic risk regulation (sometimes called macroprudential regulation) serves to protect the financial system's ability to so operate.[5]

As explained below, any regulatory framework for achieving that objective will be imperfect and have tradeoffs. That is because systemic shocks are inevitable and we do not yet know enough about how such shocks spread to prevent their transmission. Systemic risk regulation therefore should include a focus on stabilizing parts of the financial system afflicted by those shocks.

(a) Systemic Shocks are Inevitable

For at least three reasons, systemic shocks are inevitable. First, some of the inevitable market failures that impair efficiency can also increase systemic risk. Second, the financial system is constantly changing, and therefore regulation will

[3] See, eg, Mary Jo White, US SEC Chair, 'Deploying the Full Enforcement Arsenal' (Council of Institutional Investors Fall Conference, Chicago, 2013) <http://www.sec.gov/News/Speech/Detail/Speech/1370539841202#.VE7m_iJ4pK4> accessed 24 September 2015; Claire A Hill and Richard W Painter, 'Why SEC Settlements Should Hold Senior Executives Liable' *New York Times* (29 May 2012) <http://dealbook.nytimes.com/2012/05/29/why-s-e-c-settlements-should-hold-senior-executives-liable/> accessed 24 September 2015 (observing two reasons for this greater deterrence: that economic actions taken against individuals not only require them to pay out of their own pockets but also impose reputational costs—a form of shaming—causing the individuals to lose social standing and jeopardizing their ability to continue working in the financial sector).

[4] See Section 3(b).

[5] This discussion is based on Steven L Schwarcz and Iman Anabtawi, 'Regulating Systemic Risk: Towards an Analytical Framework' (2011) 86 Notre Dame Law Review 1349; Steven L Schwarcz, 'Regulating Complexity in Financial Markets' (2009) 87 Washington University Law Review 211; and Steven L Schwarcz, 'Systemic Risk' (2008) 97 Georgetown Law Journal 193.

occasionally lag financial reality. Finally, as examined in detail in Section 2 of this chapter, regulation does not adequately limit the incentives of corporate managers to engage their firms in risk-taking that could have systemic consequences.

(i) Certain Inevitable Market Failures Can Increase Systemic Risk

Some of the inevitable market failures that impair efficiency can also increase systemic risk. For example, increasing financial complexity has created information failures that even disclosure cannot remedy.[6] The task of deciphering a prospectus, hundreds of pages long and full of detailed technical and legal phraseology, is usually burdensome even for the most sophisticated institutional managers—so they often over-rely on credit ratings, especially if other financial institutions are investing in the same types of securities. Bounded human rationality, including cognitive limitations and time horizons for decision-making, also limits the effectiveness of even otherwise ideal laws.[7] And the increasing dispersion of financial risk is undermining monitoring incentives.[8]

In combination, these information failures can increase systemic risk in several ways. Inadequate transparency and inadequate monitoring can cause firms to overinvest, leading to systemic shocks such as price bubbles and bankruptcies. Inadequate transparency (as we saw with some of the more complex asset-backed securities), especially when coupled with bounded rationality, can lead to panics, causing financial market prices to collapse.

Another type of market failure—principal–agent failure—can also increase systemic risk. This failure is typified by a manager—and increasingly with financial complexity, including a middle manager such as an analyst—sacrificing a firm's long-term interests to make short-term personal gains. For example, senior analysts may recommend that their firms invest in highly leveraged (and thus risky) securities, such as ABS collateralized debt obligations (CDOs), in order to make personal bonuses. They 'earn' the bonuses because these are high-yield securities with ostensibly minimal risk, as evidenced by heuristic[9] models such as VaR[10] and rating-agency ratings. The models can

[6] See Steven L Schwarcz, 'Disclosure's Failure in the Subprime Mortgage Crisis' (2008) Utah Law Review 1109 (observing that investors did not fully understand certain complex asset-backed securities notwithstanding securities-law compliant disclosure; and arguing that disclosure alone is inadequate to remedy asymmetric information and other information failures); Steven L Schwarcz, 'Rethinking the Disclosure Paradigm in a World of Complexity' (2004) University of Illinois Law Review 1.

[7] See, eg, Anabtawi and Schwarcz, 'Regulating Systemic Risk: Towards an Analytical Framework' (n 5).

[8] Steven L Schwarcz, 'Marginalizing Risk' (2012) 89 Washington University Law Review 487.

[9] I use this term in its broad sense, to refer to simplifications of reality that allow us to make decisions in spite of our limited ability to process information.

[10] VaR, or Value at Risk, is a measure of the probable loss in an investment portfolio given certain parameters such as time and probability of loss.

obscure the reality that the risk may be relatively low but, if it occurs, the consequences are very high—a so-called 'black swan' event. Senior executives often lack the technical background, and the time, to second-guess the models.

Principal–agent failure is theoretically, although less pragmatically, susceptible to legal solutions. The obvious solution is to require systemically important firms to pay their managers under longer-term compensation arrangements, possibly including clawbacks. To some extent, this is now beginning to be done in the US. But it still has several flaws. One is that existing regulation focuses on senior executive compensation, whereas the greater problem may lie with middle manager compensation. Middle managers are almost always paid under short-term compensation schemes, misaligning their interests with the long-term interests of the firm.[11] Complexity exacerbates this problem by increasing information asymmetry between technically sophisticated middle managers and the senior managers to whom they report.[12] Another flaw is that financial managers can work in money centres worldwide, so effective regulation would need to be global.

Market realities can also increase the magnitude of these systemic shocks. For example, credit markets often provide short-term funding of long-term capital needs (which economists sometimes refer to as 'maturity transformation') because the interest rate on short-term debt is usually lower than that on long-term debt. This sacrifice of stability for lower cost can create the financial market equivalent of a bank run if, due to investor anxiety, a firm is unable to roll over, or refinance, its short-term debt. I later observe that shadow banking in particular disproportionately relies on maturity transformation.

(ii) In a Changing Financial System, Regulation Can Lag Reality

Another reason why systemic shocks are inevitable is that the financial system is constantly changing. As a result, systemic risk regulation will often lag financial reality.[13]

[11] See Steven L Schwarcz, 'Conflicts and Financial Collapse: The Problem of Secondary-Management Agency Costs' (2009) 26 Yale Journal on Regulation 457.

[12] For example, as the VaR model for measuring investment portfolio risk became more accepted, financial firms began compensating secondary managers not only for generating profits but also for generating profits with low risks, as measured by VaR. See, eg, Philippe Jorion, *Value at Risk: The New Benchmark for Managing Financial Risk* (3rd edn, McGraw-Hill Education 2009) 568. Secondary managers turned to investment products with low VaR risk profile, like credit-defaults swaps that generate small gains but only rarely have losses. They knew, but did not always explain to their superiors, that any losses that might eventually occur would be huge. See Schwarcz, 'Conflicts and Financial Collapse' (n 11).

[13] This time lag may be exacerbated by the increasing complexity of the financial industry and financial products. See n 39 and accompanying text.

Most are aware by now that future financial crises are unlikely to resemble, and may have very different causes than, past crises; thus regulatory reform can be misguided if it represents politically motivated reactions to a past crisis. That awareness, unfortunately, does not always prevent politically motivated regulation. For example, the Dodd-Frank Act focuses heavily on preventing future mortgage-lending problems because mortgage lending was at the heart of the financial crisis. Professor Anabtawi and I have observed, however, that the mortgage-lending problem itself was not special; rather, it followed a broader generic pattern that closely parallels the margin lending that was at the heart of the Great Depression.[14]

There is, however, a more subtle problem. Even otherwise salutary financial regulation is often tethered to the financial architecture—the particular design and structure of financial firms, markets, and other related institutions—existing at the time the regulation is promulgated.[15] This type of grounded regulation has value as long as it is updated as needed to adapt to changes in the financial architecture. This helps to explain the success of the Uniform Commercial Code (UCC), a uniform state-law statute that benefits from ongoing monitoring and updating by the non-partisan American Law Institute and the Uniform Law Commission.

But ongoing monitoring and updating can be costly and is subject to political interference at each updating stage. Without ongoing monitoring and updating, financial regulation tethered to today's financial architecture will quickly become outmoded, causing unanticipated consequences and allowing innovations to escape regulatory scrutiny. This occurred in 2008, for example, when the pre-crisis financial regulatory framework, which assumed the dominance of bank-intermediated funding, failed to adequately address a collapsing financial system in which the majority of funding had become non-bank intermediated.[16]

[14] See Schwarcz and Anabtawi, 'Regulating Systemic Risk'(n 6) 1356–57, 1406–07.

[15] See eg, Anita Anand, Michael Trebilcock, and Michael Rosenstock, 'Institutional Design and the New Systemic Risk in Banking Crises' in Anita Anand (ed), *Systemic Risk, Institutional Design and the Regulation of Financial Markets* (OUP 2016) (describing how short-term asset-backed commercial paper was typically exempt from disclosure requirements because the purchasers were predominantly large institutional investors whose sophistication was thought to obviate the need for extensive disclosure).

[16] As a supplementary approach to regulating a dynamically changing financial system, I have advocated regulation that focuses also on the system's underlying, and thus less time-dependent, economic functions—the provision, allocation, and deployment of capital. See Steven L Schwarcz, 'Regulating Financial Change: A Functional Approach' (2016) 100 Minnesota Law Review <http://ssrn.com/abstract=2469467> (forthcoming) accessed 24 September 2015. Compare with Robert C Merton and Zvi Bodie, 'A Conceptual Framework for Analyzing the Financial Environment' in Dwight B Crane, KA Froot, Scott P Mason, André Perold, RC Merton, Z Bodie, ER Sirri, and P Tufano (eds), *The Global Financial System: A Functional Perspective* (Harvard Business School Press

(iii) Excessive Corporate Risk-taking Can Trigger Systemic Shocks

Yet another reason why systemic shocks are inevitable is that regulation does not currently—and is unlikely to, at least in the near future—adequately limit the incentives of corporate managers to engage their firms in risk-taking that could trigger systemic shocks. As mentioned, excessive corporate risk-taking is widely regarded to have been a principal cause of the financial crisis.[17]

Regulators and policy-makers have not yet systematically examined how to control excessive corporate risk-taking to limit its potential systemic consequences. Section 2 of this chapter addresses this issue in detail, first inquiring into the failure to prosecute managers for risk-taking that led to the financial crisis and thereafter examining how excessive corporate risk-taking should be regulated.

(b) Regulation therefore should Protect the Financial System against the Impact of Systemic Shocks

Section 2(a) above has shown that systemic shocks are inevitable. The regulation of systemic risk therefore should include—and this Section 2(b) focuses on—the goal of protecting the financial system against the impact of those shocks. An obvious way to achieve that goal would be to prevent their transmission. Unfortunately, we do not yet—and indeed, might never—know enough about how systemic shocks are transmitted to prevent that.[18]

Systemic risk regulation therefore should help to stabilize parts of the financial system afflicted by systemic shocks.[19] The complexities of the financial system include not only cognitive complexity—that things are just too complex to understand[20]—but also temporal complexity—a 'tight coupling' within markets in which events tend to move rapidly into a crisis mode with

1995) (viewing 'financial innovation as driving the financial system toward the goal of greater economic efficiency').

[17] See n 1 and accompanying text.

[18] This discussion is based on Steven L Schwarcz, 'Controlling Financial Chaos: The Power and Limits of Law' (2012) Wisconsin Law Review 815; and Steven L Schwarcz and Iman Anabtawi, 'Regulating *Ex Post*: How Law Can Address the Inevitability of Financial Failure' (2013) 92 Texas Law Review 75.

[19] This type of *ex post* regulation, of course, is second best to preventing systemic shocks. The discussion below of *ex post* regulation is based on Schwarcz, 'Regulating Complexity in Financial Markets' (n 5).

[20] Compare with Schwarcz, 'Regulating Complexity in Financial Markets' ibid at n 15 ('[T]he more complicated a system becomes, and the more interconnected, … the odds of a breakdown in a portion of the system increases (because of complexity)').

little time or opportunity to intervene.[21] In these ways, complexities in the financial markets resemble those found in complex engineering systems. Chaos theory, which is used to address engineering system complexity, can also inform financial system complexity. One aspect of chaos theory is deterministic chaos in dynamic systems, which recognizes that the more complex the system, the more likely it is that failures will occur. Thus, the most successful (complex) systems are those in which the consequences of failures are limited. There are at least two ways that financial regulation could accomplish this: by ensuring liquidity to systemically important firms and markets, and by requiring those firms and markets to be more internally robust.[22]

The extent to which regulation should require systemically important firms and markets to be more internally robust is unclear. In the case of firms, the Basel Accords, and national implementing legislation, impose capital and liquidity requirements. It may be too early, however, to assess how effective those requirements will be, or whether they might be too strict. The Basel Accords certainly failed to protect banks in connection with the financial crisis. And some argue that those types of requirements may be economically counterproductive.[23]

An important but only partly answered question is how regulation should require systemically important markets to be more internally robust. The primary response to date is to provide for so-called circuit breakers to protect markets from 'flash crashes', which appear to be at least partly caused by high-speed automated trading. Formal member-sponsored equity markets may also have member-provided liquidity requirements. The Dodd-Frank Act introduces another approach to making systemically important markets more internally robust. Title VIII of that Act requires the Financial Stability Oversight Council to identify systemically important financial market utilities (SIFMUs), subjecting them to heightened regulatory standards. SIFMUs must, among other requirements, maintain liquid assets at least equal to

[21] See Richard Bookstaber, *A Demon of Our Own Design: Markets, Hedge Funds, and The Perils of Financial Innovation* (Wiley 2008) 156 (applying the engineering term 'tight coupling' to the context of finance).

[22] Requiring systemically important firms to be more internally robust can also help to deter systemic shocks in the first place, by preventing such firms' failures that could trigger systemic shocks. At least existing regulatory requirements to make these firms more internally robust are more microprudential, however; they focus on protecting individual firms, as opposed to protecting the financial system per se.

[23] See, eg, Eduardo Porter, 'Recession's True Cost is Still Being Tallied' *New York Times* (22 January 2014) at B1 <http://www.nytimes.com/2014/01/22/business/economy/the-cost-of-the-financial-crisis-is-still-being-tallied.html> accessed 24 September 2015 (observing that regulations that require financial institutions to increase capital cushions to buffer against risks and potential losses have been criticized for cutting into global economic output and reducing jobs).

(a) the cost of implementing their resolution plan or (b) six months' current operating expenses, whichever is greater. They must also adopt plans addressing recovery, resolution, credit loss allocation, and recapitalization after stress events. This approach is certainly valuable, but its application to financial market utilities is limiting. Because these entities only facilitate the mechanical functions of transferring, clearing, and settling payments and securities, the approach does not help to protect market pricing. I next discuss how a liquidity provider of last resort could help to provide that protection.

Systemic risk regulation could also help to stabilize parts of the financial system afflicted by systemic shocks by ensuring liquidity to systemically important firms and markets. This effectively entails a liquidity provider of 'last resort'.[24] The Federal Reserve Bank, of course, historically served as such a liquidity provider to banks and other financial firms; however, the Dodd-Frank Act restricted its power under § 13(3) of the Federal Reserve Act to serve in that capacity, in order to limit moral hazard. I personally believe that restriction is the Dodd-Frank Act's greatest mistake.

A better way of limiting moral hazard would be to privatize at least part of any provided liquidity. For example, regulation could require systemically important firms to pay into a systemic risk fund, designed for that purpose—which, in essence, is how banks pay for their FDIC deposit insurance. Such a requirement was originally in the bill that became the Dodd-Frank Act. It was deleted, however, because certain members of Congress felt that the very creation of a systemic risk fund would itself increase moral hazard.

To the contrary, however, such a fund should decrease moral hazard. The requirement to pay into the fund would help to internalize externalities.[25] The likelihood that systemically important firms will have to make additional contributions to the fund to replenish bailout monies should motivate those firms to monitor each other and help control each other's risky behaviour.[26] Because their own funds would be at risk, for example, fund contributors would have incentives to inform regulators when other firms take unwise risks.[27] If the required contributions to the fund are risk-adjusted, fund contributors would also have incentives to report firms that are underpaying.[28]

[24] Such a liquidity provider should provide funding only to solve temporary liquidity problems; it should not attempt to bail out insolvent firms.

[25] This type of regulation ideally should be global to avoid prejudicing the competitiveness of firms subject to US regulatory requirements.

[26] See Schwarcz, 'Controlling Financial Chaos' (n 18).

[27] Jeffrey N Gordon and Christopher Muller, 'Confronting Financial Crisis: Dodd-Frank's Dangers and the Case for a Systemic Emergency Insurance Fund' (2011) 28 Yale Journal on Regulation 156 (calling for a systemic emergency insurance fund that is funded by the financial industry).

[28] ibid.

In an era of disintermediation, it is also critical to focus on providing liquidity to critical capital markets as necessary to keep them functioning.[29] This task could be performed by a market liquidity provider of last resort, ideally in the form of a combined public-private enterprise. I have elsewhere explained in detail how such a liquidity provider could help to stabilize panicked financial markets, without creating moral hazard.[30] In brief, a market liquidity provider could either choose to purchase market securities, at a price deeply discounted from the original market price and also much lower than the estimated intrinsic value of the securities purchased but still high enough to stabilize market prices above the panicked free-fall level.[31] Alternatively, a market liquidity provider could attempt to stabilize the market by entering into derivatives contracts to strip out risks that the market has the greatest difficulty hedging—in effect, the market's irrationality element—thereby stimulating private investment. By hedging—and not actually purchasing securities directly—the market liquidity provider would appear to be taking less investment risk, and thus its function may be seen as more politically acceptable.[32]

By providing a lifeline to financial institutions, a lender of last resort can foster 'moral hazard' by encouraging these entities to be fiscally reckless. In contrast, a market liquidity provider, especially if it acts at the outset of a market panic,[33] can profitably invest in securities at a deep discount from the original market price and still provide a floor to how low the market will drop.[34] Buying at a deep discount will mitigate investor moral hazard. Furthermore, by focusing on markets, a market liquidity provider can minimize the too-big-to-fail dilemma faced by a lender of last resort to institutions.

[29] Steven L Schwarcz, 'Markets, Systemic Risk, and the Subprime Mortgage Crisis' (2008) 61 Southern Methodist University Law Review 212.

[30] See, eg, Steven L Schwarcz, 'Too Big To Fail?: Recasting the Financial Safety Net' in Lawrence E Mitchell and Arthur Wilmarth, Jr (eds), *The Panic of 2008* (Edward Elgar 2010).

[31] Say, eg, that the intrinsic value of a type of mortgage-backed securities (or MBS) is estimated to be in the range of 80 cents on the dollar. If the market price of those securities had fallen significantly below that number, say to 20 cents on the dollar, the market liquidity provider could purchase these securities at, say, 60 cents on the dollar, thereby stabilizing the market and still making a profit. To induce a holder of the MBS to sell at that price, the market liquidity provider could, for example, agree to pay a higher 'deferred purchase price' if the securities turn out to be worth more than expected.

[32] Compare with Floyd Norris, 'U.S. Bank Bailout to Rely in Part on Private Money' *New York Times* (9 February 2009) A1 (observing that having the government purchase the distressed MBS securities directly would be a 'politically perilous course').

[33] The timing of purchases will be critical. The market liquidity provider should try to act at the outset of a market panic, before market prices collapse too far. On the other hand, the market liquidity provider should be careful not to act when price fluctuations are normal.

[34] The market liquidity provider, and therefore taxpayers, would profit by buying securities at a much lower price than their intrinsic value.

By stabilizing markets, the likelihood of firm-level failure is diminished, thereby reducing the incidences in which a lender of last resort to institutions is needed. In economic terms, therefore, any safety-net subsidies created by a marker liquidity provider of last resort should be much smaller than those created by a lender of last resort.

In summary, systemic shocks are inevitable. Regulation therefore should be designed not only to try to reduce those shocks but also to protect the financial system against their unavoidable impact. This could be done by applying chaos theory to help stabilize the financial system. I next focus on trying to prevent excessive corporate risk-taking, which is one of the leading triggers of systemic shocks and widely regarded to have been a principal cause of the financial crisis.

3. Perspectives on Regulating Excessive Corporate Risk-taking, a Leading Trigger of Systemic Shocks

Agency theory suggests that targeting managers in their personal capacity would be an optimal deterrent to excessive corporate risk-taking. Yet few managers have been prosecuted for the excessive corporate risk-taking that led to the financial crisis. Section 3(a) shows why managerial prosecution is not—and is unlikely to become—a credible deterrent. Thereafter, Section 3(b) examines how else excessive corporate risk-taking could, and should, be regulated.

(a) Why Have So Few Managers been Prosecuted for Excessive Corporate Risk-taking that Led to the Financial Crisis?

To understand why post-financial crisis prosecution has focused so heavily on firm-level liability, and not personal liability, consider the changes that may be impeding the imposition of personal liability for excessive corporate risk-taking.[35]

[35] This discussion is based on Steven L Schwarcz, 'Excessive Corporate Risk-Taking and the Decline of Personal Blame' (2015) 65 Emory Law Journal <http://ssrn.com/abstract=2553511> (forthcoming) accessed 24 September 2015.

(i) Systemic Risk is Complicating What Risk-taking is 'Excessive'

Until the financial crisis, it seemed relatively easy to identify excessive corporate risk-taking by taking into account the consequences of corporate risk-taking on investors, primarily shareholders. Because of its potential for widespread public harm, systemic risk is complicating that analysis.

What constitutes 'excessive' risk-taking depends on the observer. Risk-taking is excessive from a given observer's standpoint if it has a negative expected value to that observer. Thus, it is reasonable to assume that investors would oppose risky business ventures that have a negative expected value to them. The problem, however, is that systemically important firms can engage in risk-taking ventures that have a positive expected value to their investors but a negative expected value to the public. That is because much of the systemic harm from such a firm's failure would be externalized[36] onto other market participants as well as onto ordinary citizens impacted by an economic collapse.

This misalignment occurs because the expected value of corporate risk-taking is traditionally viewed only from the standpoint of a firm's investors. That perspective ignores (non-investor) externalities caused by the risk-taking. Because myriad externalities result from corporate risk-taking, it would not be feasible to take all those externalities into account in regulating risk-taking. But systemic externalities that harm the real economy should be taken into account.

Until systemic externalities are required to be taken into account, managers who engage their firms in risk-taking that has potentially systemic consequences may not at the time be engaging in legal wrongdoing.

(ii) Decision-making is Becoming More Decentralized

Another reason for the decline of personal liability may be the increasingly decentralized nature of decision-making at large financial services firms, which makes it difficult to assign personal liability for excessive risk-taking. Senior executives do not even get involved in the design of potentially risky financial products, such as CDOs.

Former Attorney General Holder has intimated that this decentralized decision-making is intended to protect managers from personal liability.[37] In

[36] This could be described as a type of 'tragedy of the commons', insofar as market participants suffer from the actions of other market participants. But it also is a more standard externality insofar as non-market participants (ie, the ordinary citizens impacted by an economic collapse) suffer from the actions of market participants.

[37] Attorney General Eric Holder, 'Remarks on Financial Fraud Prosecutions at NYU School of Law' (2014) http://www.justice.gov/opa/speech/attorney-general-holder-remarks-financial-fraud-prosecutions-nyu-school-law accessed 3 August 2016 ('[C]orporations are structured to blur lines

reality, though, it may well be intended to maximize corporate efficiency and innovation. Decentralization is said to (i) encourage motivation and creativity; (ii) allow many minds to work simultaneously on the same problem; and (iii) accommodate flexibility and individualization.[38] Business scholars also argue that decentralized decision-making is necessary in a globalized economy, providing firms with much needed flexibility to deal with rapidly changing market conditions.

Whatever the intention, a side-effect of decentralized decision-making is to make it more difficult to assign risk-taking responsibility, and thus to impose personal liability for excessive risk-taking.

(iii) The Law Increasingly is Lagging Financial Innovation

Another change is that the law increasingly lags financial innovation as the financial industry and financial products become more complex. Even when regulators acquire industry information, it may be of only limited relevance to the current situation. The increasing income disparity, now more than two-to-one, between financial industry employees and their government regulatory counterparts[39] may also be lengthening that time lag by making it more difficult for financial regulators to understand and process complex information once obtained.

Because of the time lag, many risky actions by financial firms will not be illegal when taken. Therefore, the executives who determine and manage those actions will not be acting illegally at the time.

(iv) Systemic Harm is Limiting Proof of Causation

Another change impeding the imposition of personal liability for excessive risk-taking is that the primary harm now caused by financial failure—systemic harm—limits the application of tort law. Tort law, which is part of what Judge Richard Posner calls public control through the common law system of privately enforced rights, has long been a fundamental tool to impose personal civil liability to remedy harm for unreasonable risk-taking. Its utility is limited, however, to remedying foreseeable harm. But systemic harm is rarely foreseeable.

of authority and prevent responsibility for individual business decisions from residing with a single person.').

[38] Thomas W Malone, 'Making the Decision to Decentralize' (2004) Harvard Business School—Working Knowledge for Business Leaders, http://hbswk.hbs.edu/archive/4020.html.

[39] Steven L Schwarcz, 'Intrinsic Imbalance: The Impact of Income Disparity on Financial Regulation' (2015) 78 Law and Contemporary Problems 97.

Systemic harm instead affects a wide range of third parties in unpredictable ways. Consider, for example, an individual who is forced to close her family-owned restaurant during a systemically caused recession. Or taking a more concrete example from the financial crisis, consider whether to impose tort liability on a manager of a financial firm who, in the expectation of a bonus, sells risky ABS CDO securities to investors, contributing to that crisis. Tort law could not—and probably should not—be used to impose personal liability on that manager for the resulting systemic harm.

(v) Shrinking of Resources is Tightening Prosecutorial Risk–Reward Assessment

Like everyone else, prosecutors have limited resources. Since the terrorist attacks of 11 September 2001, several government agencies that investigate the financial industry have lost resources to anti-terrorism investigations. And since the Madoff fraud, the SEC has concentrated on Ponzi-like schemes, further diverting resources.

Being under pressure to spend their resources for maximum impact, prosecutors are choosing to prosecute clear-cut fraud cases. They also are choosing to prosecute firms, not individuals. Firms are much more likely to settle, or to enter into deferred prosecution agreements,[40] as a cost of doing business.

Moreover, pursuing individuals can be very costly. For example, the rate of successful prosecutions of individuals is very low. Some believe this reflects a self-reinforcing trend: as prosecutors spend less time engaged in actual litigation, their trial skills can diminish. Juries are also more reluctant to hold individuals liable. At least in part because of these costs, personal liability is now rarely pursued in complex financial cases, and then primarily through civil settlements that do not admit wrongdoing.

For the reasons explained above, the prosecution of corporate managers for excessive risk-taking is unlikely, under our existing regulatory framework, to be successful. Section 3(b) next examines how else that risk-taking could, and should, be regulated.

(b) How Else Could Excessive Corporate Risk-taking be Regulated?

I next consider five alternative methods of regulating excessive corporate risk-taking. First, I show why imposing firm-level liability is not a credible

[40] A deferred prosecution agreement, or DPA, is a contractual arrangement between a firm and the government that enables the firm to avoid prosecution in return for agreeing to act responsibly in the future.

deterrent.[41] Second, I examine whether there should be a managerial duty to the public.[42] Third, I suggest that the principle of limited liability should be re-examined in the context of shadow-banking firms. Fourth, I explore the concept of ring-fencing, or cordoning off, risky ventures. Finally, I consider so-called 'Too-Big-to-Fail' (TBTF) regulation.

(i) Imposing Firm-level Liability is not a Credible Deterrent

Being managed by individuals, firms themselves are only second-best targets of deterrence.[43] Although numerous firms have been fined very substantial amounts for activities related to the financial crisis,[44] some experts view these fines, from the perspective of multiple-year corporate earnings, as simply the 'cost of doing business'.[45] Firm-level liability can also inadvertently harm third parties, such as the prosecution of accounting giant Arthur Andersen which caused tens of thousands of employees to lose their jobs. Targeting managers in their personal capacity is widely viewed as a greater,[46] if not also a more optimal,[47] deterrent to corporate risk-taking than firm-level liability.

[41] This discussion is based on Schwarcz, 'Excessive Corporate Risk-Taking and the Decline of Personal Blame' (n 35).

[42] This discussion is based on Steven L Schwarcz, 'Keynote Reflections: The Public Governance Duty' (2015) 50 Georgia Law Review 1 (2015) <http:// ssrn.com/ abstract=2585551> accessed 24 September 2015. It also is based on my forthcoming article, 'Misalignment: Corporate Risk- Taking and Public Duty' <http:// ssrn.com/ abstract=2644375> accessed 24 September 2015.

[43] See, eg, Claire A Hill and Richard W Painter, 'Why SEC Settlements Should Hold Senior Executives Liable' *New York Times* (29 May 2012) <http://dealbook.nytimes.com/2012/05/29/why-s-e-c-settlements-should-hold-senior-executives-liable/> accessed 24 September 2015 (arguing that when penalties are assessed only against an entity, the individuals responsible have little incentive to change their behaviour; and thus, in order to change that incentive, individuals should also be personally liable); Clair Hill and Richard W Painter, 'Berle's Vision Beyond Shareholder Interests: Why Investment Bankers Should Have (Some) Personal Liability' (2010) 33 Seattle University Law Review 1173 (arguing that high-level bankers should be held personally liable).

[44] See, eg, Richard McGregor and Aaron Stanley, 'Banks Pay Out $100bn in U.S. Fines' *Financial Times* (25 March 2014) <http://www.ft.com/cms/s/0/802ae15c-9b50-11e3-946b-00144feab7de.html#axzz3Eds2zwdl> accessed 24 September 2015 (quoting Tony Fratto of Hamilton Place Strategies as stating that the fines were 'very substantial').

[45] McGregor and Stanley, ibid (quoting Professor Anat Admati of Stanford University Knight School of Business). Professor John Coffee similarly claims that 'the SEC is settling cheaply with entities and ignoring individuals—a policy of parking tickets for securities fraud.' See John C Coffee, 'Securities Enforcement: What Has Happened? Why are Folks Upset? What Can Be Done?' (Columbia University Law School First Annual Securities Regulation and Enforcement Institute, New York City, 2012).

[46] See, eg, Mary Jo White, US SEC Chair, 'Deploying the Full Enforcement Arsenal' (Council of Institutional Investors Fall Conference, Chicago, 2013) <http://www.sec.gov/News/Speech/Detail/Speech/1370539841202#.VE7m_iJ4pK4> accessed 24 September 2015 (observing two reasons for this greater deterrence: that economic actions taken against individuals not only require them to pay out of their own pockets but also impose reputational costs—a form of shaming—causing the individuals to lose social standing). The reputational costs might also include, of course, the inability to continue working in the financial sector.

[47] Some argue that adding the threat of personal liability to the threat of firm-level liability should be the optimal deterrent. See, eg, Cedric Argenton, Eric van Damme, and Sigrid Suetens,

Many nonetheless view firm-level liability as a valuable deterrent when it is imposed through deferred prosecution agreements (DPAs). Assistant Attorney General Breuer has argued, for example, that firm-level DPAs can bring large settlements and oversight that can have great punitive and deterrent effect. He explains that a deferred prosecution agreement is a powerful tool because

> when a company enters into a DPA with the government … it almost always must acknowledge wrongdoing, agree to cooperate with the government's investigation, pay a fine, agree to improve its compliance program, and agree to face prosecution if it fails to satisfy the terms of the agreement. All of these components of DPAs are critical for accountability.[48]

Professor Arlen also observes that a DPA can incentivize firms to monitor, police, and deter crime by creating or improving internal compliance programmes under the threat of firm-level sanctions.[49]

But the fact that firm-level liability in the form of DPAs can be a valuable deterrent does not prove it is a sufficient deterrent. Some question whether DPAs provide adequate sanctions.[50] Others question whether firms always comply with them. Professor Brandon Garrett has found, for example, that at least eight large banks have continued since 2001 to engage in actions prohibited by the DPAs.[51]

'Optimal Deterrence of Illegal Behavior Under Imperfect Corporate Governance' (2014) European Economic Association & Econometric Society 1 <http://www.eea-esem.com/files/papers/EEA-ESEM/2014/2301/collusion%20under%20agency%20theory%2020140123.pdf> accessed 24 September 2015 (arguing that personal liability is needed in addition to firm-level liability to reach the optimal level of deterring corporate moral hazard); A Mitchell Polinsky and Steven Shavell, 'Should Employees Be Subject to Fines and Imprisonment Given the Existence of Corporate Liability?' (1993) 13 International Review of Law and Economics 239, 246–48.

[48] Lanny A Breuer, Assistant Attorney General for the Criminal Division, US Department of Justice, 'The Role of Deferred Prosecution Agreements in White Collar Criminal Law Enforcement' (The Association of the Bar 2012).

[49] Jennifer Arlen, 'Corporate Criminal Liability: Theory and Evidence' (2012) NYU Center for Law, Economics and Organization, Law & Economics Research Paper Series: Working Paper No 11-25, 169. Compare with Wulf A Kaal and Timothy A Lacine, 'The Effect of Deferred and Non-Prosecution Agreements on Corporate Governance: Evidence from 1993–2013' (2014) 70 Business Lawyer 61 (arguing that deferred and non-prosecution agreements have increased substantially in recent years and have led to broad changes and improvements to corporate governance).

[50] See, eg, Mike Koehler, 'The Foreign Corrupt Practices Act Under the Microscope' (2012) 15 University of Pennsylvania Journal of Business Law 1 (DPAs 'allow egregious instances of corporate conduct to be resolved too lightly. Because the government does not file actual charges to which the company must plead, such conduct is often resolved without adequate sanctions and without achieving maximum deterrence.').

[51] Brandon L Garrett, *Too Big to Jail: How Prosecutors Compromise With Corporations* (Belknap Press 2014). Garrett further observes that the DPAs implemented from 2001 to 2012 have been largely ineffective due, in part, to fines that have lacked any meaningful impact.

It also is uncertain whether prosecutors would attempt—and if they did, whether they legally would have the right—to apply DPAs to deter excessive corporate risk-taking, even risk-taking that results in systemic harm. DPAs are normally applied only to deter crime and other illegal actions. Excessive corporate risk-taking, however, is not (and should not necessarily be) illegal. It therefore remains uncertain whether firm-level liability, even in the form of DPAs, is a sufficient deterrent to control and internalize the costs of excessive corporate risk-taking.

(ii) Should there be a Public Governance Duty?

As discussed, there is a fundamental misalignment between the risk-taking interests of individual market participants and societal interests in controlling systemic harm.[52] One regulatory response has been the post-crisis prosecution of systemically important firms for excessive risk-taking. But this response has been inadequate for several reasons, including that, being managed by individuals, firms themselves are second-best targets of deterrence, and firm-level liability can inadvertently harm third parties.[53]

To better control systemic risk, excessive corporate risk-taking should be regulated at the managerial level. But what would it mean to prosecute managers for excessive corporate risk-taking? The threshold problem is that, as mentioned, systemic risk is complicating what that concept means.[54] A systemically important firm may well decide to engage in a transaction that is expected to be profitable—and thereby favourable to its investors and thus appropriate corporate risk-taking under existing corporate governance law—even though doing so could increase systemic risk, since much of the harm from a resulting systemic collapse would be externalized onto other market participants as well as onto ordinary citizens impacted by an economic collapse.[55]

Because corporate risk-taking can impact the public in addition to impacting investors, one way of controlling excessive risk-taking would be to require the managers of a systemically important firm to run the firm as agents not merely for the investors but also for the public. To that extent, such managers would not only have a private corporate governance duty to investors but also a 'public governance duty' to society not to engage in excessive risk-taking that could systemically harm the public.[56]

[52] See n 36 and accompanying text. [53] See nn 42–46 and accompanying text.

[54] See Section 3(a). [55] See n 36 and accompanying text.

[56] See Schwarcz, 'Misalignment: Corporate Risk-Taking and Public Duty' (n 51). Some argue that a fiduciary duty to the public is already required under Canadian law, after *BCE Inc. v 1976*

By explicitly taking into account systemic risks to the public, this public governance duty would go much further, for example, than the duty of existing corporate risk committees. Even the Dodd-Frank Act risk-committee mandate at most indirectly suggests that risk committees consider the public interest.[57]

This reformulation of corporate governance law raises several practical questions: (1) How should a public governance duty be legally imposed? (2) How should managers assess the public costs and private benefits of a risk-taking activity? (3) How should managers balance those costs and benefits when deciding whether the firm should engage in a given risk-taking activity? (4) How should a public governance duty be enforced? (5) Weighing the goals of protecting the public against systemic externalities and encouraging the best people to serve as managers, to what extent should managers performing their public governance duty have the protection of a business judgment rule as a defence to liability? (6) To what extent should managers be protected under directors and officers liability insurance? I attempt to answer these questions in a separate article.[58]

(iii) Should Limited Liability Remain the Norm, Especially for Shadow-banking Firms?

Narrowing limited liability for at least certain firm managers can limit conflicts that encourage excessive risk-taking. Corporate limited liability protects a firm's equity investors from the firm's liabilities, except for the capital invested. Although limited liability can create moral hazard, leading to excessive corporate risk-taking, it also encourages equity-capital investment by

Debentureholders [2008] 3 S.C.R. 560 (Can.), in which the court stated that '[w]here conflicting interests arise, it falls to the directors of the corporation to resolve them in accordance with their fiduciary duty to act in the best interests of the corporation.... There are no absolute rules and no principle that one set of interests should prevail over another. In each case, the question is whether, in all the circumstances, the directors acted in the best interests of the corporation, having regard to all relevant considerations, including—but not confined to—the need to treat affected stakeholders in a fair manner, commensurate with the corporation's duties as a responsible corporate citizen.'

[57] This mandate, promulgated in Federal Reserve Regulation YY, requires that systemically important firms form a risk committee chaired by an independent director and have a member with 'risk-management expertise comparable to the company's structure, risk profile, complexity, activities, [and] size.' It also mandates (emphasis added) that 'The level of risk management expertise possessed by the risk committee of a company should rise in accordance with a company's rising threat of *systemic risk to the economy*.' It does not, however, specifically require the committee to take systemic risk to the economy into account. See 12 CFR § 252.20–22, 30–35 (2015), part of Regulation YY promulgated by the Federal Reserve to carry out § 165(h) of Dodd-Frank Wall Street Reform and Consumer Protection Act (Pub L 111– 203, HR 4173) (Dodd-Frank).

[58] See Schwarcz, 'Misalignment: Corporate Risk-Taking and Public Duty' (n 51).

addressing investor risk aversion. Empirically, scholars have been uncertain how those factors should be balanced.[59]

That balance shifts radically, however, in the context of shadow banking. (Shadow banking is a loose term that refers to the decentralized provision of financing outside of traditional banking channels, and thus without the need for traditional modes of bank intermediation between capital markets and the users of funds.) For two reasons, limited liability can be a uniquely fertile source of systemic externalities for shadow-banking firms.[60]

First, managers of shadow-banking firms are likely to take greater risks than managers of other limited liability firms. The relatively small firms, such as hedge funds, that operate in the shadow-banking system are often managed directly by their primary investors. Because such investor-managers typically are entitled to a significant share of their firm's profits, they have strong incentives to take high risks that could generate outsized profits. Yet if a risky action exposes their firm to significant liability for externalized harm, limited liability protects those investor-managers from losing more than their invested capital. This is radically unlike the management incentives in non-shadow-banking firms, in which senior managers tend to share only indirectly in profits, such as through stock options.

Even more significantly, the failure of a shadow-banking firm is more likely than that of a non-bank to have systemic consequences. Like traditional banks, shadow-banking firms engage in financial intermediation on which the real economy is dependent. Because all financial intermediaries—including shadow-banking firms and traditional banks—tend to be highly interconnected, the failure of a shadow-banking firm could trigger the failures of other financial intermediaries. Such a chain of failures would be the epitome of a systemic event, especially if it materially reduces the availability of financial intermediation. Additionally, shadow banking's disproportionate reliance on short-term funding of long-term projects not only increases the likelihood of a shadow-banking firm's failure but also can increase the systemic consequences of that failure. Economists have identified the failure of shadow-banking firms to roll over short-term debt as a contributing factor to the recent financial crisis.[61]

[59] This discussion is based on Steven L Schwarcz, 'The Governance Structure of Shadow Banking: Rethinking Assumptions About Limited Liability' (2014) 90 Notre Dame Law Review 1 <http://ssrn.com/abstract=2364126> accessed 24 September 2015.

[60] For more on shadow banking's systemic risk implications, see Anita Anand, Michael Trebilcock, and Michael Rosenstock, Chapter 1 in this volume; see also Weitseng Chen, Chapter 6 in this volume.

[61] Sandra C Kreiger, Executive Vice President, New York Federal Reserve Bank, 'Reducing the Systemic Risk in Shadow Maturity Transformation' (Global Association of Risk Professionals 12th

A potential solution to this problem is to impose personal liability on investor-managers with the power to 'control' shadow-banking firms by narrowing their limited liability protection—perhaps to double liability or some other multiple of their investment. This would not be unfair to shareholders because it would only impact those in a capacity to control the firm. And it should not unduly discourage equity-capital investment. Even if they are risk averse, owner-managers with the power to control their firms could choose to govern to minimize their potential liability (and the liability of those owner-managers would not be open-ended but limited to, eg, double liability).

(iv) Should Ring-fencing be used to Control Corporate Risk-taking?

'Ring-fencing' is often touted as a potential regulatory way to control risk in banking, finance, public utilities, and insurance.[62] The UK has been ring-fencing banks by legally separating certain of their risky assets from their retail banking operations. Regulators in the US have been considering ring-fencing systemically important financial institutions (SIFIs), including banks, to reduce systemic risk. The 'Volcker Rule' is also a form of ring-fencing in that it prohibits systemically important firms from conducting activities viewed as risky, such as running a private equity fund. Congress has been considering enacting a ring-fencing scheme proposed in federal 'covered bond' legislation, which would parallel European ring-fencing of certain secured transactions. State regulators often require the ring-fencing of utility companies by legally separating their risky assets and operations from the public utility function. And the National Association of Insurance Commissioners (NAIC) has been proposing the increased ring-fencing of insurance companies.

But what is 'ring-fencing'? Because it is proposed in different contexts as a solution to different problems, ring-fencing is inconsistently defined; and even within a given context, it is often ill-defined. By examining its functions, ring-fencing can be understood as legally deconstructing a firm in order to more effectively reallocate and reduce risk. The deconstruction can occur in various ways. For example, the firm could be made more internally viable, such as by separating risky assets from the firm, preventing the firm from engaging in risky activities or investing in risky assets, and ensuring that the firm is able to operate on a standalone basis even if its affiliates fail. The firm

Annual Risk Management Convention 2011) <http://www.newyorkfed.org/newsevents/speeches/2011/kri110308.html> accessed 24 September 2015.

[62] This discussion is based on Steven L Schwarcz, 'Ring-Fencing' (2013) 87 Southern California Law Review 69 <http://ssrn.com/abstract=2228742> accessed 24 September 2015.

could also be protected from external risks, such as third-party claims, involuntary bankruptcy, and affiliate abuse.[63]

Consider whether SIFIs should be ring-fenced. Ring-fencing can apply to SIFIs in two ways: by protecting the publicly beneficial activities, if any, performed by SIFIs; and by protecting against the failure of SIFIs that are so large and contractually interconnected with other SIFIs (including banks) that their failure could trigger a systemic collapse. First examine whether ring-fencing should be used to protect the publicly beneficial activities performed by bank-SIFIs. Then examine non-bank SIFIs.

The need to ring-fence banks would certainly not be as strong, for example, as the need to ring-fence public utilities. Public utilities not only provide critical services such as power, clean water, and communications but are also typically monopolies—and hence the only entities able to provide these services. Ring-fencing the utility helps assure the continuity of those services. In contrast, the market for banking services, at least in the US (in contrast to the UK), is competitive. If some risky banks become unable to provide critical services, other banks should be able to provide substitute services.

The argument that ring-fencing should be used to protect the publicly beneficial activities performed by non-bank SIFIs is therefore even more dubious. As a result of disintermediation, non-bank SIFIs have begun to perform at least some financial intermediation services that previously were performed by banks. It does not appear, however, that any of those services are of the type that should justify ring-fencing. Non-bank SIFIs do not take deposits, and, at least in the US, they are legally restricted from doing so. Non-bank SIFIs do not operate payments systems. The only traditional banking activity that non-bank SIFIs are performing is the intermediation of credit, by providing financing to business. Although this activity is beneficial to the public, there is no evidence suggesting that ring-fencing regulation is needed to protect it. A wide range of non-bank firms engage in disintermediated financing, and those that find aspects of ring-fencing desirable as a business matter are already able to contractually ring-fence themselves.

(v) Should Regulation Limit Too-Big-to-Fail Firms?

Another potential way to regulate excessive risk-taking is to limit the chance that so-called too-big-to-fail (TBTF) firms will engage in risky projects

[63] There are many practical questions associated with ring-fencing. For example, which firms should be subject to ring-fencing? Which 'risky' assets should be separated from the firm, and how should that separation occur? Which 'risky' activities and asset investments should the firm not engage in, and how should that engagement be prevented? Which affiliate 'risks' should the firm be protected from, and how should that protection be implemented?

without worrying about failing, since managers of these firms know, or at least believe, that the government would never let the firms fail. As mentioned, the Dodd-Frank Act restricts the Federal Reserve's power to bail out firms, in order to limit such morally hazardous behaviour. TBTF regulation also focuses on reducing the TBTF nature of systemically important firms, exemplified by the Dodd-Frank Act's requirement that systemically important firms must file so-called living wills, setting forth how they could liquidate with minimal systemic impact.[64]

I am somewhat sceptical of TBTF regulation. As observed, restricting the Fed's power to bail out failing firms is likely to increase systemic risk. I also question the efficacy of the living-will requirement. In my many years as a workout and bankruptcy lawyer, I rarely saw a firm's failure that accurately reflected, much less closely resembled, expectations about the firm when it was profitable. Living wills also do not prevent the concurrent failure of multiple otherwise TBTF firms from, collectively, having a systemic impact; the financial crisis demonstrated that such a concurrence is likely when the causes of the failures are interconnected.

4. Conclusion

Systemic shocks are inevitable. Regulation should therefore be aimed at protecting the financial system from the impact of those shocks. Regulation also needs to focus on reducing a leading, but under-theorized, source of systemic shocks: the incentives of corporate managers to engage their firms in excessive risk-taking. Although it may not be feasible to reduce those incentives by prosecuting managers for that risk-taking, there are several regulatory alternatives. This chapter argues that at least two of these alternatives—mandating a public governance duty, and narrowing limited liability protection for owner-managers of shadow-banking firms—are especially worth pursuing.

[64] TBTF regulation and the regulation of systemically important firms to make them more internally robust (and thereby better able to absorb systemic shocks) also overlap, such as regulation imposing capital and liquidity requirements. I have already addressed that other regulation. See nn 22–24 and accompanying text (discussing the extent to which regulation should require systemically important firms to be more internally robust, including imposing capital and liquidity requirements).

3

Law, Financial Instability, and the Institutional Structure of Financial Regulation

Dan Awrey[*]

1. Introduction

There is a large and diverse body of academic and policy literature examining the institutional structure of financial regulation. Broadly speaking, this literature can be subdivided into at least three distinct, if often intertwined, strands. The first strand examines the information, coordination, agency, and other transaction costs and benefits of different structural models. These models include the historically prevalent 'institutional' and 'functional' models, along with the 'integrated' and 'objectives-based' models which have emerged more recently in response to the challenges of regulating modern financial markets and institutions.[1] The second strand examines the dynamics

[*] This chapter is based on research undertaken in connection with two larger projects. The first is the 'Legal Theory of Finance' project funded by the Institute for New Economic Thinking in which the author is a co-principal investigator along with Katharina Pistor and Brigitte Haar; see Katharina Pistor, 'A Legal Theory of Finance' (2013) 41:2 Journal of Comparative Economics 315; Dan Awrey, 'Toward a Supply-side Theory of Financial Innovation' (2013) 41:2 Journal of Comparative Economics 401; and Dan Awrey, 'Law and Finance in the Chinese Shadow Banking System' (2015) 48:1 Cornell International Law Journal 1. The second project will shortly culminate in the publication of a book, entitled *Principles of Financial Regulation*, by Oxford University Press, on which the author is a co-author along with John Armour, Paul Davies, Luca Enriques, Jeffrey Gordon, Colin Mayer, and Jennifer Payne. I am indebted to my collaborators on both of these projects for their comments, advice, and support. All errors remain my own.

[1] See, for example, Martin Cihak and Richard Podpiera, 'Is One Watchdog Better Than Three? International Experience with Integrated Financial Sector Supervision' (2006) IMF Working Paper 06/57 <http://www.imf.org>; Jose de Luna Martinez and Thomas Rose, 'International Survey of Integrated Financial Sector Supervision' (2003) World Bank Policy Research Working Paper 3096 <http://www.worldbank.org>; Richard Abrams and Michael Taylor, 'Issues in the Unification of Financial Sector Supervision' (December 2000) IMF Working Paper 00213<http://www.imf.org>; Charles Goodhart, Philipp Hartmann, David Llewellyn, Liliana Rojas-Suarez, and Steven

Law, Financial Instability and the Institutional Structure of Financial Regulation. First Edition. Dan Awrey. © Dan Awrey 2016. Published by Oxford University Press.

of regulatory competition between multiple regulatory authorities responsible for the oversight of different but overlapping aspects of corporate governance, securities law, or financial regulation within a single jurisdiction.[2] A related strand examines the dynamics of regulatory competition at the international level.[3] The third strand, meanwhile, examines the evolving global regulatory architecture: exploring questions around the role of international institutions such as the International Monetary Fund (IMF) and World Bank, the nature and effectiveness of so-called 'soft law' institutions and regulatory networks, and the feasibility and desirability of greater international regulatory integration and convergence.[4] While not always explicitly, each of these strands of literature can ultimately be understood as exploring variants of the same fundamental question: what role, if any, does institutional structure play in advancing the objectives of financial regulation?

The objective of financial regulation which has arguably attracted the most attention in the aftermath of the global financial crisis is the maintenance of financial stability.[5] The crisis vividly demonstrated how risks arising within

Weisbrod, *Financial Regulation: Why, How, and Where Now?* (Routledge 1998); and Michael Taylor, *Twin Peaks: A Regulatory Structure for the New Century* (Centre for the Study of Financial Innovation 1995).

[2] See, for example, Mark Roe, 'Delaware's Competition' (2003) 117 Harvard Law Review 588; Howell Jackson, 'Centralization, Competition, and Privatization in Financial Regulation' (2001) 2:2 Theoretical Inquiries in Law 649; and John Coffee, 'Competition versus Consolidation: The Significance of Organizational Structure in Financial and Securities Regulation' (1995) 50 Business Law Journal 447.

[3] See, for example, Frederick Tung, 'Passports, Private Choice, and Private Interests: Regulatory Competition and Cooperation in Corporate, Securities, and Bankruptcy Law' (2002) 3:2 Chicago Journal of International Law 369; John Coffee, 'Racing towards the Top? The Impact of Cross-Listings and Stock Market Competition on International Corporate Governance' (2002) 102 Columbia Law Review 1757; Roberta Romano, 'The Need for Competition in International Securities Regulation' (2001) 2:2 Theoretical Inquiries in Law 387; John Coffee, 'The Future as History: The Prospect for Global Convergence in Corporate Governance and Its Implications' (1999) 93 Northwestern University Law Review 641; Merritt Fox, 'Securities Disclosure in a Globalized Market: Who Should Regulate Whom?' (1997) 95 Michigan Law Review 2498; and Stephen Choi and Andrew Guzman, 'National Laws, International Money: Regulation in a Global Capital Market' (1997) 65:5 Fordham Law Review 1855.

[4] See, for example, Roberta Romano, 'For Diversity in the International Regulation of Financial Institutions: Critiquing and Recalibrating the Basel Architecture' (2014) 31 Yale Journal on Regulation 1; Jeffrey Gordon and Colin Mayer, 'The Micro, Macro and International Design of Financial Regulation' (29 April 2012) Columbia Law & Economics Working Paper No 422 <http://www.ssrn.com>; Chris Brummer, *Soft Law and the Global Financial System: Rule Making in the 21st Century* (Cambridge University Press 2012); Anne-Marie Slaughter, *A New World Order* (Princeton University Press 2004); John Eatwell and Lance Taylor, *Global Finance at Risk: The Case for International Regulation* (WW Norton & Company 2000); and Ngaire Woods (ed), *The Political Economy of Globalization* (MacMillan Palgrave 2000).

[5] The objectives of promoting consumer and investor protection have also figured prominently in the post-crisis policy debate.

one market, institution, or jurisdiction can quickly spread, triggering instability within other parts of the financial system. The crisis also demonstrated how historical distinctions between different markets and institutions—often used as a blueprint for designing the institutional structure of financial regulation—have in many cases been rendered obsolete by the forces of financial innovation.

In response, policy-makers in the United States (US), United Kingdom (UK), and European Union (EU) have adopted a number of significant institutional reforms. In the US, the crisis has lead to the creation of the Financial Stability Oversight Council (FSOC). In the UK, it has lead to the abolishment of the integrated Financial Services Authority (FSA), the introduction of a new objectives-based institutional structure, and the creation of a new Financial Policy Committee (FPC) within the Bank of England. And in the EU, the crisis has provided the impetus for a series of wholesale institutional reforms including the creation of three new European 'supervisory'[6] authorities (ESAs), the European Systemic Risk Board (ESRB), and the European Banking Union. Finally, the crisis has also spurred a number of institutional reforms at the international level, including perhaps most significantly the transformation of the moribund former Financial Stability Forum into the newly reinvigorated Financial Stability Board (FSB). The primary driver behind these domestic and international reforms has been to ensure that regulatory authorities are able to more effectively identify, monitor, and respond to potential threats to financial stability.

Given the scale of these reforms, one might think that policy-makers possess a clear understanding of how the institutional structure of financial regulation can help promote greater financial stability. In reality, however, the relationship between institutional design and the promotion of regulatory objectives such as financial stability is poorly understood. This chapter seeks to enhance our understanding of this relationship by examining a variable which, somewhat paradoxically, is both one of the most important mechanisms by which regulatory authorities seek to promote financial stability and a potentially significant, if often overlooked, source of financial instability. This variable is the *law*. The law—defined broadly as including both public law and regulation and private contracts enforced in public courts—can contribute to financial instability in at least three ways. First, strong law and

[6] The use of the term 'supervisory' by the European Commission to describe these authorities is ultimately inaccurate. While these authorities have the power to adopt legally binding rules in many areas, responsibility for supervising compliance with these rules falls predominantly on the competent authorities within individual member states.

regulation can spur regulatory arbitrage: incentivizing the pursuit of correlated business strategies, and channelling capital and risk into less well-developed and regulated parts of the financial system. Second, in a world of incomplete contracting and potential externalities, strong contractual rights can be a source of structural inflexibility: rendering strict enforcement of these contracts individually rational, but socially undesirable. Third, the law plays a number of important and yet poorly understood roles in supporting confidence in money and other 'money-like' financial claims. By the same token, however, differences in the legal or regulatory treatment of financial claims used as economic substitutes for more conventional forms of money, which may be immaterial during periods of high market confidence and stability, may prove significant during periods of market turmoil. These differences can incentivize run-like behaviour by market participants, thus triggering or exacerbating instability. As we shall see, examining the relationship between law and financial instability across each of these three dimensions holds out a number of potentially important insights in terms of the optimal institutional structure of financial regulation.

This chapter proceeds as follows. Sections 2 and 3 begin by providing some much needed conceptual clarity around what we mean by both 'law' and 'financial stability'. Section 4 examines in greater detail some of the different ways in which the law can contribute to financial instability. Section 5 then examines what lessons these insights into the relationship between law and financial instability might yield in terms of the optimal institutional structure of financial regulation. There are four principal takeaways from this chapter. First, distinctions between different types of markets, institutions, or economic functions are less important than regulatory objectives in designing the institutional structure of financial regulation. Second, irrespective of other structural choices, there exists a strong case for allocating responsibility for financial stability to a single regulatory authority and for positioning this authority at the apex of the institutional hierarchy.[7] Third, promoting financial stability requires a coordinated approach toward identifying, monitoring, and responding to both *micro*prudential and *macro*-prudential risks. Fourth, in a world where capital and risk flow relatively freely across borders, the institutional structure of financial regulation at the domestic level may be less important than an effective global regulatory architecture.

[7] See Armour et al. (n *) Chapter 27.

2. What is 'Law'?

Examining the relationship between law and financial instability demands that we first understand what we mean when we talk about 'the law'. Distinguished legal scholars and philosophers have dedicated their entire careers to exploring this important and highly contested question.[8] For the purposes of this chapter, however, it is sufficient to adopt a somewhat less theoretical—more pragmatic—definition.

This definition views the law as consisting of two basic elements. The first element is made up of the primary and secondary legislation, regulation, and other policy instruments adopted by public authorities with the objective of imposing binding constraints on the behaviour of private market participants. Pursuant to this view, while the Basel Capital Accords for example would *not* be viewed as law, the legislation transposing these international standards into domestic law unequivocally would. The second element is then made up of the legally enforceable contractual and institutional arrangements through which private market participants carry on their business activities. As we shall see, this definition is entirely instrumental: reflecting the interaction between public law and private ordering at the heart of the financial system and, ultimately, the relationship between law and financial instability.

3. What is 'Financial Stability'?

Examining the relationship between law and financial instability also demands that we understand what we mean when we talk about 'financial stability'. The concept of financial stability is often understood in terms of the avoidance or containment of 'systemic' risk. Scholars and policy-makers have advanced a number of different definitions of this important and inchoate concept. Many definitions refer in abstract and general terms to the existence of negative spillovers or externalities.[9] Other definitions, somewhat tautologically, focus on risks which undermine 'stability' or 'confidence' in the financial system.[10] Yet others focus more precisely on events or circumstances which

[8] See, for example, HLA Hart, *The Concept of Law* (Clarendon Press 1961) 89–96 and Hans Kelsen, *Introduction to the Problems of Legal Theory: A Translation of the First Edition of the Reine Rechtalehre or Pure Theory of Law* (Clarendon Press 1997).

[9] See FSB, 'Guidance to Assess the Systemic Importance of Financial Institutions' Report to the G20 Finance Ministers and Central Bank Governors (FSB October 2009) <http://www.financialstabilityboard.org>.

[10] See Monica Billio, Mila Getmansky, Andrew Lo, and Loriana Pelizzon, 'Econometric Measures of Systemic Risk in the Finance and Insurance Sectors' (July 2010) National Bureau of Economic Research Working Paper 16223 <http://www.nber.org>.

impair the functioning of the financial system to the point where they disrupt the flow of capital and other financial services to the real economy, thereby undermining economic growth and broader social welfare.[11] Ultimately, these definitions share a number of similarities. Perhaps most importantly, they each envision the transmission of risks from within specific financial markets or institutions to the broader financial system and, in many cases, to the consumers, businesses, taxpayers, and governments which this system is designed to support.[12]

Another important similarity shared by these definitions is that they focus on the harmful *effects* generated by the crystallization of systemic risk. From a policy perspective, however, it may be useful to compliment this 'effects-based' definition of systemic risk with one which focuses on its potential *causes* and most likely *transmission mechanisms*. This is especially true if policy-makers want to identify, monitor, and respond to potential threats to financial stability before these harmful effects materialize. In this vein, Monica Billio, Mila Getmansky, Andrew Lo, and Loriana Pelizzon identify four sources of systemic risk: leverage, liquidity, losses, linkages.[13] These sources can interact with one another to generate systemic risk in a variety of different ways. The use of leverage, for example, makes the balance sheets of market participants more sensitive to adverse price movements, thereby increasing the probability of financial distress and insolvency. Where a large number of market participants use leverage to finance the holding of similar assets, meanwhile, correlated deleveraging can undermine market liquidity, thereby driving down prices and potentially forcing further deleveraging. Conversely, liquidity shocks within the markets used as sources of leverage—for example, wholesale funding or financial collateral markets—can trigger forced deleveraging and fire sales in other asset markets, thereby precipitating the spread of illiquidity and losses throughout the financial system.

Viewed from this '*cause*-based' perspective, it is possible to identify at least three basic mechanisms for the transmission of systemic risk. First, the financial distress or insolvency of a market participant can have a *direct* impact on the stability or solvency of its shareholders, creditors, and other counterparties (the so-called 'domino' effect). Intuitively, this domino effect is likely to be a function of the systemic importance of the relevant market participant as measured by the number, value, and nature of its economic interconnections

[11] See ECB, 'Financial Networks and Financial Stability' Financial Stability Review (ECB June 2010) 155 <http://www.ecb.europa.eu>.

[12] See also, Steven Schwarcz, Chapter 2 in this volume and Anita Anand, Michael Trebilcock, and Michael Rosenstock, Chapter 1 in this volume.

[13] Billio et al. (n 10).

with other financial markets and institutions. Second, the actions of market participants in attempting to avoid financial distress or insolvency—for example, by deleveraging or selling assets—can have an *indirect* impact on the stability or solvency of other, otherwise unconnected, market participants utilizing similar financing models or holding similar assets (the so-called 'contagion' effect). Third, observing the financial distress or insolvency of one institution, market participants may draw adverse inferences about the stability or solvency of other institutions perceived to be utilizing similar financing models or holding similar assets (the so-called 'informational contagion' effect).[14] This perception, in turn, can become a self-fulfilling prophecy as counterparties seek to minimize their direct and indirect exposures to these market participants by withdrawing funding and liquidity, thereby exacerbating—or even triggering—their distress or insolvency.

Having briefly identified some of the principal causes, effects, and transmission mechanisms of systemic risk, it is important to also say something about how to effectively *measure* it. Commonly used metrics of systemic risk can be subdivided into two categories: those which seek to measure the risks posed by individual markets and institutions, and those which seek to measure broader macroeconomic imbalances. In terms of the first category, scholars and policy-makers will typically measure the leverage employed by banks and other financial institutions,[15] along with the size of each institution's largest counterparty exposures.[16] Where possible, they may also attempt to identify correlated holdings, business strategies, or counterparties across financial institutions with the objective of estimating the joint probability of financial distress or insolvency within a given network.[17] In terms of the second category, meanwhile, scholars and policy-makers often seek to use changes in gross domestic product, inflation, interest rates, and monetary aggregates;[18] imbalances between credit, equity, and property markets;[19] tight

[14] See Viral Acharya and Tanju Yorulmazer, 'Information Contagion and Bank Herding' (2008) 40:1 Journal of Money, Banking and Credit 215.

[15] See John Geanakoplos, 'Solving the Present Crisis and Managing the Leverage Cycle' (2010) 16:1 Federal Reserve Bank of New York Economic Policy Review 101 and Robert Merton and Zvi Bodie, 'Deposit Insurance Reform: A Functional Approach' (1993) 38 Carnegie-Rochester Conference Series on Public Policy 1.

[16] In order to measure systemic risk within financial *markets*, in contrast, scholars and policy-makers might measure correlated holdings and investment strategies, along with levels of liquidity within both asset and underlying funding markets.

[17] See IMF, 'Global Financial Stability Report: Responding to the Financial Crisis and Measuring Systemic Risks' (IMF April 2009) <http://www.imf.org>.

[18] Rodrigo Alfaro and Mathias Drehmann, 'Macro Stress Tests and Crises: What Can We Learn?' (2009) Bank for International Settlements Quarterly Review 29.

[19] See Claudio Borio and Mathias Drehmann, 'Assessing the Risk of Banking Crises–Revisited' (2009) Bank for International Settlements Quarterly Review 29.

coupling between different markets,[20] or illiquidity within domestic sovereign debt markets[21] as potential indicators of the build-up of systemic risk.[22]

4. Why Does Law Matter for Financial Stability?

Absent from these conventional accounts of the causes of financial instability—and thus from conventional metrics for effectively measuring it—is any meaningful attempt to account for the essential role of the law within the structure of the financial system. Indeed, conventional economic theory has long been influenced by the view that while the law plays an important role in helping market participants make credible commitments to one another, it is nevertheless fundamentally *exogenous* to finance and, thus, financial stability.[23] Not surprisingly, economic theory has thus tended to abstract away from the law and legal institutions, along with the political, historical, and cultural context in which the law is made and evolves over time. Yet there is ultimately no escaping the fact that financial markets and institutions are not naturally occurring economic phenomena—they are *made*. They are made of private contracts which create the financial claims we often refer to as 'equity', 'debt', and 'derivatives'. They are made of the private rules—for example, exchanges, alternative trading platforms, and standardized contracts—created by market participants in order to foster deep and liquid markets for these claims. And, importantly, they are made of the public laws and legal institutions which prescribe the regulatory environment within which financial markets and institutions must operate, and which ensure the effective enforcement of financial contracts. Together, these contracts, private rules, and public laws

[20] See Mark Kritzman, Yuanzhen Li, Sebastien Page, and Roberto Rigobon, 'Principal Components as a Measure of Systemic Risk' (2011) 37:4 Journal of Portfolio Management 112.

[21] See Xing Hu, Jun Pan, and Jiang Wang, 'Noise as Information for Illiquidity' (2013) 68 Journal of Finance 2223.

[22] For those seeking further information on these and other metrics, the US Office of Financial Research has published a useful survey examining different methodologies for measuring systemic risk, see Dimitrios Bisias, Mark Flood, Andrew Lo, and Stavros Valavanis, 'A Survey of Systemic Risk Analytics' Office of Financial (5 January 2012) Research Working Paper 0001 <http://www.treasury.gov/ofr>.

[23] This view is most evident in the literature exploring the relationship between legal rules and financial development; see, for example, Simeon Djankov, Rafael La Porta, Florencio Lopez-de-Silanes, and Andrei Shleifer, 'The Law and Economics of Self-Dealing' (2008) 88:3 Journal of Financial Economics 430; Rafael La Porta, Florencio Lopez-de-Silanes, and Andrei Shleifer, 'What Works in Securities Laws?' (2006) 61:1 Journal of Finance 1; Rafael La Porta, Florencio Lopez-de-Silanes, Andrei Shleifer, and Robert Vishny, 'Law and Finance' (1998) 106:6 Journal of Political Economy 1113; and Rafael La Porta, Florencio Lopez-de-Silanes, Andrei Shleifer, and Robert Vishny, 'Legal Determinants of External Finance' (1997) 52:3 Journal of Finance 1131.

create a complex web of rights and obligations between market participants, between market participants and the state, and between states.[24] Indeed, in a very real way, these rights and obligations *are* the financial system.

The global markets for interest rate, currency, credit, equity, and other swaps offer an illustrative example. The emergence and growth of these markets in recent decades can be largely attributed to the development of standardized contracts by market participants working under the auspices of organizations such as the International Swaps and Derivatives Association (ISDA).[25] ISDA has also played an important role in developing private rules—for example, auction settlement and determination committees for credit default swaps (CDS)—which ensure the smooth and orderly functioning of these markets.[26] By the same token, the growth of swap markets can also be attributed to public law and regulation. Perhaps most importantly, swaps enjoy an explicit carve-out from the automatic stay and fraudulent preference provisions under corporate insolvency laws in many jurisdictions, thereby enabling market participants to enforce close-out netting and related financial collateral arrangements upon a termination event or event of default.[27] In the wake of the crisis, public law has also been used to incentivize the shift of many standardized swaps from bilateral to centralized clearing.[28] In the end, it is difficult to envision what these markets would look like—assuming that they would even exist—in the absence of any one of these contractual or regulatory frameworks.

As the swap example clearly illustrates, the rights and obligations which make up the financial system are often structurally interdependent. We would thus expect changes in one part of the system to precipitate changes elsewhere. Perhaps most importantly, changes in public law and regulation can spur private contractual and institutional innovation. These private innovations can also drive changes in the law: whether in order to ensure these innovations' enforceability or to ameliorate their harmful effects. As Katharina Pistor has observed, law and finance are thus engaged in a dynamic process in which private contracts and rules emerge and evolve in response

[24] Katharina Pistor, 'Towards a Legal Theory of Finance' (2013) European Corporate Governance Institute Law Working Paper No 196 <http://www.ecgi.org> 8.

[25] See Glenn Morgan, 'Market Formation and Governance in International Financial Markets: The Case of OTC Derivatives' (2008) 61 Human Relations 637.

[26] See Dan Awrey, 'The Limits of Private Ordering Within Modern Financial Markets' (2015) 34:1 Review of Banking and Financial Law 183.

[27] See Mark Roe, 'The Derivatives Players' Payment Priorities as Financial Crisis Accelerator' (2011) 63 Stanford Law Review 539. Until recently, swaps have also been effectively exempt from public securities laws in a number of core jurisdictions.

[28] See, for example, Title VII of the Dodd-Frank Wall Street Reform and Consumer Protection Act, Pub L No 111-203, § 971, 124 Stat 1376 (2010) (Dodd-Frank).

to changes in public laws, and in which public laws respond to the problems generated by these innovations.[29] Viewed from this perspective, the law becomes of first order importance in terms of explaining the behaviour and interactions of market participants and, ultimately, the structure of the financial system.[30] By effectively ignoring the law, mainstream economics has thus deprived itself of a potentially important variable for understanding why the structure of the financial system changes over time and, thus, the causes of financial instability.

All this is not to suggest that conventional economics has not made a significant contribution to our understanding of the financial system and of the causes of financial instability. What it does do, however, is highlight the importance of theoretical choices and the inherent dangers of excluding important explanatory variables. As Milton Friedman suggested, these choices are ultimately what demarcate the thin line between the 'crackpot' and the 'scientist'.[31] From Friedman's positivist perspective, however, the exclusion of important explanatory variables is essentially unproblematic so long as the relevant theory possesses strong predictive power. Following this logic, the best theories are those which generate the most accurate predictions on the basis of the fewest number of independent variables.[32] Inevitably, however, this logic leaves such theories vulnerable to changes in underlying causal dynamics, and to interdependencies between different and potentially excluded variables. Yet understanding these dynamics and interdependencies is often of clear theoretical and practical importance. Indeed, if a variable such as the law is both important and evolving, then a theory which abstracts away from this variable is unlikely to be highly predictive over any significant period of time.[33]

We thus return to our original question: what is the relationship between law and financial instability? Drawing on examples from the recent financial crisis, the remainder of this section examines in very broad terms three ways in which the law can contribute to financial instability. This examination is not intended to be exhaustive. Rather, it is designed to provide the foundation for our subsequent exploration of the impact this relationship in terms of the optimal institutional structure of financial regulation.

[29] Pistor (n *) 315. [30] ibid at 3.

[31] See Milton Friedman, 'The Methodology of Positive Economics' in *Essays in Positive Economics* (University of Chicago Press 1966) 25. For a critique of Friedman's positivist methodology, see Dieter Helm, 'Predictions and Causes: A Comparison of Friedman and Hicks on Method' (1984) 36 Oxford Economic Papers 118.

[32] Friedman (n 31).

[33] Implicit within this idea is the possibility that a variable which was previously unimportant can, owing to a change of circumstances, subsequently become very important indeed.

(a) Regulatory Arbitrage

As described above, changes in public law and regulation can spur private innovation. This type of innovation—often referred to as 'regulatory arbitrage'—can be understood as a product of the competitive forces at the heart of a global market economy. These forces compel market participants to identify and pursue strategies designed to minimize the private costs imposed by public law and regulation across the range of activities and jurisdictions in which they operate. Broadly speaking, these strategies involve either the development of new contractual or institutional structures which reduce the impact of this law and regulation, or shifting activities to financial markets or institutions subject to less burdensome legal or regulatory regimes. In effect, these strategies seek to exploit inconsistencies between the economic function of a contractual or institutional structure and its legal or regulatory treatment.[34]

Importantly, where these strategies prove successful, the same competitive forces which provided the initial impetus for this regulatory arbitrage also incentivize other market participants to imitate it. This imitation can result in market participants pursuing highly correlated arbitrage strategies: driving the flow of capital and risk into potentially less well developed, poorly regulated segments of the financial system. These flows can contribute to financial instability in a number of ways. First, the flow of capital and risk into the darker corners of the financial system—or even just across national borders—can make it considerably more costly for regulatory authorities to engage in effective oversight. As a result, these authorities may be in a relatively poor position to identify, monitor, or respond to potential threats to financial stability. Second, large one-way flows of capital and risk can themselves be a source of instability—especially where these flows are followed by rapid, uncoordinated reversals. Third, where the markets and institutions into which this capital and risk are channelled involve greater leverage or higher levels of credit, maturity, or liquidity transformation than those from which they originated, these flows can be understood as increasing the fragility of the financial system.

The development and growth of US structured finance markets in the years prior to the recent financial crisis provides a compelling example of how regulatory arbitrage can contribute to financial instability. Structured finance or 'securitization' is a process whereby the cash flows generated by illiquid assets such as mortgages and loans are pooled together, restructured, and sold as more liquid asset-backed securities (ABS). As documented by David Jones,

[34] See Victor Fleischer, 'Regulatory Arbitrage' (2011) 88 Texas Law Review 227.

the structure of US securitization markets prior to the crisis was characterized by three core features.[35] The first feature was the sale of loans from originating lenders or sponsoring dealers to bankruptcy remote 'special purpose vehicles' (SPVs). In theory, the banks and other financial institutions which originated the underlying loans could achieve many of the economic benefits of structured finance by issuing 'covered' bonds secured against the underlying loan pool. In practice, however, securitization typically took place though SPVs which both held the loans and issued ABS to investors. In many cases, SPVs were also used to make the underlying loans: so-called 'remote origination'. Amongst other implications, the sale of loans to SPVs had the effect of removing these assets from the balance sheets of both the originating lenders and sponsoring dealers for regulatory and financial reporting purposes.

The second feature was structural subordination. Structural subordination involves the allocation of losses experienced by the underlying loan pool amongst different species—or 'tranches'—of ABS issued by an SPV. The relationship between the different tranches is often described in terms of a waterfall: with tranches higher up in the waterfall entitled to repayment before those further toward the bottom. In effect, structural subordination contemplates that the first losses in a loan pool up to a specified threshold will be allocated to the bottom or 'junior' tranche, while any subsequent losses will be absorbed by progressively more 'senior' tranches further up the SPV's capital structure. Each junior tranche thus serves as a form of credit enhancement for more senior tranches.[36]

The third and in many respects most important feature of structured finance was and is its financing model. Sponsoring dealers typically finance the acquisition of loans from originating lenders via their wholesale funding operations.[37] SPVs, meanwhile, finance the purchase or origination of loans by issuing asset-backed commercial paper (ABCP) to institutional investors.[38] SPVs can also use ABCP to bridge any liquidity mismatch between the cash flows generated by the loan pool and scheduled payments of principal and interest to ABS investors. To protect investors against liquidity shortfalls stemming from the breakdown of the ABCP market, sponsoring dealers then typically provide backstop guarantees often referred to as 'liquidity puts'.[39]

[35] See David Jones, 'Emerging Problems with the Basel Capital Accord: Regulatory Capital Arbitrage and Related Issues' (2000) 24 Journal of Banking and Finance 35.

[36] ibid.

[37] See Zoltan Pozsar, Tobias Adrian, Adam Ashcraft, and Hayley Boesky, 'Shadow Banking' (2013) 19:2 Federal Reserve Bank of New York Economic Policy Review 1.

[38] Jones (n 35).

[39] In a comprehensive survey of the US ABCP market just prior to the financial crisis, Viral Acharya, Phillip Schnabl, and Gustavo Suarez found that approximately 74 per cent of ABCP was

This financing model is notable for two reasons. First, sponsoring dealers and SPVs rely on relatively liquid, short-term liabilities in the form of ABCP and other wholesale funding to finance the holding of illiquid, longer-term loans and to make payments to ABS investors. Structured finance thus involves significant levels of credit, maturity, and liquidity transformation. Second, despite historically being characterized as 'off-balance sheet' items for regulatory and accounting purposes, the provision of liquidity puts to SPVs exposes sponsoring dealers to the risk of disruption within ABCP and other wholesale funding markets.

Between 1985 and 2008, the total outstanding amount of ABS issued and outstanding in the US grew from approximately $1.2 billion to over $1.9 *trillion*.[40] There is little doubt that this growth reflected the significant economic benefits of structured finance.[41] At the same time, however, it also reflected the fact that financial institutions exploited structured finance for the purposes of regulatory arbitrage. Indeed, the core features of structured finance—the use of bankruptcy remote SPVs and remote origination, tranching, and liquidity puts—were each used by originating lenders and sponsoring dealers to reduce their regulatory capital charges under Basel II.[42] David Jones, for example, has demonstrated how financial institutions could in certain circumstances use these features to reduce the risk weighting on a full resource whole loan from 100 per cent to 0 per cent.[43] Predictably, the resulting capital treatment in many cases did not reflect these institutions' economic exposure to the underlying assets. This was particularly the case where sponsoring dealers provided SPVs with backstop liquidity puts or other guarantees, thus effectively shifting the tail risk associated with the breakdown of wholesale funding markets from ABCP and ABS investors to sponsoring dealers.[44]

The core features of structured finance played an important role in the thick of the recent financial crisis. As a preliminary matter, the information problems stemming from the use of bankruptcy remote, off-balance sheet SPVs served to reduce the intensity of both regulatory oversight and market-based discipline imposed on originating lenders and sponsoring dealers. These information problems were often exacerbated by the use of complex

covered by these liquidity or credit guarantees; Viral Acharya, Phillip Schnabl, and Gustavo Suarez, 'Securitization Without Risk Transfer' (2013) 107 Journal of Financial Economics 515.

[40] Securities Industry and Financial Markets Association, 'US ABS Issued and Outstanding' (updated as of 5 January 2015) <http://www.sifma.org>. Figures exclude agency ABS.

[41] For a description of these benefits, see Gary Gorton and George Pennacchi, 'Financial Intermediaries and Liquidity Creation' (1990) 45:1 Journal of Finance 49.

[42] See Acharya, Schnabl, and Suarez (n 39) and Jones (n 35). [43] Jones (n 35).

[44] See Darrell Duffie, 'The Failure Mechanics of Dealer Banks' (2010) 24:1 Journal of Economic Perspectives 51.

tranche structures.[45] The use of SPVs also necessitated the reliance on fragile wholesale funding, leaving SPVs vulnerable to widespread market disruption.[46] Compounding matters, when wholesale funding markets broke down during the crisis, the liquidity puts and other guarantees provided by sponsoring dealers to SPVs created enormous 'wrong way' risk: putting immense pressure on dealers at a time when their balance sheets were already under considerable strain. Indeed, as Zoltan Pozsar and others have observed, these guarantees were one of the primary mechanisms by which the disruption within the ABCP market spread to dealers and, ultimately, the broader financial system.[47]

Viewed from this perspective, insofar as the widespread use of bankruptcy remote SPVs, remote origination, structural subordination, and liquidity puts were motivated by the desire to minimize the impact of the risk-weighted capital requirements imposed under Basel II, regulation can be seen as having been a significant driver of transaction structures which, with the benefit of hindsight, clearly contributed to financial instability. What is more, the relationship between regulatory arbitrage and financial instability is far from unique to structured finance. The emergence, growth, and eventual instability of US money market funds, for example, followed a broadly similar pattern.[48] Looking forward, the dramatic growth of the Chinese shadow banking system in the wake of the crisis may eventually pose comparable problems.[49]

(b) Contractual Inflexibility

A second way in which the law and legal institutions can contribute to financial instability stems from contractual inflexibility in states of the world where the costs of *ex post* renegotiation are prohibitively high. It is all but inevitable that the contracts written by market participants will fail to identify every potential future state of the world, let alone prescribe the optimal constellation of rights and obligations in each state. At the same time, market participants are unlikely to possess high-powered incentives to address the potential negative externalities which the exercise of these rights or performance of these obligations may impose on third parties. The combination

[45] Robert Barlett III, 'Inefficiencies in the Information Thicket: A Case Study of Derivatives Disclosures During the Financial Crisis' (2010) 36:1 Journal of Corporation Law 1.

[46] Pozsar et al. (n 37). [47] ibid.

[48] See Alton Gilbert, 'Requiem for Regulation Q: What It Did and Why It Passed Away' (1986) Federal Reserve Bank of St. Louis Review 22 <http://research.stlouisfed.org> and Timothy Cook and Jeremy Duffield, 'Money Market Mutual Funds: A Reaction to Government Regulation or a Lasting Innovation?' (1979) 65 Federal Reserve Bank of Richmond Economic Review 15.

[49] Awrey, 'Law and Finance in the Chinese Shadow Banking System' (n *).

of contractual incompleteness and potential externalities can lead to structural rigidity: erecting substantial barriers to *ex post* renegotiation in response to changing circumstances, or with a view to preventing financial instability.[50] This inflexibility is often compounded by acute coordination problems, especially where claims are dispersed amongst a large number of market participants.[51]

Perhaps the most straightforward example of how this inflexibility can trigger instability arises form the contractual rights of bank depositors to withdraw their savings on demand. While the exercise of these rights in response to the perception that a bank is on the brink of failure may be individually rational, the correlated exercise of these rights brings with it the risk of a destabilizing bank run. Writing a complete state-contingent contract amongst all the relevant stakeholders to address this problem is not a realistic option. Neither is real-time judicial intervention to fill the contractual gaps and prevent instability. The most common solution to this problem is thus for public authorities to intervene through the provision of lender of last resort programmes and deposit guarantee schemes. Notably, however, the moral hazard generated by these public regulatory interventions can itself contribute to financial instability by incentivizing socially excessive risk-taking.

The failure of global insurance giant AIG during the recent crisis offers another example of how contractual inflexibility can contribute to financial instability. The proximate cause of AIG's failure was the activities of its subsidiary AIG Financial Products (AIGFP).[52] AIGFP was an important player in the growing CDS market, with an overall derivatives exposure of $2.66 trillion in 2007, including a significant exposure to collateralized debt obligations (CDOs) linked to the US subprime mortgage market.[53] The CDS contracts underwritten by AIG typically contemplated that the counterparties would collateralize their residual net exposures to one another. Importantly, they also contemplated that one counterparty could require the other to post additional collateral upon the occurrence of certain prescribed trigger events. These trigger events included a downgrade in the credit rating of a

[50] See Kate Judge, 'Fragmentation Nodes: A Study in Financial Innovation, Complexity and Systemic Risk' (2012) 64 Stanford Law Review 657 and Anna Gelpern and Adam Levitin, 'Rewriting Frankenstein Contracts: Workout Prohibitions in Residential Mortgage-Backed Securities' (2009) 82 Southern California Law Review 1075.

[51] Judge; Gelpern and Levitin ibid.

[52] See Congressional Oversight Panel, 'The AIG Rescue, Its Impact on Markets, and the Government's Exit Strategy' (10 June 2010) Oversight Report 19–33.

[53] ibid 23.

counterparty, a downgrade in the credit rating of the underlying CDOs, and a decrease in the market value of these CDOs or other reference obligations.[54]

The deterioration of the US subprime mortgage market in 2007–08 predictably led to a marked decrease in the liquidity and market value of CDOs linked to subprime assets, along with downgrades in these CDOs' credit ratings. These developments precipitated demands from AIG's CDS counterparties for additional collateral. These collateral calls put pressure on AIG's cash position, ultimately resulting in a downgrade in AIG's own credit rating, thereby triggering further collateral calls. In the end, Goldman Sachs, Société Générale, Deutsche Bank, and other counterparties demanded over $30 billion in additional collateral from AIG in the months leading up to its failure.[55] Together with the corresponding run by AIG's securities lending counterparties, these collateral calls had the effect of draining liquidity from AIG during a period of extreme market volatility.[56] Notably, much like conventional bank runs, these uncoordinated demands for additional collateral helped to effectively bring about a result which—in the absence of massive government intervention[57]—would have left these counterparties in the disadvantageous position of being unsecured creditors in the estate of AIG. Contractual collateral triggers under these CDS contracts thus played an important role in AIG's failure. What is more, these eve-of-bankruptcy collateral calls would likely not have been legally enforceable had it not been for the carveouts enjoyed by CDS and other swaps from the automatic stay and fraudulent preference provisions under US bankruptcy laws.

AIG's instability was triggered by a relatively small number of its outstanding CDS contracts: 125 out of a total of approximately 44,000.[58] Looking forward, however, it is not difficult to envision any number of circumstances in which the high degree of contractual standardization associated with CDS, swaps, and many other financial contracts could in theory trigger or exacerbate even more widespread instability as market participants—responding to similar incentive structures—pursued correlated strategies which, while individually rational, had the collective effect of destabilizing one or more systemically important markets or institutions.[59]

[54] ibid 29. [55] Roe (n 27). [56] Congressional Oversight Panel (n 52) 19–33.

[57] It is also notable that the economic effect of this public intervention, like deposit insurance, was to make the parties which triggered the run whole (in the case of AIG by purchasing the assets underlying the CDS); see ibid at 73–77.

[58] ibid at 24. [59] Pistor (n *) 326.

(c) Law and Moneyness

A third way in which the law can play a role in fomenting financial instability is by providing for the differential legal treatment of financial claims used as economic substitutes for money. During periods of relative certainty and ample liquidity, one could be forgiven for thinking that the financial system was essentially flat. This 'flatness' would manifest itself in at least two ways. First, we would observe relatively tight credit spreads between financial claims issued by borrowers of varying degrees of creditworthiness. Second, and as a corollary, we would observe many financial claims issued by *private* borrowers being viewed as effective substitutes for both fiat money and sovereign debt. Indeed, as Gary Gorton, Andrew Metrick, and others have noted, this is precisely what we observed within wholesale funding, derivatives, and other markets during the heady days leading up to the global financial crisis.[60]

One of the potential explanations for this expanded conception of 'moneyness' is that during these periods of high market confidence and stability, market participants discount the importance of differences in the legal treatment of substitute financial claims which only have an impact on outcomes in adverse states of the world. These laws generally fall into one of two categories. The first category includes those laws which apply in the vicinity of, at, or following a firm's insolvency. This category includes, for example, general corporate insolvency laws. The second category includes those laws which relax the constraints—or otherwise substitute for the application—of these insolvency laws. Examples of legal regimes falling into the second category include lender of last resort facilities, deposit guarantee schemes, and special resolution regimes for banks and other financial institutions. Also included are financial collateral rules and carveouts from automatic stay and fraudulent preference rules for derivatives and repurchase agreements which together facilitate closeout netting.

Once again, demand deposits provide an illustrative example of the impact of these legal regimes. We tend to think of demand deposits as economically equivalent to legal tender—literally as 'cash in the bank'.[61] In reality, however, demand deposits are often unsecured contractual liabilities owed by the bank to its depositors. In most states of the world, this distinction has little practical importance: we use cash and bank deposits interchangeably in our everyday lives. Where a bank finds itself on the brink of insolvency, however,

[60] See Gary Gorton and Guillermo Ordonez, 'Collateral Crises' (2014) 104:2 American Economic Review 343 and Gary Gorton and Andrew Metrick, 'Securitized Banking and the Run on Repo' (2013) 104:3 Journal of Financial Economics 425.

[61] For an example of this view in legal scholarship, see Robert Proctor (ed), *Good on Payment Obligations in Commercial and Financial Transactions* (Sweet & Maxwell 2009) 6.

this distinction—essentially between the highly secure property rights in cash and the unsecured contractual rights of a depositor against a potentially insolvent bank—becomes highly determinative of both the value of these otherwise equivalent claims and, ultimately, the behaviour of depositors. While in 'good' states of the world the financial system may appear relatively flat, the revealed preferences of depositors in seeking to withdraw their deposits in 'bad' states thus reveal its inherent legally constructed hierarchy.

Most jurisdictions attempt to resolve this problem as it exists in relation to demand deposits by providing some form of deposit guarantee scheme. In effect, these schemes strive to ensure that depositors can transform their unsecured deposits into cold hard cash in adverse states of the world, thus legally engineering near perfect economic substitutability and disincentivizing destabilizing run-like behaviour.[62] In many other financial markets and institutions, however, where the functional equivalent of deposit insurance is not available, the tendency of market participants to discount differences in the legal treatment of substitute financial claims in adverse states of the world can contribute to instability. Perhaps most importantly, this discounting can contribute to what should by now be a familiar pattern of capital flowing into relatively fragile markets and institutions during periods of high market confidence, only to flow out in a rapid, uncoordinated, and destabilizing fashion during periods of market uncertainty or turmoil as market participants shift capital into safer, more stable markets and institutions farther up the hierarchy. Looking back at the recent crisis, instability within both money market funds[63] and the market for repurchase (or 'repo') agreements[64]—both of which emerged as substitutes for conventional bank deposits—can be viewed as illustrative of this pattern. Looking ahead, the rise of peer-to-peer payment systems such as PayPal, crypto-currency exchanges, and so-called 'mobile money' platforms may cause similar problems insofar as they perform storage and liquidity functions equivalent to demand deposits without benefiting from deposit insurance schemes, emergency liquidity assistance programmes, and other prudential regulatory regimes supporting conventional deposit-taking banks.[65]

[62] Of course, the extent to which individual deposit guarantee schemes actually achieve this objective is a function of institutional design. For example, the UK's deposit guarantee scheme prior to the crisis has been widely criticized for its relatively low cap and the use of depositor co-insurance; see Armour et al. (n *) Chapter 12.

[63] ibid Chapter 20.

[64] See Gorton and Metrick (n 60).

[65] See Dan Awrey and Kristin van Zwieten, 'Law and Liquidity in the Shadow Payment System' (2015) (working paper on file with authors).

The objective of this section has not been to offer an exhaustive account of the myriad of ways in which the law can contribute to financial instability. Nor is it to argue that, in any of these cases, the law is the most important variable in triggering or exacerbating instability. Rather, it is simply to point out the fact that the law is an important and often neglected part of the story. By paying closer attention to contractual, legislative, and regulatory frameworks which together comprise the structure of the financial system, we may therefore be able to better understand the causes of financial instability.

5. Law and Financial Instability: Implications for the Institutional Structure of Financial Regulation

The relationship between law and financial stability explored in the previous section has a number of important policy implications. Perhaps most importantly, it provides regulatory authorities with a useful framework for understanding what types of information to collect from market participants, where to look within the financial system for potential sources of systemic risk, and, ultimately, how their own substantive policy decisions may have an impact on financial stability. This relationship also has potentially important implications in terms of the institutional structure of financial regulation. The global financial crisis was viewed by many as exposing fundamental weaknesses in the institutional structure of financial regulation in many jurisdictions. In the US, for example, the emergence of gaps in its highly fragmented regulatory structure was seen as allowing the risks generated by the growth of wholesale funding, structured finance, and derivatives markets to go largely unchecked.[66] In the UK, the integrated management structure of the FSA was widely perceived as leading to its myopic focus on conduct of business regulation at the expense of prudential supervision.[67] And in the EU, the loosely structured Lamfalussy 'Level 3' committees were exposed as fundamentally inoperable under the strains of a complex and rapidly evolving cross-border crisis.[68] More broadly, regulatory authorities on both sides of the Atlantic failed to adopt a coordinated approach toward the identification, monitoring, and response to potential threats to financial stability.

[66] Financial Crisis Inquiry Commission, *Final Report of the National Commission on the Causes of the Financial and Economic Crisis in the United States* (US Government Printing Office 2011).

[67] FSA, *The Turner Review, A Regulatory Response to the Global Banking Crisis* (March 2009) 7.

[68] See 'Report of the High Level Group on Financial Supervision in the EU' (February 2009) <http://www.ec.europa.eu>.

In the wake of the crisis, policy-makers have adopted a number of institutional reforms designed to address these perceived weaknesses. In the US, the FSOC has been established in order to improve coordination and information flow amongst the Federal Reserve Board, Federal Deposit Insurance Corporation (FDIC), Securities and Exchange Commission (SEC), Commodity Futures Trading Commission (CFTC), and other federal agencies. The FSOC's mandate includes the collection of information from regulatory authorities, monitoring potential threats to financial stability, identifying gaps in regulation which could pose risks to financial stability, and making recommendations to US lawmakers and regulatory authorities.[69] It also serves as a forum for the resolution of jurisdictional disputes among FSOC members. While the FSOC does not have direct responsibility for the oversight of regulated markets or institutions, it is responsible for designating systemically important non-bank financial institutions, financial market utilities, and payment, clearing, and settlement activities.[70] It is also responsible for approving decisions of the Federal Reserve Board to restrict the activities of, mandate the disposal of assets owned by, or shut down, firms which pose a 'grave threat' to financial stability.[71]

In the UK, the post-crisis reforms targeting the institutional structure of financial regulation have been far more fundamental in nature. The FSA has been abolished and its responsibilities divided up between the Bank of England and two new regulatory authorities: the Prudential Regulatory Authority (PRA) and Financial Conduct Authority (FCA). Under this objectives-based 'twin peaks'[72] structure, the PRA—a subsidiary of the Bank of England—is responsible for the prudential regulation of banks, insurance companies, and other complex investment firms. The FCA, meanwhile, is responsible for conduct of business regulation across all regulated firms. This new institutional structure thus contemplates that many firms will be regulated by both the PRA and FCA. Crucially in this regard, the PRA is empowered to restrict the FCA from taking any action with respect to a firm authorized by the PRA where it believes that such action would either threaten financial stability or result in the failure of a firm authorized by the PRA in a way which would have an adverse impact on the UK financial system.[73] Finally, in response to perceived failures of macroprudential oversight in the run up to the crisis, a new Financial Policy Committee (FPC) has been created under the auspices of the Bank of England. Like the FSOC, the Bank of England and FPC have

[69] Dodd-Frank s 112. [70] ibid ss 112, 113. [71] ibid s 121.

[72] See Michael Taylor, *Twin Peaks: A Regulatory Structure for a New Century* (Centre for the Study of Financial Innovation 1995).

[73] Financial Services Act 2012, c 21, s 3I.

been charged with responsibility for identifying, monitoring, and responding to potential threats to financial stability.[74] The FPC has also been given explicit authority to direct the FCA and PRA to exercise their functions so as to ensure the implementation of measures designed to protect financial stability.[75]

Like the UK, the EU has also undertaken a number of fundamental institutional reforms in the wake of the financial crisis. As part of these reforms, the Lamfalussy Level 3 committees have been replaced by three pan-European ESAs: the European Securities and Markets Authority (ESMA), European Banking Authority (EBA), and European Insurance and Occupational Pension Authority (EIOPA). Unlike their predecessors, these ESAs have been given the power to write legally binding technical standards in several areas.[76] Once endorsed by the European Commission, these standards have the status of regulations or decisions under EU law.

Joining these new authorities within Europe's institutional architecture is the European Systemic Risk Board (ESRB). The ESRB is responsible for macroprudential oversight of the European financial system and, in this capacity, for identifying, monitoring, and assessing potential systemic risks.[77] Unlike the three ESAs, however, the ESRB has very few formal legal powers. In effect, its powers are limited to issuing recommendations and warnings to European institutions, member states, and national supervisory authorities.[78] These powers are supported by the imposition of a comply or explain obligation on all recipients.[79] If the ESRB is not satisfied with any explanation it receives, it can then refer the matter to the European Council, the European Parliament's Economic and Monetary Affairs Committee or, where appropriate, the EBA, ESMA, or EIOPA.[80] It can also make its recommendations or warnings public.

The creation of the ESAs and ESRB represents a significant shift in the institutional structure of financial regulation within the EU. Arguably of far greater significance, however, has been the creation of the so-called 'European

[74] ibid ss 2, 9A, 9C, and 9G. [75] ibid s 9H.

[76] See Directive 2010/78/EU of the European Parliament and of the Council of 24 November 2010 amending Directives 98/26/EC, 2002/87/EC, 2003/6/EC, 2003/41/EC, 2003/71/EC, 2004/39/EC, 2004/109/EC, 2005/60/EC, 2006/48/EC, 2006/49/EC, and 2009/65/EC in respect of the powers of the European Supervisory Authority (European Banking Authority), the European Supervisory Authority (European Insurance and Occupational Pensions Authority) and the European Supervisory Authority (European Securities and Markets Authority) Text with EEA relevance.

[77] See Regulation (EU) No 1092/2010 of the European Parliament and of the Council of 24 November 2010 on European Union macro-prudential oversight of the financial system and establishing a European Systemic Risk Board, Art 3(1).

[78] ibid Art 16. [79] ibid Art 17(1). [80] ibid Art 17(2).

Banking Union'. The European Commission (EC) has framed the creation of the Banking Union as a response to three intertwined problems.[81] The first problem stems from the EC's attempts to promote the development of a single market in financial services within the EU, and the resulting increase in both the number and size of cross-border banks and other financial institutions in recent decades.[82] The costs of supervising these complex and interconnected institutions are extremely high. Moreover, as became clear during the financial crisis, the cross-border operations of these institutions can become channels for the transmission of risk from one jurisdiction to another. The second problem stems from the historical fragmentation of responsibility for supervising cross-border banks and other financial institutions amongst national supervisors. These supervisors often possess very different levels of institutional capacity, resulting in dramatic differences in the intensity of prudential supervision. Compounding matters, 'home' and 'host' supervisors often possess radically divergent incentives, thereby undermining effective cross-border coordination and crisis response. Third, and perhaps most importantly, the European sovereign debt crisis demonstrated the existence of pernicious feedback effects between the financial health of banks and other financial institutions and the fiscal health of the sovereign states in which these institutions are established and upon which they rely for both explicit and implicit support.

The Banking Union introduces two principal mechanisms designed to address these problems. The first is the Single Supervisory Mechanism (SSM).[83] The SSM grants the European Central Bank (ECB) exclusive competency to perform a number of specified tasks in relation to the prudential supervision of Eurozone banks.[84] These tasks include the authorization of banks,[85] monitoring their compliance with prudential regulatory requirements,[86]

[81] See EC, *A Roadmap Towards a Banking Union* (COM 2012) 510 <http://eur-lex.europa.eu/legal-content/EN/TXT/?uri=CELEX:52012DC0510>.

[82] For a detailed discussion of the growth trend and determinants of cross-border banking in Europe, see Franklin Allen, Thorsten Beck, Elena Carletti, Philip Lane, Dirk Schoenmaker, and Wolf Wagner, *Cross-Border Banking in Europe: Implications for Financial Stability and Macroeconomic Policies* (Centre for Economic Policy Research 2011) Chapter 2.

[83] The EC has recently announced plans to introduce a third mechanism—a single European deposit guarantee scheme; see 'A Stronger Banking Union: New Measures to Reinforce Deposit Protection and Further Reduce Banking Risks' (EC 24 November 2015) <http://europa.eu/rapid/press-release_IP-15-6152_en.htm>.

[84] Council Regulation (EU) No 1024/2013 conferring specific tasks on the European Central Bank concerning policies relating to the prudential supervision of credit institutions (15 October 2013) (the 'SSM Regulation'), Art 4(1).

[85] ibid Arts 4(1)(a) and 14 and Recital 20.

[86] ibid Arts 4(1)(d) and 4(1)(e). European law for these purposes includes European directives, national laws transposing these directives, and European regulations with direct application to member states; ibid Art 4(3).

conducting supervisory reviews and stress tests,[87] and carrying out supervisory tasks in relation to recovery plans.[88] The SSM operates on the basis of a dual track—or 'differentiated'—supervisory system. Under this system, the ECB is responsible for setting the supervisory handbook for all credit institutions established in the Eurozone.[89] The ECB is then *directly* responsible for the supervision of a relatively small number of these banks—currently 123—deemed to be systemically 'significant'.[90] For banks not deemed systemically significant, the ECB's role is restricted to overseeing the consistent application of the single handbook by national supervisors.[91] At the same time, the ECB has the power to assume direct supervisory responsibility for these 'less significant' banks in certain specified circumstances.[92]

Viewed in isolation, the creation of the SSM drives a jurisdictional wedge between responsibility for the prudential *supervision* of the Eurozone's largest banks and the legal and fiscal responsibility for their *resolution*. In designing the Banking Union, however, the European Council was constrained by Article 127(6) of the Treaty on the Functioning of the European Union, which only empowers it to confer tasks on the ECB relating specifically to 'prudential supervision'. This necessitated the creation of a second mechanism, independent of the ECB, and founded on a separate legal basis. This mechanism would become known as the Single Resolution Mechanism (SRM).[93] The SRM shifts responsibility for the resolution of banks supervised directly by the ECB from national resolution authorities to a newly created Single Resolution Board (SRB). Under the oversight of the EC and European Council, the SRB then has access to a wide range of tools designed to rehabilitate, restructure, or wind down failing banks. It will also ultimately have access to a €55 billion resolution fund capitalized by contributions from the banking industry.

There is little doubt that the creation of the Banking Union, ESRB, ESAs, FPC, and FSOC have significantly altered the institutional structure of financial regulation in the EU, UK, and US. Yet the question remains: will these multiple institutional reforms serve to promote financial stability? The remainder of this section explores what insights our earlier examination of the

[87] ibid Art 4(f). [88] ibid Art 4(1)(i). [89] ibid Art 6(5)(a).

[90] ibid Art 6(4). [91] ibid Arts 6(5) and 6(6).

[92] First, the ECB may unilaterally deem a credit institution to be of systemic significance where it has established banking subsidiaries in two or more participating member states and its cross-border assets or liabilities represent a significant component of its total assets; ibid Art 6(4). Second, the ECB may, after consulting with national supervisors, assume direct supervisory responsibility for less significant credit institutions where it deems it necessary in order to ensure the consistent application of high supervisory standards; ibid Art 6(5)(b).

[93] See Regulation (EU) No 806/2014 establishing uniform rules and a uniform procedure for the resolution of credit institutions and certain investment firms (15 July 2014).

relationship between law and financial instability might hold out in relation to this all-important question.

(a) Regulatory 'Labels' versus 'Objectives'

The institutional structure of financial regulation in most jurisdictions has historically reflected distinctions between different categories of financial institutions, markets, and products. These distinctions have given rise to a wide range of institutional structures characterized by the fragmentation of regulatory oversight amongst multiple specialist regulatory authorities. The so-called 'institutional' model, for example, contemplates the division of regulatory responsibility on the basis of distinctions between different types of firms: for example, banks, brokerage firms, or insurance companies. The 'functional' model, in contrast, contemplates the division of responsibility on the basis of distinctions between different financial activities: for example, deposit-taking, commercial lending, mortgage underwriting, or derivatives trading. While the distinctions between these different models are often blurred in practice, they ultimately share the same fundamental characteristic. Specifically, each of these models allocates regulatory responsibility—and with it, in many instances, the applicable substantive regulatory regime—on the basis of a legally constructed *label*: whether it be a 'bank', 'broker-dealer', 'security', 'future', or other similar regulatory construct.

The complex institutional structure of financial regulation in the US prior to the financial crisis perhaps best epitomizes this labels-based approach. Responsibility for the oversight of federally chartered 'banks', for example, fell to the Federal Reserve Board in conjunction with the FDIC and Office of the Comptroller of the Currency. Concomitantly, however, another federal agency—the now defunct Office of Thrift Supervision—was responsible for the oversight of a specific type of bank known as a 'thrift' or 'savings and loan'. In the area of capital markets regulation, meanwhile, oversight was split between the SEC and CFTC on the basis of what were often hard to parse distinctions between 'securities' and 'futures'.[94] From 2004 to 2008, the SEC was also responsible for the prudential supervision of several large investment

[94] See Willa Gibson, 'Are Swaps Agreements Securities or Futures? The Inadequacies of Applying the Traditional Regulatory Approach to OTC Derivatives Transactions' (1999) 24 Journal of Corporation Law 379; Thomas Russo and Marlisa Vinciguerra, 'Financial Innovation and Uncertain Regulation: Selected Issues Regarding New Product Development' (1990) 69 Texas Law Review 1431; and David Gilberg, 'Regulation of New Financial Instruments Under the Federal Securities and Commodities Laws' (1986) 39 Vanderbilt Law Review 1599.

banks under the Consolidated Supervised Entities (CSE) programme by virtue of their status as 'broker dealers'.[95]

The crisis brought the shortcomings of such labels-based approaches into sharp relief. At their core, these shortcomings stem from the inability of these approaches to keep up with the pace of financial innovation and, specifically, the development of new markets and institutions which blur the lines between traditional 'banking', 'securities', 'insurance', and other regulatory constructs. The emergence and growth of structured finance, for example, has both strengthened and rendered more complex the relationships between retail and commercial banking, securities markets, and wholesale funding markets. Many derivatives, meanwhile, simultaneously exhibit characteristics of securities, insurance, and debt instruments. And while money market mutual funds may be structured as investment funds, their functions—and risks—largely mirror those of conventional deposit-taking banks.

These and other similar developments pose a number of potentially significant regulatory challenges. First, as vividly demonstrated by the growth of structured finance, derivatives markets, and money market mutual funds in the decades leading up to the crisis, the inevitable gaps in regulation created by these labels provide fertile ground for regulatory arbitrage. As we have seen, this arbitrage can sow the seeds of financial instability. Second, the regulatory path dependence created by these labels can result in the allocation of responsibility to regulatory authorities with little established expertise in a particular type of regulation or supervision. The allocation of responsibility for the oversight of large investment banks under the CSE programme to the SEC—a capital markets regulator with almost no expertise in micro-prudential supervision—is a glaring example how this path dependence can contribute to suboptimal outcomes. Third, insofar as more than one label can theoretically be applied to a given market or institution, the resulting overlap of regulatory responsibility can give rise to turf wars such as the one amongst the SEC, CFTC, and Federal Reserve Board over the regulation of OTC derivatives. Conversely, the use of these labels runs the risk of framing how regulatory authorities view the scope of their responsibilities, with the possible result that no authority sees itself as having primary responsibility for new market developments or financial stability. Finally, and perhaps most importantly, the fragmentation of responsibility under labels-based approaches makes it more difficult for regulatory authorities to see the entire field—thus undermining their ability to identify, monitor, and effectively respond to potential risks at the *system* level.

[95] See Alternative Net Capital Requirements for Broker-Dealers that Are Part of Consolidated Supervised Entities, Exchange Act Release No 34-49830, 69 Fed Reg 34,428 (21 June 2004).

So how well does the recent raft of structural reforms address these challenges? The institutional reforms adopted in the US arguably hold out the most promise.[96] This promise stems from the creation of the FSOC, and the subtle shift it signals towards an institutional structure based not on regulatory labels but the *objective* of promoting financial stability. While the basic allocation of regulatory responsibilities among the phalanx of US regulatory authorities remains essentially intact, the creation of the FSOC can be understood as providing a forum for these authorities to share information with one another, to identify and evaluate potential threats to financial stability, and to coordinate regulatory action in response to these threats. The FSOC also provides a forum for identifying and, theoretically, eliminating gaps or inconsistencies in the regulatory regimes adopted by different regulatory authorities which might otherwise provide the basis for destabilizing regulatory arbitrage. Importantly, once the FSOC has identified a potential threat to financial stability, its authority to designate non-bank financial institutions as 'systemically important' endows it with a potentially powerful tool to subject these institutions to consolidated prudential regulation and supervision under the oversight of the Federal Reserve. The creation of the FSOC thus provides a clear locus of responsibility and authority for the maintenance of financial stability. Accordingly, while it is still far too early to tell whether the FSOC will be able to overcome decades of inter-agency rivalry and suspicion which have often undermined effective coordination, its creation provides some reason for cautious optimism that the institutional structure of financial regulation in the US may now be better aligned with the objective of promoting greater financial stability.

At the other end of the spectrum, arguably, are the structural reforms recently introduced in the EU. As a preliminary matter, the division of responsibilities amongst the EBA and ECB, ESMA, and EIOPA have been drawn up largely along traditional labels-based, 'institutional' lines. While various mechanisms have been established to promote coordination and take forward cross-sectoral issues, this division of regulatory responsibility is nevertheless vulnerable to the emergence of gaps and inconsistencies as financial markets and institutions continue to evolve over time. It is also vulnerable to the same coordination problems and conflicts of interest which plagued the former Lamfalussy Level 3 committees.

[96] While the UK's shift toward a more objectives-based model is also promising, the former FSA's integrated structure meant that regulatory labels were a less pronounced feature of the UK's institutional architecture.

History suggests that these gaps and inconsistencies will be exploited by market participants for the purposes of regulatory arbitrage.[97] Differences in the capital adequacy regimes imposed on European banks and insurance companies, for example, have spurred the development of so-called 'collateral swap' markets, thereby strengthening the economic linkages between the banking and insurance sectors.[98] Compounding matters, while responsibility for the design of substantive regulation has increasingly been allocated to the ESAs, responsibility for supervision and enforcement of this regulation still largely rests with the regulatory authorities in individual member states. This continued fragmentation of regulatory and supervisory responsibility erects potentially significant obstacles to the identification, monitoring, and effective response to threats to financial stability within the EU.

In theory, responsibility for identifying and monitoring these threats falls to the newly created ESRB. Like the FSOC, the ESRB provides a forum for pan-European regulatory information sharing and coordination with the objective of promoting greater financial stability. Unlike the FSOC, however, the ESRB has very few formal legal powers. Indeed, its most potent power is arguably to issue a public warning: a warning which may or may not be heeded by regulatory authorities with the power to take more meaningful action. The ESRB's relative impotence is likely to be compounded by its complex governance structure, which includes voting representatives from each member state, the ECB, and other European agencies. Viewed from this perspective, it seems unrealistic to expect the ESRB to be able to resolve inter-agency (or inter-member state) conflicts, eliminate gaps or inconsistencies between regulatory regimes or, more broadly, to mount an effective response to potential threats to financial stability.

(b) Financial Stability versus Other Regulatory Objectives

The question of whether it is more desirable to allocate regulatory responsibility on the basis of labels or objectives is essentially a question about the optimal *horizontal* structure of financial regulation. Arguably more important, however, is the *vertical* structure. Collectively, the financial regulatory authorities within a given jurisdiction will inevitably be tasked with responsibility for pursuing multiple regulatory objectives. These objectives can include consumer and investor protection, market efficiency, competition,

[97] See Awrey, 'Toward a Supply-side Theory of Financial Regulation' (n *); Fleischer (n 34); Jones (n 35); Gilbert (n 48), and Cook and Duffield (n 48).
[98] Awrey, 'Toward a Supply-side Theory of Financial Regulation' (n *).

the prevention of financial crime, the microprudential safety and soundness of financial institutions and, of course, the maintenance of financial stability.[99] These regulatory authorities—along with their political masters—must then make complex and important decisions about how to allocate their scarce financial, human, and other resources in pursuit of these objectives. In many cases, these objectives may also come into direct conflict with one another: for example, where the imposition of stricter microprudential regulation would introduce barriers to entry which would threaten to undermine vigorous competition. One of the most important roles of financial policymakers is thus to strike a socially desirable balance between what are often competing regulatory objectives.

Crucially, the existence of multiple and potentially competing regulatory objectives does not necessarily mean that all objectives should be accorded equal weight in the process of designing, implementing, and enforcing financial regulation. Indeed, in the wake of the financial crisis, a strong case can be made for viewing the maintenance of financial stability as the most important regulatory objective. This case rests on three principal grounds. The first is the sheer scale and scope of the social harm generated by financial instability. While a true and accurate accounting of the social costs of the financial crisis is all but impossible, most estimates range in the *trillions* of dollars once lost growth and productivity are taken into account.[100] Second, financial stability can be viewed as a condition precedent to the effective pursuit of other regulatory objectives. Put differently, we would expect widespread financial instability to undermine the safety and soundness of individual institutions, weaken levels of consumer and investor protection, and impede effective competition for financial services. Third, unlike many other regulatory objectives, financial stability has no natural (non-regulatory) constituency to champion it. The absence of any natural constituency is especially apparent during periods of economic growth, where none of the financial services industry, consumers of financial products and services, or elected officials are likely to support regulatory intervention which—while potentially avoiding or containing financial instability in the long run—may serve to undercut short-run profits, returns, or tax revenues.

Once we view financial stability as residing at the apex of a hierarchy of regulatory objectives, the next question becomes how this status should be reflected within the institutional structure of financial regulation. One

[99] Armour et al. (n *) Chapter 3.

[100] For an analysis of the costs to the US alone, see for example Tyler Atkinson, David Luttrell, and Harvey Rosenblum, 'How Bad Was It? The Costs and Consequences of the 2007–09 Financial

intuitively appealing approach would simply be to mirror this hierarchy within the institutional structure by allocating responsibility for financial stability to a single regulatory authority and then giving this authority the power to override the policy decisions of other regulatory authorities in the interests of financial stability. Indeed, this approach may be particularly appealing in light of our earlier examination of some of the different ways in which the law can potentially foment financial instability. Thus, for example, this authority could be given the power to compel information from other regulatory authorities and market participants with a view to determining whether regulatory arbitrage or contractual inflexibility posed a potential threat to financial stability. It could also monitor the patterns of use and growth of money-like claims within the financial system. Where this information revealed a potential threat, this authority could then compel other regulatory authorities to close any gaps or inconsistences in their regulatory regimes, redesign regulations which may contribute to future instability, or take other preventative action to address these threats.

Measured against this standard, recent structural reforms in the US once again hold out some not inconsiderable promise. As we have already seen, the creation of the FSOC has introduced a clear locus of responsibility for the maintenance of financial stability within the otherwise highly fragmented US regulatory architecture. Simultaneously, however, the FSOC's primary legal power—the designation of a non-bank financial institution as systemically important—is both somewhat Draconian and, perhaps more significantly, not a particularly well tailored response to many potential threats to financial stability. It is difficult to envisage, for example, how this power could have been employed to proactively address the types of problems which emerged within structured finance, repo, or derivatives markets in the midst of the recent crisis.

Like the FSOC, the creation of the FPC can be understood as introducing a clear locus of responsibility for financial stability within the UK's new regulatory architecture. In this respect, the FPC stands in sharp contrast with the former tripartite agreement on financial stability among the Bank of England, HM Treasury, and FSA,[101] which was widely criticized in the aftermath of the financial crisis for failing to engender effective inter-agency coordination.[102]

Crisis' (July 2013) No 20 Federal Reserve Bank of Dallas Staff Papers <http://www.dallasfed.org/assets/documents/research/staff/staff1301.pdf>.

[101] See Memorandum of Understanding between HM Treasury, the Bank of England, and the Financial Services Authority (2006).

[102] See for example, House of Commons Select Committee on Treasury 24 January 2008, Fifth Report, paras 269–75.

Importantly, unlike the FSOC, the FPC has been given the legal authority to direct the FCA and PRA to exercise their functions so as to ensure the implementation of measures designed to protect financial stability.[103] The PFC has published statements articulating its general policy toward the use of this authority in relation to sectoral capital requirements,[104] counter-cyclical capital buffers,[105] loan-to-value and debt-to-income requirements on residential mortgages,[106] and leverage ratio requirements.[107] The creation of the FPC is thus a relatively straightforward example of an approach that seeks to embed the special status of financial stability as a regulatory objective within the vertical structure of financial regulation.

The recent structural reforms within the EU present a somewhat more complicated picture. On one level, the creation of the ESRB might be viewed as establishing a locus of responsibility for the maintenance of financial stability broadly analogous to the FSOC and FPC. On another level, the ESRB's status as essentially a soft law institution might be expected to undermine its influence within the EU's increasingly complex regulatory architecture. The allocation of regulatory responsibility for financial stability has been further complicated by the creation of the European Banking Union. In practice, however, it seems likely that the assumption of responsibility for supervising the Eurozone's largest and most important banks—including, importantly, the exercise of discretion with respect to the application of macroprudential capital buffers[108]—will cement the ECB's status at the apex of Europe's monetary and financial system. Accordingly, while certainly far from perfect, the EU's new regulatory architecture may ultimately prove more effective than initial appearances might suggest. The most obvious vulnerability of this approach is that the scope of the ECB's supervisory mandate does not extend beyond deposit-taking banks and their affiliates, thus raising an important question regarding the allocation of regulatory responsibility for identifying, monitoring, and responding to threats to financial stability emanating from *outside* the conventional banking system.

[103] Financial Services Act 2012, c 21, s 9H.

[104] See 'Bank of England Policy Statement: The Financial Policy Committee's Powers to Supplement Capital Requirements' (Bank of England January 2014) <http://www.bankofengland.co.uk>.

[105] ibid.

[106] See 'Bank of England Policy Statement: The Financial Policy Committee's Powers Over Housing Tools' (Bank of England July 2015) <http://www.bankofengland.co.uk>.

[107] See 'Bank of England Policy Statement: The Financial Policy Committee's Powers Over Leverage Ratio Tools' (Bank of England July 2015) <http://www.bankofengland.co.uk>.

[108] SSM Regulation, Art 5.

(c) Microprudential versus Macroprudential Stability

One of the most costly and important lessons of the financial crisis was that systemic risk should not be understood as the straight sum of the risks posed by the financial institutions which comprise this system.[109] It is thus not sufficient for regulatory authorities to simply monitor the safety and soundness of individual institutions: this *microprudential* supervision must be accompanied by, and integrated with, a rigorous assessment of potential *macroprudential* risks.[110] While the definition of macroprudential risk is still somewhat inchoate, it can broadly be understood as encompassing at least two distinct categories of risk.[111] The first category is comprised of *cross-sectional* risks generated by the various direct and indirect transmission mechanisms which create complex and often hard to detect linkages among and between different types of financial institutions and markets. The second category is comprised of *time series* risks generated by procyclicality within the financial cycle, or arising by virtue of the interactions between the financial and business cycles.[112]

Importantly, the regulatory strategies designed to address microprudential risks can in some cases exacerbate macroprudential risks. The procyclicality associated with risk-weighted capital requirements for banks is perhaps the most infamous example.[113] Another illustrative example are the carveouts from automatic stay and other insolvency rules for derivatives and repurchase agreements. These carveouts enable counterparties of a failing institution to terminate their derivatives and repo agreements in certain prescribed circumstances, seize (as necessary) and liquidate any posted collateral, net out gains and losses on different agreements, and retain any eve-of-bankruptcy payments.[114] The result is a de facto reprioritization of claims within the failing

[109] See Anand et al. (n 12).

[110] See, for example, Andrew Crockett, 'Marrying the Micro- and Macro-prudential Dimensions of Financial Stability' (11th International Conference of Banking Supervisors, 18 September 2000); Claudio Borio, 'Towards a Macroprudential Framework for Financial Supervision and Regulation?' (2003) 49 CESifo Economic Studies 181; Samuel Hanson, Anil Kashyap, and Jeremy Stein, 'A Macroprudential Approach to Financial Regulation' (2011) 25 Journal of Economic Perspectives 3; and Robert Hockett, 'The Macroprudential Turn: From Institutional "Safety and Soundness" to Systemic "Financial Stability" in Financial Supervision' (2014) 15 University of Virginia Law & Business Review 201.

[111] See Armour et al. (n *) Chapter 23.

[112] See Claudio Borio, 'The Financial Cycle and Macroeconomics: What Have We Learnt?' (2014) 45 Journal of Banking and Finance 182.

[113] See Armour et al. (n *) Chapters 11 and 23.

[114] See Frank Partnoy and David Skeel, 'The Promise and Peril of Credit Derivatives' (2007) 75 University of Cincinnati Law Review 1019; Franklin Edwards and Edward Morrison, 'Derivatives and the Bankruptcy Code: Why the Special Treatment?' (2005) 22 Yale Journal on Regulation 91;

institution's capital structure, with derivatives and repo counterparties effectively enjoying a form of 'super priority' over other creditors.[115] Notably, one of the primary policy rationales for these carveouts was the microprudential objective of preventing the 'domino' effect: the risk that failure of one financial institution could precipitate the instability or failure of other institutions with which it has direct economic exposures.[116] At the same time, however, the moral hazard stemming from the introduction of these carveouts generates a number potentially significant macroprudential risks. Perhaps most importantly, insofar as this moral hazard leads to reduced market discipline[117] or increased leverage[118] within derivatives and repo markets, these carveouts can *ceteris paribus* be viewed as exacerbating rather than mitigating the threat of financial instability.

So what insights can we take away from this possible tension between microprudential regulatory strategies and macroprudential risk in terms of the optimal structure of financial regulation? First, it suggests that the regulatory authority responsible for financial stability should have access to all firm-level information collected and generated by the authorities responsible for microprudential supervision. Second, it suggests that the authority responsible for financial stability should be closely involved in the design of microprudential regulation. Third, this authority should have the power to intervene at any point before or after the implementation of microprudential regulation if it can make out a case that this regulation may have a negative impact on financial stability.

In theory, perhaps the most straightforward way to operationalize these insights would be to integrate responsibility for microprudential and

Stephen Lubben, 'Derivatives and Bankruptcy: The Flawed Case for Special Treatment' (2009) 12:1 University of Pennsylvania Journal of Business Law 61; and Roe (n 27).

115 See Roe (n 27).

116 See UNIDROIT, *Principles on the Operation of Close-out Netting Provisions* (2013) Principle 4 and accompanying commentary <http://www.unidroit.org/instruments/capital-markets/netting>. As explained in the commentary to Principle 4:

> A third justification [for the safe harbours] is the avoidance of systemic risk. This element flows partly from the second justification. In deteriorating market conditions, the ability to terminate contracts and thus to limit exposures is important in guarding against the situation where the failure by one of the parties to perform its obligations causes its counterparty likewise to become unable to perform its obligations vis-à-vis third parties.

See also, Philipp Paech, 'The Value of Insolvency Safe Harbours' (2016) Oxford Journal of Legal Studies (forthcoming).

117 See Roe (n 27).

118 See Riz Mokal, 'Bankruptcy, Systemic Risk, and the Bankruptcy Treatment of Financial Contracts' (2015) 10 Brooklyn Journal of Corporate, Financial and Commercial Law (forthcoming).

macroprudential regulation and supervision.[119] In practice, of course, full integration may not be feasible. Encouragingly, however, the post-crisis structural reforms in each of the US, UK, and EU reflect at least some positive movement in this direction. The UK is arguably best positioned in this regard: with the incorporation of the PRA and FPC under the umbrella of the Bank of England, along with the ability of the FPC to direct both the PRA and FCA, likely to lead to a high level of de facto integration. In the US and EU, the creation of the FSOC, ESRB, and European Banking Union similarly recognize the need for greater structural integration in order to identify, monitor, and respond to potential threats to financial stability. Nevertheless, significant questions remain. In the US, these questions revolve around whether the FSOC will be able to promote effective cross-sectional information flow and inter-agency coordination. As we have seen, the FSOC's ability to intervene in the event that it views microprudential regulation as posing a threat to financial stability is also relatively limited. In the EU, meanwhile, these questions revolve around the complex governance structure and legal impotence of the ESRB, along with the relatively narrow subject matter scope of the ECB's mandate under the SSM.

(d) Domestic versus Global Stability

The global financial crisis demonstrated how rapidly financial instability within one jurisdiction can spill over into others. It also demonstrated how the decisions of domestic regulatory authorities in terms of both substantive law and the intensity of supervision and enforcement can have a significant impact on the flow of capital and risk across borders. Put differently: in a world where domestic financial and economic systems are highly interconnected, the ability of domestic regulatory authorities to maintain financial stability is inherently constrained. In this world, we might expect the institutional structure of financial regulation at the domestic level to ultimately be somewhat less important than an effective *global* regulatory architecture.

The risks posed by the increasing globalization and interconnectedness of the financial system have been one of the primary drivers behind the development of a growing number of international regulatory bodies. This developing global regulatory architecture includes high level agenda setters such as the G20 Group of Finance Ministers and Central Bank Governors and its offshoot the FSB, international standard setters such as the Basel Committee

[119] Full integration may also not be desirable insofar as responsibility for financial instability is conferred upon central banks, thus potentially giving rise to problems of microprudential forbearance.

on Banking Supervision, and venerable international institutions such as the IMF and World Bank.[120] While the composition, governance, mandates, and legal authority of these institutions vary widely, the establishment of each can ultimately be understood as motivated, at least in part, by the common desire to enhance international regulatory coordination in the interests of promoting greater financial stability.

There can be little doubt that the key players within this emerging global regulatory architecture have played an important role in the wake of the financial crisis: coordinating the development of new international standards in several important areas,[121] establishing new frameworks for the cross-border resolution of systemically important financial institutions,[122] and launching a host of new initiatives designed to enhance cross-border information flow and macroprudential risk assessment.[123] Ultimately, however, any optimism associated with these developments must be tempered by the fact that, with the notable exception of the IMF, these players by and large lack the legal power to compel domestic regulatory authorities to take action in response to potential threats to financial stability. Instead, the emerging global regulatory architecture is structured almost exclusively through informal, non-binding agreements often referred to as 'soft law'.[124] This, in turn, exposes the vulnerability of this architecture: while the threat of negative spillovers provides the most compelling rationale for international regulatory coordination, these same spillovers threaten to drive a wedge between domestic interests as some jurisdictions become net importers of financial instability and others net exporters.[125] In the absence of more credible international commitments, regulatory coordination is thus most likely to evaporate at the precise moment that it is most urgently required: in the thick of a rapidly evolving cross-border crisis.

So where do we go from here? One way to strengthen the credibility of international commitments would be a legally binding treaty. Barry Eichengreen,

[120] See Brummer (n 4) for a more detailed description of these institutions and their mandates.

[121] See, for example, Basel Committee on Banking Supervision (BCBS), 'Basel III: A Global Regulatory Framework for More Resilient Banks and Banking Systems' (BCBS June 2011) <www.bis.org/publ/bcbs189.pdf>; BCBS, 'Basel III Leverage Ratio Framework and Disclosure Requirements' (BCBS January 2014) <http://www.bis.org/publ/bcbs270.htm>; and 'Liquidity Coverage Ratio (LCR)' (BCBS January 2013) and 'Net Stable Funding Ratio (NSFR)' (BCBS October 2014) <http://www.bis.org/bcbs/basel3.htm>.

[122] See, for example, FSB, 'Key Attributes of Effective Resolution Regimes of Financial Institutions' (FSB October 2014) <http://www.financialstabilityboard.org>.

[123] See, for example, FSB, A Global Legal Entity Identifier for Financial Markets (8 FSB June 2012) <http://www.financialstabilityboard.org>.

[124] Brummer (n 4). [125] ibid.

for example, has proposed the creation of a treaty-based World Financial Organization analogous to the World Trade Organization.[126] John Eatwell and Lance Taylor, meanwhile, have advanced a more radical proposal to create a supranational regulatory authority responsible for the supervision of globally systemically important financial institutions.[127] At least for the foreseeable future, it seems unlikely that these or other 'hard law' proposals will be able to generate sufficient political support from domestic constituencies to get off the ground.[128] As a result, one might reasonably question whether we find ourselves caught between the relative impotence of soft law and the intractable political obstacles to the emergence of more credible international commitments. Nevertheless, while global treaties and supranational regulators may be politically infeasible, this does not preclude the possibility of strengthening the credibility of international commitments on a more incremental scale. In this respect, perhaps the most obvious place to start would be those elements of the global regulatory architecture designed to promote effective cross-border information flow, thereby ensuring that domestic regulatory authorities are in a position to identify and monitor global threats to domestic financial stability.

6. Conclusion

There are those who view the institutional structure of financial regulation as fundamentally less important than substantive law in advancing regulatory objectives. Indeed, in a great many cases, this is undoubtedly true. At the same time, while a well designed institutional structure is unlikely to singlehandedly advance regulatory objectives, a poorly designed structure can undermine effective information flow and coordination, contribute to suboptimal policymaking, and obstruct the identification, monitoring, and response to new issues and emerging threats.

The institutional structure of financial regulation is particularly important in advancing the objective of financial stability. This is partly because many of the potential sources of financial instability transcend the historical distinctions between 'banking', 'securities', and 'insurance' which have often served as the blueprints for the institutional structure of financial regulation.

[126] Barry Eichengreen, 'Not a New Bretton Woods but a New Bretton Woods Process' (6 November 2008) <http://www.voxeu.org>.

[127] Eatwell and Taylor (n 4).

[128] Although many would have said the exact same thing about the European Banking Union a few short years ago.

Importantly, it is also because one of the potential sources of financial instability is the law itself. This makes effective information flow and coordination between the regulatory authorities responsible for writing, monitoring, and enforcing compliance with these laws extremely important. To the extent that is serves to enhance (or impede) effective information flow and coordination, the institutional structure of financial regulation can thus be understood as playing a meaningful role in advancing (or undermining) the objective of financial stability.

This chapter has examined some of the myriad of different ways in which the law can contribute to financial instability, focusing specifically on regulatory arbitrage, contractual inflexibility, and the role of the law in supporting the creation of money-like claims. It then examined what insights the relationship between law and financial instability might yield in terms of the optimal institutional structure of financial regulation. There are four principal takeaways. First, regulatory objectives are likely to provide a more robust basis for the allocation of regulatory responsibility than inherently arbitragable labels. Second, promoting financial stability should be viewed as residing at the apex of a hierarchy of regulatory objectives. This hierarchy should be reflected in the vertical structure of financial regulation. Third, promoting financial stability requires a coordinated approach towards the identification, monitoring, and response to both microprudential and macroprudential risks. Finally, in an increasingly globalized and interconnected financial system, the institutional structure of financial regulation at the domestic level may be less important than an effective global regulatory architecture.

4

Further Assessment of the Iron Law of Financial Regulation

A Postscript to Regulating in the Dark

Roberta Romano

1. Introduction

In 'Regulating in the Dark',[1] I contended that there is an 'Iron Law' regarding foundational US financial regulation: (i) enactment is invariably crisis driven, adopted at a time when there is a paucity of information regarding what has transpired, (ii) resulting in off-the-rack solutions often poorly fashioned to the problem at hand, (iii) with inevitable flaws given the dynamic uncertainty of financial markets, (iv) but arduous to revise or repeal given the stickiness of the status quo in the US political framework of checks and balances. The ensuing one-way regulatory ratchet generated by repeated financial crises has produced not only costly policy mistakes accompanied by unintended consequences but also a regulatory state whose cumulative regulatory impact produces a layering of additional regulations which, over time, becomes an increasingly ineffective regulatory apparatus.

This postscript analyses the experience with regulators' implementation of Dodd-Frank since the publication of 'Regulating in the Dark'. The analysis bolsters the article's contention regarding the inherent problems in

[1] Roberta Romano, 'Regulating in the Dark' in Cary Coglianese (ed), *Regulatory Breakdown: The Crisis of Confidence in U.S. Regulation* (The University of Pennsylvania Press 2012). This chapter is an updated version of the 'Postscript' part of 'Regulating in the Dark and a Postscript Assessment of the Iron Law of Financial Regulation' published at (2014) 42 Hofstra Law Review 25 and of 'Pitfalls in the Iron Law of Financial Regulation: A Postscript to Regulating in the Dark' in Robert Waldburger, Peter Sester, Christoph Peter, and Charlotte M Baer (eds), *Law & Economics Festschrift für Peter Nobel zum 70 Geburtstag* (Stämpfli Verlag AG 2015), and is reproduced by permission.

Further Assessment of the Iron Law of Financial Regulation: A Postscript to Regulating in the Dark. First Edition. Roberta Romano. Published by Oxford University Press.

crisis-driven financial legislation and the corresponding benefit for improving decision-making that would be obtained from employing, as best practice, the legislative tools of sunsetting and experimentation to such legislation and its implementing regulation. While it would be foolhardy to claim that application of those tools would produce an optimal regulatory policy, it is plausible to conclude that their use would advance means-ends rationality by better coupling the two, substantially raising the quality of decision-making by providing a feedback loop measuring and remedying regulatory errors. The depressing travails of Dodd-Frank's implementation, which make plain the statute's shortcomings, will, it is to be hoped, focus attention on how, going forward, we can achieve more effective financial regulation by including in crisis-driven legislation, the safeguards of sunsetting and experimentation.

2. Dodd-Frank Act: A Regulatory Morass

Four years after enactment, all 280 of Dodd-Frank's specified rule-making deadlines had elapsed with 45 per cent having been missed, and of the Act's 398 rule-making requirements, slightly more than half, 52 per cent had been finalized, while nearly one-quarter (24 per cent) had not yet even been proposed.[2] Of course, the vast number of required rules and complexity of issues would of their own accord impede implementation. But rule-making has also moved at a glacial pace due to intensive lobbying by affected parties who, given the stakes in the legislative delegation to agencies of the task of reconfiguring financial markets and institutions, have quite understandably sought to shape regulatory outcomes to their advantage.

The regulatory morass occasioned by Dodd-Frank might on first impression suggest to some that sunsetting is inapposite for the complexity of contemporary emergency legislation because its delegated rule-making would not, in fact, be in place in time to be assessed when a sunset review would have to commence. I draw a contrary conclusion. In my judgement, the protracted rule-making experience of Dodd-Frank only further strengthens the case for sunsetting. First, the stakes for interested parties would be lowered, and hence lobbying less intense and prolonged, if regulation had to be reassessed and put to a legislative vote at a future date.[3] The affected parties would be assured

[2] 'Dodd-Frank Progress Report' (DavisPolk 18 July 2014) 2 <http://www.davispolk.com/Dodd-Frank-Rulemaking-Progress-Report/> accessed 18 August 2015. See Dodd-Frank Wall Street Reform and Consumer Protection Act (Pub L 111– 203, HR 4173) (Dodd-Frank).

[3] Experimentation could provide a further benefit of mitigating concerns expressed by commentators that rule-makers subject to a cost-benefit standard, such as the SEC, cannot meet the rigours of judicial review, following the invalidation of the proxy access rule discussed in Romano,

of a second chance to make their case, so to speak, at a time when far more information would be available to indicate whether proponents' claims or critics' concerns were well-founded, and they could be assured that at a specified point in time unintended adverse consequences could be attended to and reversed or mitigated by legislation adopting (or more likely, instructing implementation of) a better regulatory solution. A specified timetable, expert counsel, and streamlined voting procedures accompanying a legislative vote on whether to retain or modify the expiring legislation and implementing regulation should go a long way to ensuring such an outcome.[4]

Second, when a rule cannot be crafted within a reasonable time frame of a multi-year interval prior to a sunset review, a fair inference is that the statutory delegation was poorly devised or entirely misconceived, in the first instance. Rule-making is not intended to be interminable. If a proposed rule has not been implemented by the time set for sunsetting, the sunset review could, of course, automatically be postponed to a specified date after implementation. But legislators could also reasonably draw a negative inference regarding a rule's appropriateness or efficacy from an agency's inability to implement it in timely fashion. A protracted implementation could plausibly suggest that a proposed rule has raised broad-based concern that it would create severe market dislocations and would fail a cost-benefit test, as opposed to its being due to dilatory tactics by interest groups, because it is reasonable to suppose that regulators have a strong incentive to implement statutory directives expeditiously to avoid being called to task by members of Congress for failure to do so.

More fundamentally Dodd-Frank and the regulatory apparatus it imposes have generated controversy, disappointment, and alarm, at nearly every turn. For instance, it fails to address key factors widely acknowledged to have contributed to the financial crisis, such as, runs on shadow banks, whose liabilities were collateralized with securitized mortgages, and government-sponsored enterprises (GSEs) that guaranteed those securitized mortgages.[5]

'Regulating in the Dark' (2012) (n 1) 90. It has been advocated that SEC rules that are adopted on an experimental or sunsetting basis could be subjected to a lower level of judicial scrutiny because a more finely tuned cost-benefit analysis could be undertaken with the knowledge gleaned from the experiment when the rule comes up for the required renewal. Eg, Zachary James Gubler, 'Experimental Rules' (2014) 55 Boston College Law Review 129; Yoon-Ho Alex Lee, 'An Options Approach to Agency Rulemaking' (2013) 65 Administrative Law Review 881.

[4] Romano, 'Regulating in the Dark' (2012) (n 1) 99–100, 111 n 17 (sketching procedures necessary to render sunsetting effective).

[5] For the critical importance of the shadow banking sector in sparking the global financial crisis, see Gary Gorton, *Slapped by the Invisible Hand: The Panic of 2007* (OUP 2010); and of the GSEs, see Viral V Acharya, T. Sabri Öncü, Matthew Richardson, Stijn Van Nieuwerburgh, and Lawrence J White, 'The Government-Sponsored Enterprises' in Viral V Acharya, Thomas F Cooley, Matthew P Richardson, and Ingo Walter (eds), *Regulating Wall Street: The Dodd-Frank Act and the*

Rather than address shadow banking and the GSEs explicitly, the focus of the statute directed at the subprime mortgage market's contribution to the crisis is a requirement that mortgage securitizers retain 5 per cent of the securities of non-qualified mortgages.[6] This provision is informed by a mistaken premise, however, as securitizers did retain risk pre-crisis, holding substantial amounts of mortgage-backed securities on their balance-sheets.[7] As Ryan Bubb and Prasad Krishnamurthy note, banks' retention of securitized mortgage risk contributed to the financial crisis, jeopardizing banks' liquidity, and ultimately solvency. Consequently, this particular Dodd-Frank provision advances a perverse regulatory strategy for it would appear to aggravate, not diminish, systemic risk created by mortgage securitizations.[8] We would appear to have learned very little from the recent crisis.

New Architecture of Global Finance (Wiley 2011). As Christopher Foote and his colleagues state, the GSEs 'were major players in the lending boom of the 2000s, even if much of [the] lending occurred outside of their traditional guarantee business [i.e., were privately originated]. Specifically, both Fannie Mae and Freddie Mac indirectly invested heavily in risky mortgages by buying AAA tranches of subprime and Alt-A mortgage-backed securities and holding these securities in their retained portfolios … in many of the boom years, … account[ing] for half of the subprime AAA-rated securities.' Christopher L Foote, Kristopher S Gerardi, and Paul S Willen, 'Why Did So Many People Make So Many *Ex Post* Bad Decisions? The Causes of the Foreclosure Crisis' (2012) Federal Reserve Bank of Boston Policy Discussion. Papers No 12–12, at 35–36. Their substantial holding of such securities led to their failure and the government's taking them over in 2008.

[6] Dodd-Frank § 941, codified at 15 USC § 78o-11.

[7] See, eg, Viral Acharya and Matthew Richardson, 'Causes of the Financial Crisis' (2009) 21 Journal of the Critical Review Foundation Inc 195, 200; Foote et al., 'Why Did So Many People Make So Many *Ex Post* Bad Decisions? The Causes of the Foreclosure Crisis' (n 5) 19 (six of top ten institutions with subprime losses 'not only securitized subprime mortgages, but also actually owned companies that originated them'). For a critique of the efficacy of this provision, as well as Dodd-Frank's requirement that mortgage originators judge an applicant as having the ability to pay for the loan, see Ryan Bubb and Prasad Krishnamurthy, 'Regulating Against Bubbles: How Mortgage Regulation Can Keep Main Street and Wall Street Safe—From Themselves' (2015) 163 University of Pennsylvania Law Review 1539.

[8] The risk retention provision may prove to be a relatively minor constraint in the overall scheme of things, however. That is because regulators have adopted the CFPB definition of a 'qualified' mortgage, which does not include a down payment requirement, has a lax debt to income ratio requirement of 43 per cent plus includes numerous exemptions from these and other requirements such as limits on interest rates and prohibition of balloon payments, for small and rural area banks (some of which are statutory), and for government agency-insured loans. Consumer Financial Protection Bureau, 'Ability-to-Repay and Qualified Mortgage Standards Under the Truth in Lending Act (Regulation Z), Final Rule; Official Interpretations' (2013) 78 Federal Register 6408. Further, the Department of Housing and Urban Development's (HUD) final rule designates all of its mortgages as qualified, and also states that its standards conform to the CFPB's definition. HUD, 'Qualified Mortgage Definition for HUD Insured and Guaranteed Single Family Mortgages, Final Rule' (2013) 78 Federal Register 75215. Although, by contrast, the definition proposed in 2011 for a qualified mortgage under the risk retention provision by bank regulators, the SEC and HUD had far more substantial requirements, such as a 20 per cent down payment and 75 per cent debt-to-income ratio, that was not to be. Department of the Treasury Office of the Comptroller of the Currency, Federal Reserve System, Federal Deposit Insurance Corp, Federal Housing Finance Agency, Securities and Exchange Commission, Department of Housing and Urban Development,

In addition, Dodd-Frank inadequately responds to the after-effects of the crisis (taxpayer bailouts of 'too-big-to-fail' financial institutions). Although legislators enacting Dodd-Frank have emphatically insisted that the statute has ended 'too-big-to-fail' and taxpayer bailouts, having included a section addressed to the resolution of large financial institutions,[9] many commentators maintain that the provision has not, in fact, resolved the 'too-big-to-fail' syndrome and could well exacerbate it.[10] The basis for such a contention is that by identifying systemically important financial institutions (SIFIs) and subjecting them to a special regime that permits their being bailed out upon approval by designated government actors, it simply codifies too-big-to-fail, and thereby does not diminish the likelihood of such an occurrence, despite legislators' contrary insistence.[11] As Peter Wallison puts the net effect of these

'Credit Risk Retention: Proposed Rule' (2011) 76 Federal Register 24090. The agencies were lobbied by legislators, the housing industry, consumer advocacy groups, and community activists to adopt for the risk retention definition of a qualified mortgage, instead, the CFPB's definition of a qualified mortgage, and they did exactly that in a reproposed rule issued in 2013, finalized, as is, in 2014. Department of the Treasury Office of the Comptroller of the Currency, Federal Reserve System, Federal Deposit Insurance Corp, Federal Housing Finance Agency, Securities and Exchange Commission, Department of Housing and Urban Development, 'Credit Risk Retention, Proposed Rule' (2013) 78 57928, 57.934; Department of the Treasury Office of the Comptroller of the Currency, Federal Reserve System, Federal Deposit Insurance Corp, Federal Housing Finance Agency, Securities and Exchange Commission, Department of Housing and Urban Development, 'Credit Risk Retention, Final Rule, 79 Federal Register 77606 (2014). All of the objections to the definition in the initial proposal were directed at loosening the standards to conform to that of the CFPB. ibid 57933. Consequently, the pool of mortgages falling into the non-qualified category for risk-retention purposes will be small, and many qualified mortgages will carry considerable default risk. As Peter Wallison and Edward Pinto put it, assessing the CFPB's definition: 'Neither Dodd-Frank nor the new QM [qualified mortgage] rule has changed anything significant. Political pressure to continue lending to borrowers with weak credit standards has trumped common sense underwriting standards.' Peter J Wallison and Edward J Pinto, 'New Qualified Mortgage Rule Setting Us Up for Another Meltdown' *Washington Times* (3 March 2013). Bubb and Krishnamurthy's critique of the risk-retention rule could, however, suggest that a lax definition is for the better from the perspective of financial institution stability. Bubb and Krishnamurthy (n 7). This is an issue that a sunset review and regulatory experimentation could help to arbitrate.

[9] Eg, Cezary, Podkul, 'Is "Too Big to Fail" Really Over? Rep. Barney Frank Says Yes But Others Disagree' *Washington Post* (15 July 2011) ('Representative Barney Frank, one of the law's chief architects … insisted several times that "too big to fail was over" and "reprimanded" a bank regulator for suggesting that banks' unique role in the economy justifies a public safety net that is "unlikely ever to be provided at zero public cost" ').

[10] Eg, Viral V Acharya, Barry Adler, Matthew Richardson, and Nouriel Roubini, 'Resolution Authority' in Viral V Acharya et al. *Regulating Wall Street* (n 5); David Skeel, *The New Financial Deal* (Wiley 2011) 129–52.

[11] Eg, Peter J Wallison, 'Dodd-Frank and Too Big to Fail Receive Too Little Attention' (1 November 2012) <http://www.aei.org/article/economics/financial-services/banking/dodd-frank-and-too-big-to-fail-receive-too-little-attention/> accessed 18 August 2015; Simon Johnson, 'Sadly, Too Big to Fail Is Not Over' *New York Times Economix* (1 August 2013) <http://economix.blogs.nytimes.com/2013/08/01/sadly-too-big-to-fail-is-not-over/?_php=true&_type=blogs&_r=0> accessed 18 August 2015.

provisions, Dodd-Frank extends the Federal Deposit Insurance Corporation's policy of paying off unsecured bank depositors to all large financial institutions, as well as non-bank institutions that are classified as SIFIs.[12]

But at the same time as ignoring or inadequately addressing critical issues related to the financial crisis, the statute will be imposing considerable costs on non-financial companies, which could well be in a multiple of billions of dollars, due to time-consuming disclosure requirements whose regulatory objectives have no connection to the financial crisis, the ostensible focus of the legislation (disclosures regarding conflict minerals, payments to foreign governments for oil and gas development, and the ratio of CEO compensation to that of the median employee).[13] Even the proponents of those provisions did not believe that the issues informing their proposals had a connection to the financial crisis: the legislative majority simply opportunistically took advantage of including provisions that were desired by key constituent interest groups and that had scant chance of independent enactment (as evidenced by the stalled progress of related bills and the subsequent controversy over those rules' implementation).[14]

[12] Wallison (n 11).

[13] The SEC's conflict minerals rule was adopted by a 3:2 vote a year after its deadline because of opposition to the costs of the proposal, with industry estimates of compliance costs in a range of $9–16 billion. Eg, Eric Savitz, 'SEC Approves Detailed Disclosure on "Conflict Minerals"' *Forbes* (22 August 2012); Peter Schroeder, 'SEC Approves Rules on "Conflict Minerals"' *The Hill* (22 August 2012). Even more controversial, the CEO compensation ratio disclosure rule was not finalized until August 2015, given the daunting complexity of computing such a figure for multinational firms at any reasonable cost, with one estimate of the aggregate cost of compliance, based on individual firms' estimates of their own compliance costs, placed at $1 billion. Eg, Statement of Tom Quaadman to the House Committee on Financial Services, Subcommittee On Capital Markets and Government Sponsored Enterprise (23 May 2013), 2013 WLNR 12667870; SEC, 'Pay Ratio Disclosure' (2015) 80 Federal Register 50104. Similarly, commentators suggested that the extractive resources company foreign government payments disclosure rule could cost issuers in the billions of dollars in countries where such disclosure was prohibited. David C Buck, John B Clutterbuck, and George J Vlahakos, 'DC District Court Vacates Dodd-Frank Disclosure Rule for Payments by Resource Extraction Issuers' Journal of National Security Law & Policy (9 July 2013) <http://www.natlawreview.com/article/dc-district-court-vacates-dodd-frank-disclosure-rule-payments-resource-extraction-is> accessed 18 August 2015.

[14] A conflicts mineral bill, which among other provisions required companies to certify their imported products were conflict mineral free, had languished in the House since its introduction in November 2009. 'Bill Summary and Status, 111th Congress (2009–10) HR 4128' *The Library of Congress* <http://thomas.loc.gov/cgi-bin/thomas> accessed 18 August 2015. Similarly, a bill requiring resource extraction issuers to disclose payments to foreign governments had not progressed beyond its introduction in September 2009. 'Bill Summary and Status, 111th Congress (2009–10) S1700' *The Library of Congress* <http://thomas.loc.gov/cgi-bin/thomas> accessed 18 August 2015. Senator Menendez, who is closely identified with organized labour and was the sponsor of the CEO pay ratio provision, Jerry Markon and Dina ElBoghdady, 'Pay Rule Still Unwritten amid Corporate Push' *Washington Post* (6 July 2013) A1, had introduced a bill requiring the pay ratio disclosure in February 2010, among other provisions concerning executive compensation, and was unable to obtain even a single cosponsor. 'Bill Summary and Status, 11th Congress (2009–10) S 3049'

Including provisions unrelated to the financial crisis in Dodd-Frank was also used strategically to secure a sponsoring legislator's vote, which a lead drafting legislator deemed necessary for the bill's passage.[15] The sorry aftermath of this political horse-trading is that the Securities and Exchange Commission (SEC) has had to devote time and resources to address rules quite unrelated to both the financial crisis and the agency's core mission, a diversion further exacerbating the delayed implementation of rules with at least an ostensible nexus to the crisis, such as those relating to security-based swaps and asset-backed securitizations, along with the Volcker rule prohibiting financial institutions' proprietary trading. Those rules' statutory deadlines have long since been missed.[16]

The present appalling legislative and regulatory state of affairs should not be a surprise for, as this chapter has emphasized, emergency financial legislation is inherently ill-suited for addressing crises, given information difficulties: the politics of financial crises requires acting before sufficient information can be developed on what might be the wisest course of action, and thereby

The Library of Congress <http://thomas.loc.gov/cgi-bin/thomas> accessed 18 August 2015. He also did not even attempt to rationalize the provision's inclusion as remedying a contributory factor to the financial crisis. In a letter dated 9 January 2011, urging the SEC to implement the pay ratio disclosure rule within the year, Senator Menendez stated that he 'wrote this provision so that investors and the general public know whether public companies' pay practices are fair to their average employees, especially compared to their highly compensated CEOs'.' In a more recent press release of March 2013 'reiterating' the need for the SEC to enact a rule, he shifted the rationale by noting that 'executive compensation schemes provided part of the fuel for the financial crash' while focusing on, as the rationale for the disclosure, 'income inequality … over the last decade', with 'soaring' CEO compared to 'workers' … stagnant wages' and declining 'middle class family income', a subject matter that, although of concern, is not thought to be connected to the global financial crisis of 2008–09. 'Menendez Calls on SEC to Expedite Adoption of CEO-to-Median Pay Disclosure Rule' (12 March 2013) <http://www.menendez.senate.gov/news-and-events/press/menendez-calls-on-sec-to-expedite-adoption-of-ceo-to-median-pay-disclosure-rule> accessed 18 August 2015.

[15] As Markon and ElBoghdady (n 14), report, the pay ratio provision was included in the bill to obtain Senator Menendez's vote. Senator Menendez was a member of the Senate committee drafting what became the Dodd-Frank legislation, and prior to the pay ratio provision's inclusion, he was quoted as expressing hesitation over supporting the bill, although the concerns he mentioned in the press report related to improving provisions related to bailouts. Jessica Brady and Anna Palmer, 'Senators, K Street Not Sold on Dodd's Reform Bill' *Roll Call* (16 March 2010).

[16] Dodd-Frank's implementation deadlines are compiled in the David Polk Regulatory Tracker <https://www.regulatorytracker.com> accessed 18 August 2015. There are, of course, additional reasons for the SEC's delayed implementation of the Volcker rule besides its having to focus attention elsewhere: the need to coordinate the drafting of a rule across multiple agencies, and the complexity of the substantive issues, which is discussed in Section 2(a). The SEC's final rule implementing the Volcker rule (coordinated with banking regulators and the CFTC) was adopted on 10 December 2013 and published in the Federal Register on 31 January 2014. Department of the Treasury Office of the Comptroller of the Currency, Board of Governors of the Federal Reserve System, Federal Deposit Insurance Corporation, and Securities and Exchange Commission, 'Prohibitions and Restrictions on Proprietary Trading and Certain Interests In, and Relationships With, Hedge Funds and Private Equity Funds' (2014) 79 Federal Register 5535.

provides an opportunity for well-positioned political actors opportunistically to advance an agenda that is tangential to the crisis at hand and may well be inapposite given the best available data.[17] That situation would be mitigated by a regime for crisis-driven legislation in which a panel of legislatively appointed experts undertakes a sunset review, providing an evaluation that would direct legislators' attention to the extant evidence of a policy's impact.

But the making of Dodd-Frank is considerably more dismal than that of well-intentioned legislators, operating in a panic, making mistakes. In a parody of the textbook behavioural response to a financial crisis, an eyewitness account of the enactment of Dodd-Frank, in which every action and reaction of Congressman Frank and his staff were tracked, relates that Congressman Frank objected to appointment of a commission to study the causes of the crisis—which was being advocated by members of Congress and commentators—as a 'distraction' and was reconciled to its creation only upon ensuring the commission's work would be completed *after* legislation responding to the crisis could be enacted.[18]

We are further provided with insight into Congressman Frank's understanding of how to respond to the financial crisis by this description of his perspective on the crisis: it was that 'the causes of the Great Crash were already well understood, and that it was due to "irresponsible financiers and anti-regulation Republicans"'.[19] Such a cartoonish contention could only be

[17] See, Eg, Roberta Romano, 'The Sarbanes-Oxley Act and the Making of Quack Corporate Governance' (2005) 114 Yale Law Journal 1521 (Sarbanes-Oxley substantive corporate governance mandates, advocated by policy entrepreneurs, were adopted despite empirical literature tending to suggest that they would be ill-conceived, as they would not improve corporate performance or audit quality, the stated statutory objective).

[18] Robert G Kaiser, *Act of Congress* (Alfred A Knopf 2013) 97–99. ('Frank persuaded [House Speaker] Pelosi' that any legislation creating a commission would 'stipulate that the commission make its final report' twenty months later so that 'it would have no impact on the legislative process, which Frank intended to complete long before then.') The author, who had known the Congressman for many years, was invited to be 'historian' of the legislation and had open access to Congressman Frank and his staff, sharing 'behind the scenes' action, throughout the legislative process. ibid x–xi.

[19] ibid 98–99.Congressman Frank apparently agreed with Mark Zandi's contention that 'indiscriminate home loans by overaggressive mortgage brokers, sloppy securitization of mortgages by banks and investment houses, and woefully inadequate government regulation were the principal causes of the financial crisis.' ibid 98. Although such factors surely contributed to the crisis, it would be wildly inaccurate to contend that they solely explain what occurred. A list of factors that commentators have identified as contributing to the financial crisis would further include government policies encouraging home ownership and in particular subprime mortgages, Eg, Peter J Wallison, 'Financial Crisis Inquiry Commission Dissenting Statement' (Yale Law School, January 2011) <http://www.law.yale.edu/documents/pdf/cbl/Financial_Crisis_Wallison.pdf> accessed 21 August 2015; low interest rate policy by the Federal Reserve, eg, John B Taylor, *Getting Off Track: How Government Actions and Interventions Caused, Prolonged, and Worsened the Financial Crisis* (Hoover Institution Press 2009); overreliance on credit rating agencies, both by private institutions' guidelines and government regulation, eg, Frank Partnoy, 'Historical Perspectives on the Financial Crisis: Ivar Kreuger, the Credit-Rating Agencies and Two Theories about the Function, and Dysfunction, of

made by a poorly informed and highly partisan political actor with a sound bite understanding of the complexity of what was, after all, a global financial crisis. Unfortunately, Congressman Frank's simple-minded view of the crisis followed straightforwardly from his world view: he was one of the representatives most to the extreme left on the US political spectrum, as indicated by his dw-nominate score, a widely used ideology measure developed from roll call votes by political scientists Keith Poole and Howard Rosenthal.[20] In the 111th Congress enacting Dodd-Frank, only 36 of 435 representatives had ideology scores to the left of Congressman Frank, and similarly, in the 110th Congress, the session prior to Dodd-Frank's enactment, only 35 representatives' scores were to his left.[21]

The failure of Dodd-Frank to address key contributing factors to the crisis related to government policies, such as the GSEs, was to be expected when an individual who had strong ideological priors, and hardly an empirically oriented problem-solver, 'alone would decide what was in, and what was out' in the shaping of the legislation in the House.[22] It was also convenient to blame the financial crisis on the private sector and political opponents for that deflected blame away from Congressman Frank's own contribution to the crisis as he was an ardent supporter of the failed housing and easy credit policies. In keeping with this synoptic characterization of Congressman Frank's perspective, he did not make an earnest effort to forge a coalition across the aisle, as that was not in his nature and he did not have to, given the large Democratic majorities in both chambers and a president from his party. Dodd-Frank was consequently enacted on a virtual party-line vote, in contrast to the typical crisis-driven legislation, which garners broad bipartisan support.[23]

Markets' (2009) 26 Yale Journal on Regulation 431, 438–42; foreign nations', particularly China's, massive demand for dollars (driving down US interest rates and making credit too easily available, thereby skewing investment decision-making), eg, Alan Greenspan, 'The Crisis' in *Brookings Papers on Economic Activity* (Brookings Institution 2010 Spring), a bubble in housing prices (ie, the key was distorted beliefs, rather than distorted incentives, which some of the aforementioned factors supported but did not cause), Foote et al. (n 5); and international financial regulation, eg, Jeffrey Friedman, 'Capitalism and the Crisis: Bankers, Bonuses, Ideology and Ignorance' in Jeffrey Friedman (eds), *What Caused the Financial Crisis?* (The University of Pennsylvania Press 2011).

[20] For a discussion of the construction of the dw-nominate scores, see Keith T Poole and Howard Rosenthal, *Ideology and Congress* (Transaction Publishers 2007) 25–30.

[21] The rank orderings can be found at: <http://voteview.com/HOUSE_SORT110.HTM> accessed 18 August 2015; and <http://voteview.com/HOUSE_SORT111.HTM> accessed 18 August 2015.

[22] Kaiser (n 18) 153.

[23] No Republicans voted for the bill in the House, although several Democrats also voted against the bill, and only three Republicans voted to agree to the conference report, the vote resolving differences across the chambers, and thus enacting the legislation. Roll Call Vote # 968 (11 December 2009) (233:202) (House bill passage); Roll Call Vote # 413 (30 June 2010) (237:192) (agreement to

There is an additional factor besides the policy preferences of the agenda setters that informs the absence of any provision concerning the GSEs. As detailed in numerous sources, the GSEs were munificent contributors to election campaigns, as well as gladhanders to constituents, such as, community organizers and activists, who in response lobbied legislators on the GSEs' behalf.[24] An extensive analysis of the GSE fiasco concludes that Congressman Frank was a 'perpetual protector of Fannie [Mae] and those in his orbit were rewarded by the company',[25] as it provided employment for Frank's friends and made sizeable contributions to his mother's non-profit organization.[26]

conference report). In the Senate, similarly, all but one Democrat and only four (three) Republicans voted for the Senate's version of the bill (conference report). Sen Vote # 162 (20 May 2010) (59:39) (Senate bill passage); Sen Vote. # 208 (15 July 2010) (60:39) (agreement to conference report). The complete voting history is reported at: <http://beta.congress.gov/bill/111th-congress/house-bill/4173/all-actions-with-amendments/?q=%7B%22search%22%3A%5B%22hr+4173%22%5D%7D> accessed 18 August 2015. Sarbanes-Oxley, by contrast, was enacted with overwhelming bipartisan support, unanimously approved in the Senate and with only three House Republican members voting against, a consensus sparked by a dramatic drop in the stock market, but nevertheless virtually unopposed. Roberta Romano, 'Does the Sarbanes- Oxley Act Have a Future?' (2009) 26 Yale Journal on Regulation 229, 238.

[24] Gretchen Morgenson and Joshua Rosner, *Reckless Endangerment: How Outsized Ambition, Greed, and Corruption Led to Economic Armageddon* (Times Books 2011) 68–71 (noting that Fannie Mae was 'highly creative when it came to 'encouraging' its higher-level executives to donate to political campaigns'); ibid 59–68 (detailing Fannie Mae's public relations campaign earmarking $1 trillion in spending on affordable housing between 1994 and 2000 which would 'commit so much money to low-income housing … that no one would dare to criticize its other activities', and placing 'partnership offices' in towns and cities throughout the country which 'cemented the company's relationships with members of Congress').

[25] ibid 69. Congressman Frank's cosy relationship with the GSEs and opposition to their being reined in pre-crisis has been extensively detailed, eg, ibid 7, 68–69, 246–47, 256–59.

[26] ibid 68–71. Senator Dodd, one of the GSEs 'most strident defenders', ibid 304, was also one of several legislators who received favoured treatment for home mortgages from Countrywide Financial, the subprime mortgage originator closely associated with the GSEs, as they had common legislative interests; it was an equally vigorous campaign contributor and lobbyist. ibid 186–87. Although Senator Dodd's voting record indicates he was to the left of the centre of his party, he was not an outlier, as was Congressman Frank, among his chamber compatriots: in the 111th Congress that enacted Dodd-Frank, there were more than twenty Democrats with a dw-nominate score to the left of his score and over thirty Democrats with a score to his right, while in the Senate of the 110th Congress, which was nearly evenly divided by party, there were twenty-one Democrats with scores to his left. The rank orderings for senators in the two Congresses, respectively, are at <http://voteview.com/SENATE_SORT111.HTM> accessed 18 August 2015; and <http://voteview.com/SENATE_SORT110.HTM> accessed 18 August 2015. As these are chamber-derived scores, one must be cautious in interpreting these data as indicating that Frank was considerably more to the left of the political spectrum than Dodd, because we cannot say whether the centre of the Senate and House Democrats would be identical placed on a left–right political scale. Poole and Rosenthal have estimated a 'joint space' model for the dw-nominate scores, using the votes of representatives who moved on to the Senate. Although this model fits House members better than it does the Senate, in the joint space ranking, Frank's being considerably far more to the left than Dodd is again borne out: there are only thirty-six members whose dw-nominate score is to the left of Frank's, while there are 169 with scores to the left of Dodd's, among all members of the 111th Congress. The legislator

Frank was, of course, not alone in his staunch support of the GSEs in the years leading up to the crisis, as the GSEs' largesse was ubiquitous.[27] This venal political environment helps in explaining Dodd-Frank's peculiar silence on the GSEs and government housing policy.[28]

While the political largesse of the GSEs has ceased with their placement under government conservatorship, there has still been no legislative response to the considerable risk to the fisc and the economy at large that they and government housing policies pose. Numerous bills since Dodd-Frank's enactment have, however, been introduced regarding the GSEs, with a bipartisan bill that would replace the GSEs with a new federal agency guaranteeing all mortgages having been voted out of a Senate committee by a close vote.[29] Some commentators have contended that the bill is a solution far worse than the problem it ostensibly seeks to solve.[30] Such criticism underscores how difficult implementing a policy to control the risk of loss generated by the GSEs and existing housing policies will be politically. But that is not why the GSEs were not addressed in Dodd-Frank; they were omitted because agenda-setting legislators had been ardent supporters of the agencies, did not consider them a problem, and would not have wanted to see policies they advocated undone.[31]

The protracted implementation of Dodd-Frank has led some commentators to assert, incorrectly in my judgement, that the regulatory process has been captured by banking interests.[32] The sheer complexity and numerosity

dw-nominate score estimates from the joint space model and an explanation of the methodology are at <http://voteview.com/basic.htm> accessed 18 August 2015.

[27] Eg, Morgenson and Rosner (n 24) 59–71. [28] See, eg, ibid 304–05.

[29] The bill was introduced by Senators Johnson (Democrat) and Crapo (Republican), and was voted out of committee by a 13:9 vote, with several members of both parties voting against it. Trey Garrison, 'Johnson-Crapo Reform Bill Voted to Senate Floor' (HousingWire, 15 May 2014) <http://www.housingwire.com/articles/30016-johnson-crapo-reform-bill-voted-to-senate-floor> accessed 18 August 2015.

[30] See Peter J Wallison and Phil Gramm, 'Worse than Fannie and Freddie' *Wall Street Journal* (17 April 2014); Garrison (n 29) (citing reservations regarding the bill by former Treasury Secretary Timothy Geithner and House Financial Services Committee Chairman Jeb Hensarling).

[31] See text to nn 26–29.

[32] Eg, Arthur E Wilmarth, Jr, 'Turning A Blind Eye: Why Washington Keeps Giving in to Wall Street' (2013) 81 University of Cincinnati Law Review 1283, 1302–05. For capture-thesis critiques of Dodd-Frank and its implementation, see Nolan McCarty, Keith T Poole, and Howard Rosenthal, *Political Bubbles: Financial Crises and the Failure of American Democracy* (Princeton University Press 2013) (statute and regulatory implementation in general); John C Coffee, Jr, 'The Political Economy of Dodd-Frank: Why Financial Reform Tends to Be Frustrated and Systemic Risk Perpetuated' (2012) 97 Cornell Law Review 1019 (regulatory implementation of executive compensation provisions). For capture-thesis explanations of the origins of the financial crisis and regulatory actions taken during it, see Adam J Levitin, 'The Politics of Financial Regulation and the Regulation of Financial Politics: A Review Essay' (2014) 127 Harvard Law Review 1951, 2041–49 (because they were captured by banks, regulators both mistakenly deregulated financial institutions and failed to regulate consumer financial products, causing the crisis, and by engaging in forbearance, had to

[number] of required rule-makings under Dodd-Frank, which at times requires coordination across multiple agencies, as earlier mentioned, would contribute to slowing down any specific rule's enactment quite apart from the additional hurdle of interest group lobbying.

It would, most certainly, be inconceivable for the financial industry not to engage in intensive lobbying over proposed rules, given the immense financial stakes. Although it would not reach the level of a fiduciary breach, it would be irresponsible for management of financial firms to not seek to defend their institutions against regulation which they believed to be both counterproductive and injurious to their firms' financial position. In fact, the notice and comment rule-making procedure under which Dodd-Frank's required rules' enactment will proceed, as established by the Administrative Procedure Act (APA),[33] intentionally encourages such a dialogue: agencies are expected to be responsive to issues raised by interested parties in rule-making deliberations and informed by their input, as the bureaucracy is thought not to be well situated to be adequately conversant with business practices and consequently not attuned to the imposition of unanticipated compliance costs.

In this regard, the SEC has persistently rejected industry requests to include *de minimis* exceptions throughout the protracted Dodd-Frank rule-making process,[34] which is inconsistent with the behaviour of a captured agency. But

bail out banks at greater cost during the crisis); James R Barth, Gerald Caprio Jr, and Ross Levine, *Guardians of Finance: Making Regulators Work for Us* (MIT Press 2012) 4–7 (suggesting regulators' lax, deregulatory policies were the principal contributors to the financial crisis, and can be explained either by regulatory capture by large banks or regulators' subscribing to simplistic free-market ideologies, and placing greater emphasis on ideology than capture explanation). The intellectual pitfall for the pre-crisis capture explanation is that it mechanically assumes that all deregulation (or all deregulation not opposed by industry) is a function of capture and ill-advised. Theoretically, this is an open-ended question and short of an empirical inquiry, it is not possible to ascertain whether the narrative is accurate.

[33] 5 USC § 553.

[34] There are, for example, no *de minimis* exceptions in the conflicts minerals and oil and gas companies' foreign government payments disclosure rules, which took nearly two years for promulgation, with compliance delayed a further year. SEC, 'Conflict Minerals' (2012) 77 Federal Register 56274 (conflict minerals rules, proposed on 15 December 2010, were finalized on 12 September 2012, with effective date 13 November 2012 and compliance date the calendar year beginning 1 January 2013); SEC, 'Disclosure of Payments by Resource Extraction Issuers' (2012) 77 Federal Register 56365 (extraction payments rules, proposed on 15 December 2010, were finalized on 12 September 2012, with effective date 13 November 2012 and compliance date for fiscal years ending after 30 September 2013). Parts of the conflicts minerals were struck down by the DC Circuit in April 2014. *Nat'l Ass'n of Mfrs v SEC*, No 13-5252 (DC Cir 14 April 2014). The SEC stayed implementation of the invalidated parts of the rule, pending further judicial proceedings. SEC, In the Matter of Exchange Act Rule 13p-1 and Form SD, Order Issuing Stay, Rel No 72079 (2 May 2014). The rule was again struck down on rehearing in *Nat'l Ass'n of Mfrs v SEC*, No 13-5252 (DC Cir 18 August 2015). The extraction disclosure rule was vacated by the District Court of the District of Columbia in July 2013, *American Petroleum Inst v SEC*, 953 FSupp 2d 5 (DDC 2013), and a rule has not yet been reissued. Oxfam America, which had sued the SEC in 2012 alleging an

most importantly, as this chapter has contended, were regulators implementing Dodd-Frank to have been captured by the extended rule-making process, then sunsetting would be even more desirable than I have maintained, because a highly public legislative reassessment, replete with hearings and independent expert analyses, would draw attention to captured agencies, and so reassert, not undermine, democratic accountability and decision-making. Moreover, the public review of agency decisions subject to sunsetting should incentivize an agency to resist industry capture from the outset, as it would be aware that its actions would necessarily be evaluated thereafter and possibly overturned.

3. Dodd-Frank and the Legacy of Crisis-Driven Legislative Responses

Crisis-driven legislation often adopts off-the-rack solutions along with open-ended delegation to regulatory agencies as legislators, who perceive a political necessity to act quickly, adopt ready-to-go proposals offered by policy entrepreneurs with whom they are typically politically aligned and to whom they afford access.[35] Dodd-Frank exemplifies the difficulties that are created by these conventional crisis-driven legislative strategies, in the Volcker rule, which prohibits banks' proprietary trading, and creation of the Consumer Financial Protection Bureau (CFPB).

(a) A Problematic Delegation: The Volcker Rule

The statutory provision known as the Volcker rule illustrates both that delegation in crisis-driven legislation can be particularly problematic and that, in turn, inapt congressional directives can contribute to protracted rule-making. The provision restricts banking entities from engaging in specific risky activity, including proprietary trading and investment in hedge funds and private equity funds, activities which have often been among banks' more profitable lines of business.[36] It has arguably been the most contentious and protracted

unreasonable delay in promulgating a final rule after proposing a rule, has again sued the agency to compel the rule-making, a suit which the SEC has sought to have dismissed. *Oxfam America Inc v SEC*, No 14-cv-13648 (D Mass 18 September 2014); Yin Wilczek, 'SEC Asks Court to Nix Lawsuit Over Resource Extraction Disclosures' (2015) Bloomberg BNA Corporate Accountability Report 488.

[35] Romano, 'Regulating in the Dark' (2012) (n 1) 88–91.

[36] Dodd-Frank § 619, 12 USC § 1851(a)(1)(2012). Non-bank institutions designated as SIFIs are not subject to the ban, but are subject to heightened capital requirements and other restrictions regarding such activities. ibid § 1851(a)(2). For the proposed rule's expected adverse impact on

implementation of Dodd- Frank's regulatory directives, no doubt exacerbated by the broad discretionary delegation; as one commentator has put it, there are 'broad gaps and ambiguities on key definitional issues', the resolution of which much rides on, not the least, banks' business models.[37] Accordingly, the lengthy gestation period has been asserted to provide the opportunity for industry capture (ie, for industry delaying tactics and resistance to wear down, or otherwise convince, regulators to adopt definitions favourable to banks).[38]

A comprehensive study by Kimberly Krawiec of pre-proposal stage agency contacts and comments regarding the Volcker rule found that the vast majority of contacts were by industry and, while the vast majority of comments were by members of the public, those comments were uninformative, non-substantive form letters (a campaign organized by public interest groups), whereas the much smaller set provided by the industry were carefully drafted, addressing technical issues related to the rule.[39] Certainly, these findings are intuitive; given the highly technical nature of the rule, the public could not be expected to provide informative comments, whereas industry representatives would have the expertise to do so.[40] While the study at times intimates that the data are consistent with a capture story, Krawiec does not conclude that the data evince capture. Rather, she notes that there were important, informed 'countervailing' voices weighing in during the pre-proposal period—senators who sponsored the rule and Paul Volcker himself—and that

banks' bottom line, see Kimberly D Krawiec, 'Don't "Screw Joe the Plummer": The Sausage-Making of Financial Reform' (2013) 55 Arizona Law Review 53, 61.

[37] ibid 67. Among the ambiguities and gaps that need interpretation are the definition of 'trading account' and the scope of statutory exemptions to the ban on proprietary trading and the ban on fund investments. ibid 65–66.

[38] ibid 69–70.

[39] ibid 58–59. This is also not a unique situation. Studies of rule-making by the Environmental Protection Agency (EPA) similarly find that pre-proposal stage contacts are overwhelmingly dominated by industry (although some of those contacts are initiated by the agency as information requests). Wendy Wagner, Katherine Barnes, and Lisa Peters, 'Rulemaking in the Shade: An Empirical Study of the EPA's Air Toxic Emission Standards' (2011) 63 Administrative Law Review 99, 125–26, 143. EPA rule-making studies further report that a majority of comments submitted during the rule-making process are by industry, ibid 129, that the number of comments from industry is positively correlated with a rule's projected cost (crudely measured as above or below $100 million), while the number of comments from the public increases with newspaper coverage (issue salience) and is unaffected by a rule's projected cost, ibid 139–40. Krawiec suggests that the latter finding may explain the higher proportion of public comments in her data (ie, that the Volcker rule is a high salience provision). Krawiec (n 36) 83.

[40] Krawiec finds one datum surprising: no sector of the financial industry, such as institutional investors, who might have been 'expected to fight any weakening' of the rule's 'protections that supposedly accrue to their benefit', participated in the pre-proposal stage. ibid 84. An explanation that I think is plausible is that the provision did not benefit investors (or as she puts more mildly, the 'benefits of the legislation to those parties were overstated' ibid).

the political science literature suggests that the input of such individuals can provide an effective counterbalance to that of industry in agency decision-making.[41] And she leaves the question open, for, as she recognizes, it is difficult to glean much in the way of a bottom line with respect to industry capture without examining the constellation of comments and contacts in the later rule-making stages, nor, more importantly, how, if at all, pre-proposal concerns raised by industry affected the proposed rule, which will be subjects of her future research.[42]

More important, an assertion that the prolonged implementation of the rule, or a finding that issues raised in the pre-proposal stage influenced the proposed rule, demonstrate industry capture would ignore the built-in source of delay, as previously noted, from the need for the rule to be coordinated across multiple regulators.[43] More importantly, it would also sweep aside what is, in fact, deep and genuine intellectual disagreement on both the efficacy and workability of the Volcker rule.[44] For example, distinguishing between illegal proprietary trading and legal market making, can, to put it mildly, be a formidable task.[45] Yet such a distinction is in the statutory formulation. Indeed, the Volcker rule's substantive requirement poses such severe implementation challenges that the UK deliberately adopted instead a retail ring-fencing approach to constrain banks' risk-taking, which requires separating into different entities an institution's retail banking and related services from its wholesale and investment banking businesses, thereby, in theory, isolating retail banking services, and hence taxpayers, from losses on trading activities and other wholesale banking risks.[46] With sunsetting, legislators'

[41] ibid 82–84. The study of EPA rule-making also does not conclude that the numerical dominance (or as the authors put it, 'imbalance') of industry contacts and comments during the rule-making process 'has a meaningful impact' on the rules, but after considering arguments why it might not have such an effect, concludes that the evidence 'does not rule out' that possibility. Wagner et al. (n 39) 147.

[42] Krawiec (n 36) 83.

[43] For a discussion of the difficulties of policy implementation when there are multiple decision points, with the Volcker rule as an example, see Peter H Schuck, *Why Government Fails So Often and How It Can Do Better* (Princeton University Press 2014) 236–38.

[44] See, eg, Charles A Piasio, 'It's Complicated: Why the Volcker Rule Is Unworkable' (2013) 43 Seton Hall Law Review 737, 738–40. It also would ignore the built-in source of delay, as previously noted, from the need for the rule to be coordinated across multiple regulators.

[45] ibid 761; Krawiec (n 36) 65–68.

[46] Timothy Edmonds, 'The Independent Commission on Banking: The Vickers Report' (3 January 2013) 3, 7 <http://www.parliament.uk/briefing-papers/SN06171> accessed 19 August 2015 (House of Commons research note explaining Independent Commission on Banking's ring-fencing recommendation and rejection of Volcker rule); 'Client Update: Financial Services (Banking Reform) Bill—Expect the Unexpected' (Debevoise and Plimpton LLP 7 February 2013) <http://www.debevoise.com/clientupdate20130207a/> accessed 19 August 2015 (UK government indicated it will implement the recommendations of the Independent Commission introduced that does so).

attention, with the assistance of an expert review panel, would be directed to reassessing the proprietary trading prohibition and a comparative assessment by experts could be undertaken concerning which approach, prohibition or ring-fencing, was more effective, as well as whether such rules make much sense in the first place. Such an inquiry would serve to raise the quality of decision-making.

Compounding the challenge of implementing the Volcker rule beyond its sheer intractability, is the fact that it is one of many Dodd-Frank 'solutions' to conjectural problems, for as former Treasury Secretary Timothy Geithner succinctly put it, 'Proprietary trading by banks played no meaningful role in the crisis.'[47] Although legislation plainly should seek to anticipate future financial crises and not solely address past ones, directing the focus of regulatory efforts on resolving known and pressing regulatory issues over speculative ones is self-evidently a more rational and prudent regulatory agenda, given scarcity in agency time and resources.

Notwithstanding a protracted drafting effort, there were still large unintended adverse consequences that became immediately apparent upon the Volcker rule's promulgation. Within a month, an interim rule was further adopted to provide an exception to the final rule's treatment of specified derivative instruments (collateralized debt obligations backed by trust-preferred securities) to mitigate an otherwise adverse impact on small and medium-sized banks, their having to take large losses writing down the securities, placing banks at risk of violating capital requirements.[48] The Rube Goldberg-like Volcker rule, which is over 900 pages, will, no doubt, produce further surprises, in addition to imposing substantial compliance costs.[49] This is yet another consideration for why sunsetting would be of value in this context.

[47] Timothy F Geithner, *Stress Test: Reflections on Financial Crises* (Crown Publishers 2014) 414. For similar views in the academic literature, see, eg, Piasio (n 44) 738–40; Charles Whitehead, 'The Volcker Rule and Evolving Financial Markets' (2011) 1 Harvard Business Law Review 39, 41–42.

[48] Rob Blackwell, 'Volcker Rule Fix Will Aid Large and Small' *American Banker* (14 January 2014); Matthew Goldstein, 'Regulators Ease Volcker Rule Provision on Smaller Banks, Dealbook' *NY Times* (14 January 2014).

[49] Steve Culp, 'Final Volcker Rule Leaves Banks Facing Compliance Hurdles' *Forbes* (17 December 2013) (summarizing lengthy set of activities companies must undertake to 'bring themselves into' compliance with the rule). In addition, in at least the immediate future, adding to the cost is the considerable uncertainty over how to comply with the rule, as the rule raises a host of interpretative questions without a transparent process for how to obtain clarity from enforcement agencies, in addition to the question whether when one agency provides an interpretation, other agencies will agree. Margaret E Tahyar, 'Volcker Rule: Observations on Interagency FAQs, OCC Interim Examination Guidelines' (Harvard Law School Forum on Corporate Governance and Financial Regulation 20 June 2014) <http://blogs.law.harvard.edu/corpgov/2014/06/20/volcker-rule-observations-on-interagency-faqs-occ-interim-examination-guidelines/> accessed 19 August 2015.

The Office of the Comptroller of the Currency (OCC) estimates the Volcker rule could cost the banking entities that it supervises upwards of $4 billion, a figure challenged by an SEC commissioner as, in all likelihood, far too low.[50] As he put it, 'Based upon the fact that this is not a serious analysis, I have no way to evaluate whether they are even in the right ballpark.'[51] Sunsetting would provide an opportunity for Congress to obtain a handle on the true scope of the cost and accordingly, revise the rule or direct regulators to do so, in order to produce a more cost-effective implementation or to adopt an entirely different approach to the problem.

One might contend that sunsetting is unnecessary for a salient rule such as the Volcker rule because it would attract congressional attention for consideration under the Congressional Review Act (CRA), under which, before a rule can take effect, it must be submitted to each chamber of Congress, for review under an expedited legislative process that permits enactment of a joint disapproval resolution, which, when signed by the President (or a veto is overridden), repeals the rule.[52] However, as evidenced by the experience under the CRA—since enactment in 1996, only one rule has been disapproved and only two other disapproval resolutions have ever been passed by one chamber[53]– the CRA is not an effective substitute for sunsetting.

[50] Jesse Hamilton, 'Volcker Rule Will Cost Banks Up to $4.3 Billion, OCC Says' *Bloomberg* (21 March 2014). SEC Commissioner Michael Piwowar's critical judgement of the OCC estimate was derived from his view of the agency's analysis as 'not rigorous'.

[51] ibid.

[52] 5 USC §§ 801–802 (2012). The joint resolution must be adopted within sixty days of the submission, subject to extension if Congress is not in session at the time. ibid § 802. The statute requires consideration in the Senate under fast-track procedures, preventing a resolution from being held up in committee or filibustered, ibid § 802(c) and (d). While there are no special procedural requirements for the House, a chamber receiving a disapproval resolution from the other chamber cannot bottle it up in committee. ibid § 802(f)(1).

[53] Morton Rosenberg, Congressional Research Service, 'Congressional Review of Agency Rulemaking: An Update and Assessment of the Congressional Review Act After a Decade' (8 May 2008) 6 (as of 31 March 2008, Congress received reports on 731 major rules and 47,540 non-major rules under the statute, 47 joint resolutions concerning 35 rules were introduced, with only one rule disapproved and two other rules disapproved by the Senate). Moreover, the one rule disapproval, the Occupational Safety and Health Association's (OSHA) 2001 ergonomics standard, is considered to be a 'unique' situation, as it was extremely controversial given estimated costs to business, over a decade in the making, including delays by Congress through appropriations riders, adopted when the Clinton presidency was a lame duck, and an altered political situation within the statutory sixty-day period for review, as the intervening election gave Republicans effective control of both chambers and the presidency. ibid 6, 14–15. Whether the standard could have been repealed without the CRA is unclear (the Republican control of the Senate was not filibuster-proof, although the disapproval resolution was supported by some Democrats), but as one commentator put it, 'Because of the unique circumstances surrounding ergonomics, we cannot generalize from the impact on the CRA on ergonomics to conclude that the CRA has a significant impact on the regulatory process … Even with [the conditions of a Republican presidency and Congress and many lame duck regulations], Congress did not attempt to overturn any of the many other major regulations issued by the

There are numerous problems with the CRA. First, the CRA permits only an up or down vote on a rule in its entirety, while at the same time prohibiting an agency from reissuing a 'similar' rule if a rule has been disapproved.[54] This structure deters legislators from voting for a disapproval resolution, out of concern that it would create an administrative vacuum,[55] which could especially be a problem with a long and complicated rule, such as the Volcker rule, where parts of the rule may be desirable to retain. Sunset review, by contrast, permits legislative tailoring: besides the yes or no approach of the CRA, a rule can be revised, or retained or repealed only in part. The ability to tailor regulation would facilitate a more deliberative review process than the CRA, by eliminating the contention that a rule must be left intact to avoid regulatory anarchy. Second, there is no mechanism under the CRA by which Congress can readily obtain additional information to assess a rule, as would be provided by a sunset review's panel of independent experts, which, again, should render decision-making of higher quality under sunsetting.[56]

Finally, and most importantly, non-compliance with the requirements of the CRA is rampant, with agencies having failed to submit to Congress for review well over 1,000 rules from 1998 to 2008, 101 substantive final rules in 2008 alone.[57] Without notice of a rule, Congress cannot review, it, yet neither the CRA, nor Congress subsequently, has devised a mechanism by which it can identify unsubmitted rules or enforce compliance.[58] Agency non-compliance, and hence absence of congressional review, would not occur under a sunsetting regime, given the starkly different default: a rule stays in existence if Congress does not act under the CRA, whereas it expires if Congress fails to act under sunsetting. In short, sunsetting provides a forcing

Clinton administration in its waning months.' Stuart Shapiro, 'The Role of Procedural Controls in OSHA's Ergonomics Rulemaking' (2007) 67 American Review of Public Administration 688, 696.

[54] Rosenberg (n 53) 22–23, 34–35.

[55] For instance, opponents of the resolution disapproving the ergonomics standard contended that it would not be possible for OSHA to write another rule were the resolution to pass. Shapiro (n 53) 696.

[56] For example, the statute requires an agency to provide a cost-benefit analysis with the submission of the rule and the Comptroller General (CG) to assess the agency's compliance with that requirement, but the CG interprets the requirement narrowly, and does not substantively evaluate the agency's analysis but simply reports whether the required cost-benefit analysis is present. Rosenberg (n 53) 3.

[57] Sean D Croston, 'Congress and the Courts Close Their Eyes: The Continuing Abdication of the Duty to Review Agencies' Noncompliance with the Congressional Review Act' (2010) 62 Administrative Law Review 907, 908 (citing figures from a 2009 report by the Congressional Research Service). As Croston notes, that estimate is likely to be an understatement, because an earlier congressional report suggested that 'thousands' of rules had not been submitted for review. ibid.

[58] For possible reasons why Congress has not acted to remedy the compliance failures, see ibid 909–11.

mechanism for action that the CRA lacks, and combined with similar fast-track legislative procedures, the possibility of a minority impeding action will be vastly reduced. Although in the abstract, the CRA is an admirable concept through which Congress could exercise substantive control over poorly devised regulation, in practice, it has failed spectacularly, as commentators have noted, interpreting its disuse as evidence of total ineffectiveness.[59]

(b) Off-the-Rack Solutions: Reshuffling Bureaucratic Boxes and the CFPB

An illustration of the inherent problematic nature of 'off-the-rack solutions' fashioned in crisis-driven legislation is Dodd-Frank's creation of the CFPB, which consolidated into one agency functions that had been allocated across seven federal agencies pre-crisis.[60] Reshuffling bureaucratic boxes is a tried and true legislative response to crises. This is because it is a high visibility 'solution'—it demonstrates that legislators are 'doing something' in a way that is relatively easy for a poorly informed public to observe—and it combines two favoured legislative responses to crises—an 'off-the-rack' response conjoined with a delegation strategy, as the agency will bear responsibility for policy failures rather than legislators.[61]

[59] Rosenberg (n 53); Croston (n 57).

[60] Leonard J Kennedy, Patricia McCoy, and Ethan Bernstein, 'The Consumer Financial Protection Bureau: Financial Regulation for the Twenty-First Century' (2011–12) 97 Cornell Law Review 1141, 1145.

[61] Romano, 'Regulating in the Dark' (2012) (n 1) 88–90. A number of financial regulatory agencies have been created in response to financial crises: the Federal Deposit Insurance Corporation in the Banking Act (Pub L 73–66, 48 Stat 162, enacted 16 June 1933), which responded to the bank failures in the 1930s and the Great Depression; the SEC in the Securities Exchange Act Securities Act of 1933 [15 USC 77e], which responded to the stock market crash of 1929 and the Great Depression; the Public Company Accountant Oversight Board in the Sarbanes–Oxley Act of 2002 (Pub L 107–204, 116 Stat 745, enacted 30 July 2002), which responded to the 2001–02 accounting scandals involving Enron and other companies; and not only the CFPB but also the Financial Stability Oversight Council in the Dodd-Frank Reform and Consumer Protection Act (Pub L 111–203, HR 4173) (Dodd-Frank). The approach has also been used in response to non-financial crises, the most recent and notable example being creation of the Homeland Security Department in the Uniting and Strengthening America by Providing Appropriate Tools Required to Intercept and Obstruct Terrorism Act of 2001 (Public Law Pub L 107–56). And it would seem to be a stock response to crises beyond US borders as well: the European Union created three new EU-level supervisory agencies in the wake of the crisis. See, eg, 'Financial Supervision Package—Frequently Asked Questions, Memo' (European Commission 2010) <http://europa.eu/rapid/press-release_MEMO-10-434_en.htm> accessed 19 August 2015. For a cogent critique of bureaucratic reorganization as a crisis response, see Richard Posner, *The Crisis of Capitalist Democracy* (Harvard University Press 2010) 171–75.

As often occurs with 'off-the-rack' legislative responses to financial crises, Dodd-Frank's administrative reorganization mismatches problem and solution because the US regulatory architecture, and in particular, absence of a designated consumer-product regulator, did not contribute to the financial crisis. For instance, housing bubbles produced severe financial crises in Iceland, Ireland, and Spain, despite the absence of subprime mortgage securitizations in those nations.[62] In addition, there were meltdowns of financial institutions operating under distinctly different regulatory architectures (eg, under both the multi-regulator, decentralized US regime and the UK's centralized one).[63] Given the simultaneous regulatory failures and crises in nations with disparate financial products, markets, and regulatory structures, it is improbable that any bureaucratic reorganization would address the causes of the recent financial crisis, let alone prevent a future one.[64]

More particularly, it is quite implausible that the recent financial crisis would have been averted had there been an independent federal agency regulating consumer financial products: in discussing in his memoir the Administration's decision to reorganize the government bureaucracy in the area of consumer protection, former Treasury Secretary Geithner does not mention the financial crisis once as a rationale or cause for the proposal. Rather, he refers to the President's passion for 'defending ordinary families from financial abuse', dating back to outrage at his credit card rates when he was a community organizer, and presidential aides' political considerations, including, pleasing the political base that was dissatisfied with Administration policies, and resonating with the public and therefore building support for the rest of the bill.[65]

[62] Carmen M Reinhart and Kenneth S Rogoff, *This Time is Different: Eight Centuries of Financial Folly* (Princeton University Press 2009) 244. For an analysis debunking the contention that the resets on exploding adjustable-rate mortgages caused a wave of foreclosures ushering in the financial crisis, see Foote et al. (n 5).

[63] While the regulatory structures differed substantially across nations, international bank capital requirements were harmonized under the Basel Accords, and elsewhere I have contended that international harmonization contributed, in some measure, to the global financial crisis, by incentivizing banks to follow similar business strategies. See Roberta Romano, 'For Diversity in the International Regulation of Financial Institutions: Rethinking the Basel Architecture' (2014) 31 Yale Journal on Regulation 1, 13–20. But the Basel Accords did not harmonize how regulators should respond to bank failures, and different regulatory architecture did not produce quicker or cleaner resolutions to the global financial crisis.

[64] In addition, most of the new agency's jurisdiction is over products and institutions that had no connection to the crisis. See, eg, Todd Zywicki, 'The Consumer Financial Protection Bureau: Savior or Menace?' (2013) 81 George Washington Law School 856, 861 ('[T]here is absolutely no evidence that failures in consumer protection actually contributed in a major way to the crisis—indeed, many of the financial service providers swept under the CFPB's umbrella, such as payday lenders and providers of cash remittances, had nothing at all to do with the financial crisis.').

[65] Geithner (n 47) 403–04. The CFPB's lax definition of a qualified mortgage (n 8) and the fact that none of the subprime products sold to consumers were newly invented in the years before the

As is also quite typical for many components of crisis-driven legislation, the idea of a single federal agency with regulatory authority specifically over consumer financial products was not a new proposal carefully tailored to address an identified problem related to the financial crisis. Rather, it had been floated as a proposal by a policy entrepreneur prior to the onset of the crisis. Then law professor Elizabeth Warren had advocated such an entity in a short 2007 article, by analogy to the federal agency protecting consumers from harm by physical products.[66] The Bush Administration had similarly proposed such an entity in a March 2008 plan to consolidate the multiple regulators of financial institutions, which had been crafted prior to the onset of the financial crisis as a strategy to improve capital market competitiveness (but then, with repositioning, urged as a solution to the financial crisis in the waning days of the Bush presidency).[67]

Warren shortly thereafter co-authored a more extensive law review article with Oren Bar-Gill which sought to provide a theoretical justification for her original proposal, fleshing out why consumers of financial products could need regulatory protection using concepts from behavioural economics.[68] Underscoring the fact that the genesis of the idea for the agency was independent of the financial crisis, the bulk of the 100-page-long article's analysis focuses on consumer credit cards, which had no role in the financial crisis, with only a page or so discussing mortgages. The Bar-Gill and Warren article was identified by the Obama Administration as the source of its inclusion of such an agency in its legislative reform proposal to address the financial crisis.[69]

The law review article did not, however, provide any institutional detail concerning the agency's structure, except to state that it should be either an independent agency or a division within an existing agency, such as the Federal Reserve or Federal Trade Commission, while the Obama Administration proposal advocated creating an independent executive branch

financial crisis, Foote et al. (n 5), further support the text's counterfactual contention that had the CFPB predated the crisis it still would have occurred.

[66] Elizabeth Warren, 'Unsafe at Any Rate: If It's Good Enough for Microwaves, It's Good Enough for Mortgages: Why We Need a Consumer Financial Product Safety Commission' (2007) 5 [Summer] Democracy 8 <http://www.democracyjournal.org/5/6528.php?page=all> accessed 19 August 2015.

[67] United States Department of the Treasury, *Blueprint for a Modernized Financial Regulatory Structure* (March 2008) 170–71.

[68] Oren Bar-Gill and Elizabeth Warren, 'Making Credit Safer' (2008) 157 University of Pennsylvania Law Review 1.

[69] United States Department of the Treasury, 'Financial Regulatory Reform: A New Foundation' <http://treasury.gov/press-center/press-releases/Pages/200961710524873O9.aspx> accessed 19 August 2015; Kennedy et al. (n 60) 1146 n 14 (idea for Administration's proposed agency derived from Bar-Gill and Warren's recommendation).

agency with a director and board of which one member would be the head of a prudential regulator.[70] The CFPB that the statute established, adapting the Administration proposal, has a unique autonomous structure for a US administrative agency: organized similarly to a cabinet department in the executive branch with a solitary director (in contrast to independent agencies that are structured as bipartisan commissions), it is, however, entirely independent of the executive as it was placed within the Federal Reserve System (Fed).[71]

Even more unique, the CFPB is also financially independent of Congress as it is not subject to the appropriations process: the director sets his own budget, which is funded by the Fed (capped at 12 per cent of the Fed's total operating expense).[72] Moreover, Federal Reserve Board governors may neither intervene in the CFPB's affairs, review or delay implementation of its rules, nor consolidate the bureau, its functions, or responsibilities with any other office or division of the Fed.[73] This regulatory setup has a bizarre whiff of a Kafkaesque bureaucracy, as the agency is formally insulated from political accountability.[74]

The CFPB's unique independent structure is combined with wide-ranging authority that is inherently in conflict with prudential regulation aimed at reducing bank failure, underscoring the reality that creation of the agency was an off-the-rack solution quite unrelated to the financial crisis. For instance,

[70] Bar-Gill and Warren (n 68) 98; United States Department of the Treasury (n 69) 58.

[71] Dodd-Frank § 1011. Moreover, in contrast to a cabinet department secretary, who serves at the whim of the President, the CFPB director, who has a fixed term, can only be removed for cause. ibid § 1011(c)(3). As Todd Zywicki describes the evolution of the agency's structure, in the House bill, the agency was to be 'a multimember commission funded in part by congressional appropriations', but that was criticized, particularly by Republicans, who objected to the expense of creating a new agency, and the response, appearing in the Senate bill, was to 'turn the agency into a bureau of the Fed'. Zywicki (n 64) 860–61.

[72] Dodd-Frank §1017. There is an inflation index adjustment, ibid §1017(a)(2)(B), and if the amount is inadequate, the director can request a further appropriation from Congress, ibid. § 1017(e). The CFPB requested less from the Fed to fund its operations than the transfer cap for fiscal year 2014 and projected it would do so as well for fiscal year 2015, whose respective budget caps are $608.4 million and an estimated $618.7 million. 'The CFPB Strategic Plan, Budget and Performance Plan and Report' (Consumer Finance Protection Bureau 2014) 20 <http://www.consumerfinance.gov/strategic-plan-budget-and-performance-plan-and-report/> accessed 19 August 2015.

[73] Dodd-Frank § 1012 (c)(2).

[74] Although the director must file semi-annual reports with Congress, there is little action Congress can take to alter policies with which it disagrees, unless the agency requires additional funds than it obtains from the Fed and fines that it imposes on regulated entities. Moreover, as discussed at text to nn 78–98, the director has been able to circumvent Congress's effort to impose accountability in the specification of criteria to be used in rule-making, which the courts could enforce, by regulating without engaging in rule-making. For an extensive criticism of the agency's structure, as rendering the CFPB as 'one of the most powerful and publicly unaccountable agencies in American history', see Zywicki (n 64) 875–99.

the statutory mission is to 'ensur[e] that all consumers have access to markets for financial products and services' that are 'fair, transparent and competitive'.[75] Such an objective suffers from the twin faults of over- and under-inclusiveness with regard to improving the financial regulatory architecture. It is under-inclusive by failing to target the market and product igniting the global financial crisis, the shadow banking sector, an institutional, not retail, market, and securitized mortgages, which were neither a consumer credit, nor even a retail, product. Yet it is over-inclusive as the CFPB is given authority to regulate all forms of consumer credit and not simply subprime mortgages, which were the only retail product implicated in the crisis (as the increase in subprime defaults was a trigger of the shadow banking run).[76]

More importantly, the CFPB's overlapping supervisory authority with banks' prudential regulators is in inherent conflict given the distinctly different missions: safety and soundness of banks and the financial system versus consumer protection. Indeed, the CFPB's supervisory process 'flip[s] the safety and soundness regulatory paradigm on its head' by directing the most intensive scrutiny to banks' most profitable financial products and services.[77] Recognizing that the differing regulatory objectives of this dual supervisory system would lead to inevitable conflict, the statute permits banks to request that agencies coordinate if there is a supervisory conflict and, if they fail to coordinate, to appeal to an ad hoc panel of three regulators, which includes one regulator from each of the agencies that failed to coordinate.[78] But this setup is not a satisfactory resolution of the supervisory tension as such an appeals process would both be costly to undertake and uncertain in outcome, given the panel composition (as it will only shift venue without resolving the turf battle the agencies could not negotiate in the first place), factors that discourage its use.

The most troubling aspect of the CFPB's unique insulation from congressional oversight, however, is that it has facilitated policy-making that evades democratic accountability and that, on occasion, has been of questionable lawfulness. Namely, the CFPB has used notice and comment rule-making only where it was mandated to adopt a rule by Congress in Dodd-Frank. On

[75] Dodd-Frank § 1021.

[76] For the contention that whatever the contribution of subprime mortgages to the financial crisis, it was entirely unconnected to consumer protection issues and implicated solely prudential—safety and soundness—regulatory concerns, because consumers were rationally responding to incentives provided by lenders who were making unwise loans, and not consumers' misunderstanding of the loan terms, see Zywicki (n 64) 910–11.

[77] Eric J Mogilnicki and Melissa S Malpass, 'The First Year of the Consumer Financial Protection Bureau: An Overview' (2013) 68 The Business Lawyer 557.

[78] Dodd-Frank § 1025(e)(3) and (4).

all other occasions, as far as I can determine, it has instead engaged in rule-making by subterfuge, through the use of guidance (statements of 'expectations') and enforcement actions. These strategies enable the agency to evade not only engaging in the informed and transparent decision-making process that Congress sought in enacting the APA, but also in having to comply with the specific criteria Congress enumerated in Dodd-Frank regarding factors it wished to inform the CFPB's rule-making, including a cost-benefit standard, as Congress did not similarly specify criteria for CFPB orders, guidance, or enforcement actions.[79]

The use of guidance and enforcement actions, rather than rule-making, to effect regulatory policy further sidesteps an important safeguard of congressional delegation which is maintained by judicial review. Political scientists have emphasized that a key mechanism by which Congress controls administrative agencies is its specification of administrative procedures.[80] Because it cannot predict what regulatory issues will arise and therefore what substantive mandates to enact or require agencies to implement, Congress designs procedures that 'assign relative degrees of importance' to constituents, to participate in, monitor, and appeal the outcome of, administrative decisions.[81] In creating the CFPB, Congress added specific procedural content going beyond APA general rule-making procedures, specifying that the agency must consider the costs and benefits not only to consumers but also to the providers and offerors of financial products and services, in its rule-making. Without judicial enforcement of those procedures, interested parties (ie, constituents) cannot constrain agency outcomes to those Congress desired and political control over agencies is crippled.[82] Using guidance to effectuate policy-making undermines the balance struck by Congress to maintain control over the agency because courts rarely characterize guidance as agency action subject to judicial review.[83]

[79] ibid § 1022.

[80] Mathew D McCubbins, Roger G Noll, and Barry R Weingast, 'Administrative Procedures as Instruments of Political Control' (1987) 3 Journal of Law, Economics & Organization 243, 244–45.

[81] ibid 244–46. [82] ibid 263.

[83] It is difficult to obtain judicial review of guidance decisions, as courts typically do not consider them to be final agency action, as required for standing by the APA, 5 USC § 704 (2012), or otherwise ripe for review. Nina A Mendelson, 'Regulatory Beneficiaries and Informal Agency Policymaking' (2007) 92 Cornell Law Review 397, 411. If an agency's guidance is viewed as having 'binding' effect, then a court may deem it a 'legislative rule' and uphold a challenge against the agency for not following the notice and comment process. Nicholas Bagley and Helen Levy, 'Essential Health Benefits and the Affordable Care Act: Law and Process' (2013) Journal of Health Politics, Policy and Law 443, 455–56. This area of law is quite murky; as one article puts it, 'the line separating policy statements from legislative rules is not crisp', ibid, and courts generally do not second-guess

What I have described critically regarding the CFPB's regulatory strategy could be considered totally prosaic as agencies regularly engage in regulatory strategies that avoid the arduous strictures of notice and comment rule-making,[84] and administrative law scholars have long debated the degree to which this should be a matter of concern.[85] But there is a critical difference between generic agencies and the CFPB that should render the CFPB's use of such tactics profoundly unsettling. An agency subject to an annual appropriations process, in contrast to the CFPB, cannot manoeuvre as freely and aggressively use such strategies because congressional committees have leverage to enforce accountability through imposition of budgetary restrictions and non-statutory directives and instructions regarding specific expenditures accompanying budget legislation.[86] The incentive effect of the CFPB's unique organizational structure upon its choice of policy tools could, as I think it should, be revisited were financial regulation subject to sunsetting.[87]

Two examples will suffice to illustrate the CFPB's questionable employment of regulatory strategies that enable it to obtain the outcome it desires regarding regulated entities' behaviour, without the use of rule-making. First, the agency staff believed that credit card add-ons, such as payment for lost wallet protection, had no value and should not be sold. This is, of course, possible,

agencies' choice of regulatory tool. Lisa Schultz Bressman, 'Beyond Accountability: Arbitrariness and Legitimacy in the Administrative State' (2003) 78 New York University Law Review 461, 534.

[84] Mendelson (n 83) 397–99.

[85] For a general discussion of the competing considerations, see, Bressman (n 83) 541–44; and for a discussion of the considerations focused on guidance documents, see Mendelson (n 83) 406–13.

[86] For a discussion of appropriations committee oversight techniques, and their use to delay the SEC's implementation of the Sarbanes-Oxley Act's internal controls provision to small firms, see Romano (n 23) 284–86. For a parallel notion that the structural accountability of an agency affects its incentives to engage in robust informed decision-making, and is a matter of policy concern, see Catherine M Sharkey, 'State Farm "with Teeth": Heightened Judicial Review in the Absence of Executive Oversight' (2014) 89 New York University Law Review 1589 (contending that the factual determinations of independent agencies that are not subject to executive oversight should receive less judicial deference because they have insufficient incentives to engage in comprehensive cost-benefit analysis, compared to agencies which know their rules must be reviewed by the Office of Information and Regulatory Affairs in the Office of Management and Budget).

[87] Congress could, of course, revisit the CFPB's structure without sunsetting. Indeed, Republicans have introduced several bills, one of which passed the House on a nearly party line vote, to restructure the agency. Consumer Financial Protection Safety and Soundness Improvement Act of 2013, HR 3193, 113th Congress, 1st Sesssion, Roll Call vote # 85 (27 February 2014) (all Republicans and ten Democrats voting for) <http://clerk.house.gov/evs/2014/roll085.xml> accessed 19 August 2015. But none have moved in the Senate and President Obama would surely veto any such legislation. As a practical matter, the many veto points in the legislative process render reorganization of the CFPB highly unlikely in the absence of another crisis or scandal leading to calls for a bureaucratic rearrangement, or perhaps, an election sweep in which the Republican Party, whose members uniformly opposed the agency's creation, took commanding control of both chambers and the presidency.

but a contested assertion.[88] Rather than adopt a rule prohibiting or restricting their sale, it brought three enforcement actions against credit card providers for improper marketing and published a list of 'expectations'—what it would look for in evaluating the product.[89] In response to those agency actions, the three largest banks, followed by other institutions (none of whom were the subject of the enforcement actions), 'voluntarily' cancelled the products.[90] It is inconceivable that the CFPB's heavy-handed use of its powers is the approach that Congress had in mind when it directed the agency to consider the 'potential benefits and costs to consumers and covered persons [financial institutions], including the potential reduction of access by consumers to consumer financial products or services resulting from such rule',[91] as it conveyed a preference that the agency engage in cost-benefit analysis and not restrict the financial products available to consumers.

Second, the CFPB staff believes that data indicate that automobile dealers charge higher interest rates to women and minorities than to white men (although it did not make public the supporting data, which was derived from proxies, not actual sales data, used to estimate discrimination because the ethnicity of car buyers is not recorded).[92] But Dodd-Frank expressly prohibited the agency from regulating automobile dealers.[93] The agency

[88] As Alan Schwartz has noted, a problem with substantive rules restricting consumer contracts (as opposed to disclosure regulation) is that both rational and irrational consumers may prefer the same contracts, such as a credit card add-on, but as the regulator can observe only contracting choices, not preferences, it cannot distinguish irrational from rational consumers by simply observing market choices. As a consequence, restricting the consumer's ability to contract (eg, purchasing the add-on), may decrease, not increase welfare, as it might be rationally chosen and not, as the regulator assumes, chosen by mistake (ie, due to cognitive bias or consumer irrationality). Alan Schwartz, 'Regulating for Rationality' (2015) The Stanford Law Review 1373.

[89] Marketing of Credit Card Add-on Products' (Consumer Financial Protection Bureau 18 July 2012) <http://www.consumerfinance.gov/f/201207_cfpb_bulletin_marketing_of_credit_card_addon_products.pdf> accessed 19 August 2015.

[90] See Karen Weise, 'The Consumer Finance Watchdog Is Having an Impact' *Bloomberg Businessweek* (10 January 2013). The three banks subject to the enforcement actions—one of which was for failure to supervise a third-party vendor and not for any failures in its own marketing—were required to pay in aggregate $101.5 million and $435 million in refunds to customers. ibid.

[91] Dodd-Frank § 1022 (b)(2)(A)(1).

[92] 'Your Car Dealer Must Be a Racist' *Wall Street Journal* (15 November 2013) A14 (editorial); Kim B Perez, 'The CFPB "Indirectly" Regulates Lending Through Auto-Dealers' (2014) 18 North Carolina Banking Institute 399, 418 (CFPB guidance bulletin relied on mathematical proxies for race and ethnicity, using Social Security Administration and Census Bureau data to estimate the probability someone is of a racial or ethnic minority based on their surname and geographic location, and then used the proxies to determine where consumers might experience discrimination based on interest rates that proxy-determined minorities received).

[93] Dodd-Frank § 1029. The statute contains exceptions to the exclusion of auto dealers from the CFPB's regulatory authority, but none of the exceptions apply to auto loans that a dealer provides through a bank or that are securitized, the subject of the guidance.

therefore adopted the tactic of providing warning or 'guidance' in a bulletin issued to banks, which are subject to its authority, that it would enforce anti-discrimination laws against banks that purchased auto loans from auto dealers, claiming that a disparate impact is sufficient to find a violation (as the agency did not have any evidence of discriminatory intent by the dealers).[94]

The guidance further suggested that banks could avoid an enforcement action if they imposed controls on, and monitored, dealer mark-ups and then took 'prompt corrective action' against miscreant dealers, or, better yet, if they charged flat fees to eliminate dealer discretion as to the interest rate, which was the industry practice regarding dealer compensation (lenders shared profits with dealers as a function of the loan's interest rate). Banks rationally responded to the 'guidance', which was provided in the shadow of an implicit supervisory threat of adverse regulatory action if they did not comply, by telling dealers that if they did not comply, they would impose flat fees (which was the CFPB's desired objective).[95]

The discrimination standard the CFPB applied in the bulletin, a disparate impact rather than disparate treatment (ie, intent) standard, is considered a controversial approach, evidenced by the federal government's litigation strategy, that in recent years, when the Supreme Court granted certiorari on a disparate impact challenge, the federal government settled to avoid a possible adverse decision that rejected the disparate impact rationale.[96] That is because the statutes under which the Supreme Court had upheld a disparate impact approach contained the word 'affect', language not contained in the fair housing statute under which those cases were brought. The fair lending statute which is the source of the CFPB's authority similarly had no such 'affect' language. However, in a recent five to four decision, the Supreme Court upheld a disparate impact approach under the fair housing statute, holding that its specific language, 'otherwise make available', had the same meaning as the 'affect' language in the statutes previously found to encompass disparate

[94] 'CFPB to Hold Auto Lenders Accountable for Illegal Discriminatory Markup' (Consumer Financial Protection Bureau 21 March 2013) <http://www.consumerfinance.gov/newsroom/consumer-financial-protection-bureau-to-hold-auto-lenders-accountable-for-illegal-discriminatory-markup/> accessed 19 August 2015; 'Indirect Auto Lending and Compliance with the Equal Opportunity Act' (Consumer Financial Protection Bureau 21 March 2013) <http://files.consumerfinance.gov/f/201303_cfpb_march_-Auto-Finance-Bulletin.pdf> accessed 19 August 2015. No doubt, the CFPB's disparate impact approach looks to a decades-old series of settlements of Department of Justice prosecutions under the fair lending laws that were based on a disparate impact standard, see Zywicki (n 64) 923, a controversial theory which the Department assiduously avoided subjecting to Supreme Court review, see text to n 96.

[95] 'Your Car Dealer Must Be a Racist' (n 92); Perez (n 92). The agency brought enforcement actions against four banks under the Bulletin. Perez (n 92) 399.

[96] Perez (n 92) 424.

impact.[97] The fair lending statute under which the CFPB has acted has no such language,[98] and it is, accordingly, uncertain whether a disparate impact standard would be upheld in this context. In addition, commentators have suggested that there will be continued litigation regarding the use of a disparate impact theory of liability under the housing statute because the Supreme Court 'impose[d] significant limitations on the application of the theory', such as requiring plaintiffs to allege, in the pleadings, more than a 'statistical disparity' but to establish a 'robust' causal link to the defendant's policies.[99]

Another problematic feature of the CFPB's action regarding auto dealer loans is the agency's interpretation in the bulletin of who is a 'creditor' under the fair lending law. Neither auto dealers' mark-ups nor indirect lenders had previously been understood to fall within the statutory definition.[100] Although the agency has contended that it was not reinterpreting or making new 'law', conveniently eliminating the need for following rule-making procedures, to an open-minded observer, the interpretation would, in fact, appear to be quite novel.[101] A final troubling aspect of the guidance is that, despite the common use of the proxy estimation technique the CFPB employed to identify discrimination, a number of researchers have found inaccuracies in the racial classifications the methodology produces.[102]

[97] *Texas Dep't of Housing and Comm. Affairs v Inclusive Communities Project, Inc, No* 13-1371 (2015) 11 (majority opinion). The federal government was not a party to the litigation (and hence could not prevent the Court's hearing of the case), but the Department of Housing and Urban Development issued a rule interpreting the statute to include disparate impact claims while the case was in the lower courts (the absence of which is another reason given for the aforementioned settlements by the federal government to avoid Supreme Court review, see text to n 96). The Supreme Court did not, however, ground its decision in the agency's position, as it could have done under its doctrine of deference to administrative rule-making.

[98] 15 USC § 1691. The Court also emphasized statutory amendments in 1988 that did not change the language despite all circuits that had decided a disparate impact case under the housing statute at the time having validated its use, circumstances which would not be relevant to the fair lending statute. *Texas Department of Housing* (n 97) 13–15 (majority opinion).

[99] Paul F Hancock and Andrew C Glass, 'Symposium: The Supreme Court Recognizes But Limits Disparate Impact in its Fair Housing Act Decision' (SCOTUSblog 26 June 2015) <http://www.scotusblog.com/2015/06/paul-hancock-fha/> accessed 23 August 2015. As the Supreme Court put it, 'a statistical disparity must fail if the plaintiff cannot point to a defendant's policy or policies causing that disparity'.

[100] Perez (n 92) 413–14.

[101] The CFPB raised the lack of novelty contention in response to a query from members of Congress concerning why it had acted on the subject by issuing a guidance rather than a rule.

[102] Kevin M McDonald and Kenneth J Rojc, 'Automotive Finance Regulation: Warning Lights Flashing' (2015) 70 The Business Lawyer 617, 619 n 14. In addition, in using this technique, the agency does not control for creditworthiness, automobile quality, length of contract or other risk factors that enter into the lending decision. ibid 619 (describing CFPB analysis in enforcement action against Ally bank after issuance of the guidance).

By engaging in backdoor rule-making through use of guidance (its supervisory authority over banks), the CFPB sought to restrict auto dealers' negotiations with customers with regard to financing terms, and to impose a significant change in their business model, as the vast majority of auto sales are financed.[103] This was done despite explicit lack of jurisdiction over the subject matter, while employing a problematic interpretation of the statute and without making publicly available the data upon which its action was based. Had the CFPB engaged in rule-making, it would have had to explain itself and publicly release the data to justify the rule (if only to seek to avoid a defeat were it to be challenged in court).[104]

It is possible that the CFPB's determinations that credit card add-ons and auto dealer interest rate mark-ups are questionable products and practices that should be prohibited are correct, although I am sceptical of such a conclusion.[105] But these are large and substantive policy matters that are most properly calibrated through rule-making, with public participation, as contemplated by Congress, in which the agency has to develop a record and publicly justify its decisions, that is, provide evidence that the credit card add-ons had no or little value and that auto dealers were discriminating.

Most important, these two examples are instances where both sunsetting and experimentation would have been of considerable benefit. Namely, sunsetting would reduce the possibility that the CFPB could persistently evade the more demanding notice and comment procedures. For if the agency were a sunset agency, then when Congress had to revisit its authorization, it could have imposed specific rule-making requirements, or restricted the scope of the CFPB's authority, and, further, re-evaluated whether the structure, or even

[103] As the *Wall Street Journal* explained, flat fees cap dealers' profits on loans and thereby limit their flexibility to lower an interest rate on one sale to compete with an offer from another dealer and to raise an interest rate on another sale to boost profits. 'Your Car Dealer Must Be a Racist' (n 92).

[104] Perez (n 92) 415. It seems probable that the cost-benefit criteria would not have been easily satisfied as the dealer compensation policy promoted by the guidance may well increase lending costs. As Perez notes, if dealer discretion on rates is maintained, then banks must engage in substantial monitoring, imposing considerable costs, which will increase the rate of interest banks require, and if instead discretion is replaced with flat fees, then dealers will lose the flexibility of trading interest rates off against purchase price, with the upshot that they will be less likely to offer lower purchase prices. ibid 426–27. Were a bank to challenge an enforcement action brought against it for not complying with the guidance, then the agency would have to justify the rule just as it would have had to do for a challenged rule-making. But no financial institution has chosen to do so, as is typical for financial institutions subject to regulatory enforcement actions, because these institutions are in continuous interaction with regulators and therefore vulnerable to retaliation on other regulatory matters.

[105] See ibid 425–26 (discussing benefits to consumers from dealer participation in lending, including data indicating that interest rates on indirect loans even with a dealer mark-up, were 1 per cent lower than rates on direct bank loans).

the existence, of the agency made much sense in the first place.[106] The agency would also have had an incentive to behave responsibly, knowing that its decisions would be publicly scrutinized by legislators during reauthorization, a context in which there could be serious consequences to the agency for questionable conduct, in contrast to their present posture. Moreover, restrictions on credit card add-ons and imposing flat fees on auto dealers are the type of regulation where well-crafted experiments could prove to be fruitful: a subset of banks could be randomly selected to adopt such policies, and another subset could be randomly selected to take a different approach, such as improved disclosure, and the findings then used to inform policy-making.[107]

It would be a mistake to conclude that implementation difficulties and problematic regulation are occasional occurrences that can be ameliorated over time, by regulators dutifully ironing out flaws, and thereby negate a need for sunsetting. Experience teaches otherwise: the status quo is sticky, whether it be legislatively or administratively formulated. Regulations are rarely revisited and it takes an inordinately long time, sometimes decades, despite a policy consensus regarding the inappropriateness of a particular regulatory solution, for legislators to address an issue.[108]

In fact, congressional mandates to agencies to re-evaluate existing regulations on a regular basis would appear to be totally ignored. A study of the statutory requirement that agencies periodically review existing rules for their impact on small business found that most of the time agencies did not even conduct the required review, and when they did, they rarely took any action beyond publishing a notice that the review had been conducted, or they revised regulations to increase, rather than reduce, as the statute intended,

[106] McCarty, Poole, and Rosenthal assert that Congress is the problem in resolving financial crises, contending that it does not enact effective reform regulation because of interest group lobbying and polarized politics. McCarty et al. (n 32). While this article similarly contends that Congress's emergency financial legislation is deeply problematic, the explanation of its failure articulated here is altogether different from theirs. Their analysis assumes that the cause of the financial crisis was a 'Republican' ideology of free markets and deregulation, and consequently, that legislative and regulatory initiatives of congressional Democrats are presumptively superior to the status quo, with the proviso that they should not provide regulatory discretion because industry will capture implementation. As students of the recent financial crisis are well aware, there is, in fact, plenty of blame to go around regarding the crisis across the political spectrum and across all institutions, public and private. Moreover, given the global scope of the crisis, with banks imploding in countries with diverse political leadership and regulatory institutions, what occurred cannot, in a simple-minded fashion, be ascribed solely to the 'ideology' of a particular domestic political party. For a list of common fundamentals across diverse nations characterizing the financial crisis, such as real estate bubbles, current account deficits, and large capital inflows (factors experienced in Iceland, Ireland, New Zealand, and Spain, as well as the United States), see Reinhart and Rogoff (n 62) 244.

[107] The concern that firms in an experiment may act strategically is briefly discussed in Romano, 'Regulating in the Dark' (2012) (n 1) 106.

[108] See ibid 86, 96.

the burden on small firms.[109] Moreover, even when regulators are repeatedly prodded by Congress to revisit a specific regulation that is thought to be flawed, regulators are inherently conservative and tend to resist.[110] And their technical staff, positioned in an organizational hierarchy in which there can be adverse professional consequences if they are not responsive to their superiors' preferences, cannot be relied upon to produce a balanced assessment concerning whether a rule should be revised or repealed, even if they have a sophisticated appreciation of a problem. It is simply in the nature of staff reports to perceive the task at hand as rationalizing agency policy; an independent review panel of experts, who are not beholden to a bureaucracy but have professional reputations at stake when advising Congress in the context of a statutory, and thereby regulatory, sunset, would ameliorate such a problem.

Agency use of experts when compelled by judicial review is no less likely to be problematic. An illustration demonstrating the difficulty of relying on internal experts' evaluation is its use by the SEC to support an effort to require mutual fund boards to have a supermajority of independent directors. After the rule was rejected by the US Court of Appeals of the DC Circuit for not having met a requisite cost-benefit standard,[111] the Commission had its Office of Economic Analysis undertake a literature review to assist in the remanded rule-making. Although the report is a careful evaluation of the literature, in a supplemental memo, the Chief Economist sought to explain away the literature, as it was inconsistent with the premise of the proposed rule. The memo explained that, despite the absence of evidence in the literature that more independent boards reduced fees or improved performance, a failure to find a relation does not mean there is no relation, given the limits of standard statistical methods.[112] This observation is correct so far as it goes, but it also proves too much, as we must do the best with the information that we have when a judgement must be made. It is self-evident that the Chief Economist felt pressed to interpret the data in the report in the supplemental memo to assist the agency's effort to build a record that would support retaining the original rule and that could pass judicial scrutiny.

It could be asserted that the Sarbanes-Oxley Act is a good contrast to Dodd-Frank because its regulatory requirements were implemented in short order after enactment. Yet Sarbanes-Oxley provides a cautionary tale for

[109] Michael R See, 'Willful Blindness: Federal Agencies' Failure to Comply with the Regulatory Flexibility Act's Periodic Review Requirement—And Current Proposals to Invigorate the Act' (2005–06) 33 The Fordham Urban Law Journal 1199, 1200, 1215–19.

[110] An illustration of this tendency from Sarbanes-Oxley is discussed in the text to nn 108–13.

[111] *Chamber of Commerce v SEC*, 443 F3d 890 (2006).

[112] Romano (n 23) 300.

relying on an agency to revisit a crisis-driven legislative directive, in the SEC's problematic implementation of section 404, the requirement that managers certify the effectiveness of their firm's internal controls, and that auditors attest to that certification.[113] Complying with section 404 was quite costly for all companies, but disproportionately far more so for smaller firms, and the SEC initially postponed the provision's application to the smallest firms (market cap under $75 million), but declined to adopt the recommendation of its own advisory committee to exempt those firms permanently.[114] Small firms had a better hearing in Congress, which threatened the SEC with budgetary restrictions were it to let the postponed application expire as planned, and in response, then-SEC Chairman Christopher Cox agreed to maintain the postponement and conduct a cost-benefit study of the statute and the budget restriction was accordingly eliminated from the appropriations bill in conference.[115]

The promised study of section 404's effects was undertaken by economists in the SEC's Office of Economic Analysis, and completed under Cox's successor, but when data indicated a negative impact on small firms, the SEC's accountants apparently found the findings objectionable, and presumably the Chairwoman did too, for the report attempts to provide a positive assessment, and only by combing through the 100-plus page study can one piece together the negative data.[116] More to the point, when in Dodd-Frank, after eliminating the provision's applicability to the smallest firms, Congress instructed the SEC to conduct a study of the compliance burden of section 404 for

[113] See Romano, 'Regulating in the Dark' (2012) (n 1) 93, 111 n 16.

[114] The saga of the SEC's approach to section 404 is detailed in Romano (n 23). The SEC's original estimate of per-firm annual compliance costs of $91,000 was wildly inaccurate, by orders of magnitude, ibid 240, and despite declining from early per-firm compliance costs in excess of $1 million, ibid, it is still well above that amount, Office of Economic Analysis at the SEC, *Study of the Sarbanes-Oxley Act of 2002 Section 404 Internal Control Over Financial Reporting Requirements* (2009) 5 <http://www.sec.gov/news/studies/2009/sox-404_study.pdf> accessed 19 August 2015.

[115] Romano (n 23) 284.

[116] Office of Economic Analysis at the SEC (n 114). Release of the SEC study was rumoured to have been delayed so that the text could put negative findings in a more positive light. Some evidence of the commission's disapprobation of the study is that publication of a scholarly paper derived from the study by SEC staff would appear to have been delayed—all staff papers having to receive agency clearance before they can be submitted to journals—as the paper is just now about to be published, five years after the SEC study was completed. Cindy R Alexander, Scott W Bauguess, Gennaro Bernile, Yoon-Ho Alex Lee, and Jennifer Marietta-Westberg, 'Economic Effects of SOX Section 404 Compliance: A Corporate Insider Perspective' (2013) 56 Journal of Accounting and Economics 267. The accountants' objections are not surprising, as the recommendation of the SEC's advisory committee to exempt small firms was vigorously opposed by the two accountants on the committee, Romano (n 23) 240 n 39, a position at one with the profession's financial interest. Eg, ibid 241 (audit fees tripled as a percentage of revenue for small public companies before and after Sarbanes-Oxley).

small firms that Dodd-Frank did not exempt (market cap between $75 and $250 million),[117] this time the analytical work was given to the Office of the Chief Accountant, ensuring the study would—as it predictably did—advise against extending the exemption to more firms.[118]

A recent article by John Coates and Suraj Srinivasan reviewing the empirical academic literature that has sought to assess the impact of Sarbanes-Oxley over the past decade, and concluding that 'On balance, research on the Act's net social welfare remains inconclusive',[119] does not alter the need for sunsetting SOX, along with other crisis-driven financial legislation. Although I believe that the article's assessment of the literature is mistaken as it both overstates potential benefits and downplays or misses research with negative findings,[120] this Postscript is not the proper forum for providing a critique

[117] Dodd-Frank § 989(G)(b).

[118] The Office of the Chief Accountant, SEC, 'Study and Recommendations on Section 404(b) of the Sarbanes-Oxley Act of 2002 for Issuers with Public Float Between $75 and $250 Million' (2011) <http://www.sec.gov/news/studies/2011/404bfloat-study.pdf> accessed 19 August 2015 (recommending against extending exemption).

[119] John C Coates and Suraj Srinivasan, 'SOX after Ten Years: A Multidisciplinary Review' (2014) 28 Accounting Horizons 627, 627.

[120] Eg, the authors omit from their review, articles indicating that Sarbanes-Oxley's cost outweighs the benefits for foreign cross-listed firms, firm samples that tend to provide cleaner results than using samples of US firms, because they can provide controls of comparable companies not affected by the statute. Eg, Xi Li, 'The Sarbanes-Oxley Act and Cross-Listed Foreign Private Issuers' (2014) 58 Journal of Accounting and Economics 21; Kate Litvak, 'The Long-term Effect of the Sarbanes-Oxley Act on Cross-Listing Premia' (2008) 14 European Financial Management 875; Kate Litvak, 'The Effect of the Sarbanes-Oxley Act on Non-U.S. Companies Cross-Listed in the US' (2007) 13 The Journal of Corporate Finance 195. In addition, despite the seemingly modest conclusion quoted above, the text of the literature review places the statute in a more positive light. This is conveyed through statements that seemingly broadly discredit prior critiques of Sarbanes-Oxley, related to its impact on corporate law, but that are then followed by qualifiers cabining the broad statements to reference only one provision, or only one out of many critics' contentions, such that a non-specialist could easily miss the caveat and pick up only the broader statement. For example, the authors state that data on firms' disclosures of material weaknesses under section 404, 'suggests that for a significant number of public companies, SOX's section 404 has functioned at least in part in a "comply or explain" fashion, contrary to strong characterizations of that part of the law as "mandating" corporate governance changes.' Coates and Srinivasan (n 119) 635. But a consumer of the SOX literature reviewing the pre-publication article, gleans from that statement the following mistaken conclusion: 'Another concern was SOX would change financial regulation from disclosure to prescriptive command-and-control. But the authors conclude that it is a "comply or explain" regime.' Peter van Doran, 'Working Papers, Corporate Accounting, SOX after Ten Years: A Multidisciplinary Review' (2014) John M Olin Center For Law, Economics, And Business Discussion Paper No 758. He missed the critical word 'part' qualifying the sentence, which was referencing a *disclosure* provision that was not one of the many mandatory corporate governance provisions that are the source of that specific criticism of Sarbanes-Oxley, nor did Coates and Srinivasan identify any of those provisions as 'comply or explain' and not mandatory ones. See, eg, Romano (n 17) (critiquing move to mandatory rules in Sarbanes-Oxley, that consisted of audit committee requirements, corporate loan prohibition, prohibition of auditor provision of non-audit services, and officer certification of financial statement accuracy).

of their literature review. Moreover, even accepting Coates and Srinivasan's assessment and conclusion, for argument's sake, only serves to bolster this chapter's advocacy of the importance of applying sunsetting and experimentation to financial regulation. Namely, the inability to conclude that SOX has produced a net benefit highlights how crisis-driven regulation would benefit from experimentation. If the SEC had structured implementation of SOX provisions, such as the independent audit committee mandates or auditor attestation requirements, as randomized experiments, then we could have more accurately measured the net benefit or cost of the requirements.[121]

Accepting their assessment and conclusion for argument's sake also underscores the need for sunsetting. Sunsetting would provide the agency with an incentive to get things right and operate with less of a closed bureaucratic mindset regarding experimentation when implementing emergency-driven legislation,[122] as the agency would be confronted with the need to develop the highest quality information available. For if, in a sunset review occurring seven to ten years after implementation (the time range of the literature review's assessment) the net benefit remained inconclusive, then substantial

[121] The review article adopts the position on regulatory experimentation that I advanced in Regulating in the Dark, Romano, 'Regulating in the Dark' (2012) (n 1) 104–06. Coates and Srinivasan (n 119) 57–58.

[122] The one instance of a randomized experimentation undertaken by the SEC, involving the short sale uptick rule, see Romano, 'Regulating in the Dark' (2012) (n 1) 113 n 21, was directed at a long-standing regulation and not undertaken to ascertain how best to implement a new, crisis-driven legislative directive. The SEC has supported pilot programmes, which are sometimes referred to as 'experiments', see, eg, Dave Michaels, 'Exchanges Get Test to Curb Dark Trading in SEC Program' *Bloomberg* (25 June 2014) <http://www.bloomberg.com/news/2014-06-24/exchanges-get-test-to-curb-dark-trading-in-sec-program.html> accessed 19 August 2015 (describing new SEC initiative to permit exchanges to test restrictions on the tick size of small stocks approach to tick size as 'experiment'), which are not experiments in the sense used here, as they do not compare a 'treated' to a controlled set of firms, chosen at random, to permit a gold standard evaluation of the programme, but they have an experimental flavour, in that as a pilot, the programme will be evaluated to determine if it should be retained. These programmes are, however, not always agency inspired. The newly launched tick size pilot programme is the result of the recommendation of an SEC advisory committee following an agency report on the impact of decimalization ordered by Congress, along with a GAO report and a report of a Treasury Department task force. 'SEC Release Number 34-72460, Order Directing the Exchanges and the Financial Industry Regulatory Authority to Submit a Tick Size Pilot Plan' (24 June 2014) 6–11 <http://www.sec.gov/rules/other/2014/34-72460.pdf> accessed 19 August 2015. Moreover, paralleling the uptick experiment, SEC pilot programmes also address long-standing regulations. The SEC's attitude to Sarbanes-Oxley requirements, as with its approach to those of Dodd-Frank, see n 34, has been to reject inclusion of industry-sought *de minimis* exemptions, even where Congress suggested the agency consider using its authority to issue waivers of requirements. See Romano (n 17) 1595 n 214 (describing SEC's rejection of *de minimis* exception to the definition of an independent director, related to an individual's or affiliate's receipt of a trivial sum from the company, used to determine compliance with the independent audit committee requirement). The postponement of section 404's application to the smallest firms is the sole exception that I could identify.

revision of the delegating statute, reversing the agency's previous endeavours, would be a more probable outcome.

4. Conclusion

The post-enactment experience of the two most recent crisis-driven statutes concerning financial regulation, Dodd-Frank and Sarbanes-Oxley, underscore the importance of including in such legislation, mechanisms to ensure that there will be a serious, comprehensive reassessment after a fixed period, and that information regarding the impact of regulatory alternatives can be gathered in the interim to aid in the reassessment. The implementation of the statutes has been replete with instances of the sort of errors that inevitably arise from crisis-driven legislation, as it is enacted at a time when information necessary to devise suitable solutions is unavailable. That state of affairs permits agenda-setting legislators to adopt preferred policy entrepreneurs' off-the-rack solutions, which are often not well-matched to the problems at hand, along with extensive, albeit poorly thought out, delegation, that result in costly market adjustments and adverse unintended consequences with questionable social benefits. Still, sunsetting and regulatory experimentation are not panaceas—legislators must conscientiously revisit the statute and its implementation, with the assistance of the analyses of independent experts, and regulatory experiments must be well-crafted to inform a reassessment. Nonetheless, sunsetting and regulatory experimentation are the best tools we possess to mitigate the perils that arise when one is regulating in the dark.

5

Reflections on Financial Crises, Regulation, and Sunsetting

Edward M Iacobucci

1. Introduction

In her chapter in this volume and its companion piece, Roberta Romano recommends greater reliance on sunsetting of legislation enacted in response to financial crises, and more experimentation in regulation.[1] This chapter will comment on her first recommendation, that legislation adopted in the midst or immediate aftermath of a financial crisis should be sunsetted; that is, it should expire within a fixed, reasonably short period of time.

Using Dodd-Frank as an example, Romano contends that crisis regulation is necessarily fashioned with insufficient information, leading to the implementation of misguided legislation.[2] Further, owing to the checks and balances that characterize the US political system, reforming such misguided legislation at a later time through amendment or repeal is not likely to occur. The result of this stickiness to the status quo is that misguided legislation tends to remain law, an undesirable and inefficient outcome. The solution to this problem, Romano argues, is to require mandatory, expert review of crisis legislation and the expiry of such legislation in the absence of legislative re-enactment.

Coffee has critiqued the suggestion that financial crisis legislation should be sunsetted on two grounds.[3] First, he argues that investors are a 'latent

[1] Thank you to Courtland Morrice for very helpful research assistance, and to Anita Anand for comments on an earlier draft. Roberta Romano, 'Further Assessment of the Iron Law of Financial Regulation: A Postscript to Regulating in the Dark' (2015) (Chapter 4 in this volume); Roberta Romano, 'Regulating in the Dark' in Cary Coglianese (ed), *Regulatory Breakdown: The Crisis of Confidence in U.S. Regulation* (The University of Pennsylvania Press 2012).

[2] Dodd-Frank § 941, codified at 15 USC § 78o-11 ('Dodd-Frank').

[3] John C Coffee Jr, 'The Political Economy of Dodd-Frank: Why Financial Reform Tends to be Frustrated and Systemic Risk Perpetuated' (2012) 97 Cornell Law Review 1019.

Reflections on Financial Crises, Regulation and Sunsetting. First Edition. Edward M. Iacobucci.

group', dominated in the normal-course competition to shape legislation and regulatory policy by more cohesive and better-funded special interest groups. This imbalance is countered, however, in times of financial crisis, because such events encourage 'political entrepreneurs' to bear the transaction costs of organizing the latent investor group to take action. This action channels itself through the enactment of crisis legislation. Second, he suggests that flaws contained within such legislation will eventually be ironed out through the administrative process that implements the legislation.

This chapter critiques the recommendation to sunset crisis legislation on largely different grounds. Sunsetting potentially makes sense because of rigidities in the legislative process that make refinement of existing legislation difficult. Accepting the premise of legislative stickiness, however, does not necessarily lead to support for sunsetting: sunsetting crisis legislation simply shifts the bias in a sticky legislative system from crisis to pre-crisis legislation, and there is reason to believe that this is not desirable. The remainder of this chapter proceeds as follows. Section 2 frames the issue as one of favouring either crisis or pre-crisis legislation. Section 3 suggests that the incremental information gleaned from the occurrence of the crisis itself and incorporated into the crisis legislation weighs in favour of the crisis legislation as against the pre-crisis legislation. Section 4 argues that the fact that there may be a tendency for legislators to overreach in the midst of a crisis, a key concern of Romano's, does not necessarily support pre-crisis legislation as the default. Section 5 discusses the costs of temporary legislation. Section 6 offers a variation on the sunset clause whereby neither the pre-crisis legislation nor the crisis legislation is the default. Rather, an alternative piece of reform, undesirable to all parties, is automatically enacted if legislative consensus is not reached. This captures the possibility of improved law-making in light of better information, while also creating a strong counterweight to legislative inertia. Section 7 concludes.

2. Framing the Issue—Crisis vs. Pre-Crisis Legislation

The title of Romano's paper indicates her views on legislation enacted during or in the immediate aftermath of a crisis: crisis legislation 'regulates in the dark'. When crisis legislation is enacted, there is a paucity of information regarding what has transpired, but there is also a politically motivated desire to be seen as 'doing something' that leads legislators to quickly enact legislation in response to the crisis. Inevitably, according to Romano, such legislation is misguided and flawed. Compounding the problem is the stickiness of existing legislation in the US political framework of checks and balances. It is for these reasons that Romano advocates sunsetting crisis-driven financial regulation. With sunsetting, there is an opportunity to review the crisis legislation through the cool heads of an expert panel with the benefit of hindsight, rather than the hot heads of politically driven legislators in the moment of crisis, and repeal of misguided reform is more likely.

Romano has suggested that sunset review be mandatory, be conducted by independent experts evaluating pre-set criteria and operating with a predetermined and guaranteed budget, and such a review must result in a floor vote on the recommendation put forward. While there are certainly advantages to this type of expert review, such expert review could take place with or without sunsetting in place. Sunsetting simply implies that unless there is Congressional consensus on the amendment or renewal of the crisis legislation, then the pre-crisis legislation will be operative going forward. While the type of review that Romano has suggested would have advantages, such review can take place without sunsetting the crisis legislation. I focus in this chapter on sunsetting per se.

It is entirely reasonable to conclude that the repeal or amendment of an existing statute in the US is difficult. As Romano highlights, it took eight years to amend Sarbanes-Oxley despite broad consensus regarding its problems. However, it is also true that passing an amended statute or renewing the crisis legislation as-is would also be difficult, regardless of the enhanced information obtained through the sunset review.[4] Accepting that sunsetting makes repeal of an existing statute more probable,[5] the result is that sunsetting essentially changes the bias in the system, away from the crisis legislation and toward the pre-crisis legislation as the default position. Therefore, it is important to an analysis of sunsetting to assess whether the status quo ante, the pre-crisis legislation that is the default rule under sunsetting, is preferable to the crisis legislation. There are reasons not to prefer the status quo ante.

[4] Sarbanes-Oxley Act of 2002 (Pub L 107–204, 116 Stat 745, enacted 30 July 2002).

[5] There is, however, academic debate as to whether sunset clauses function successfully (either in that legislative provisions actually expire or in that meaningful legislative reconsideration results). See John E Finn, 'Sunset Clauses and Democratic Deliberation: Assessing the Significance of Sunset Provisions in Antiterrorism Legislation' (2010) 48 Columbia Journal of Transnational Law 442; John Ip, 'Sunset Clauses and Counterterrorism Legislation' (2012) Public Law 74 in the counterterrorism context; more generally Richard C Kearney, 'Sunset: A Survey and Analysis of the State Experience' (1990) 50 Public Administration Review 49 and Vern McKinley, 'Sunrises without Sunsets: Can Sunset Laws Reduce Regulation' (1995) 18 Regulation 57.

3. Incorporating Better Information

Romano stresses the role of gaining information post-crisis, which allows a sober assessment of the costs and benefits of the crisis legislation in light of the better information obtained. More broadly, Gersen argues that temporary legislation is advantaged relative to permanent legislation because it specifies a 'window of opportunity' for legislators to incorporate enhanced information into their policy judgements.[6] According to Ranchordas, in highly innovative industries sunsetting sets the stopwatch on legislation that is likely to become obsolete as information is gained.[7] In essence, these are Bayesian arguments: we should update our prior views of optimal legislation in light of new information. However, it is not clear why greater information accumulation pushes for sunsetting. That is, in the present context, why the default rule should be the pre-crisis legislation rather than the crisis legislation.

As good Bayesians, we should update our views on the status quo when a crisis hits. It is true that there may be multiple reasons for a crisis, and with time more information will be available to shed light on these reasons, but the pre-crisis regulatory structure is clearly one possibility. Moreover, the emergence of a crisis should offer some information about the specific infirmities of the pre-crisis status quo. This is not to say that one crisis will offer a complete set of information, nor that time will not yield better information, but rather that the crisis legislation is better informed than the pre-crisis legislation, and thus from a Bayesian perspective is at least presumptively better.

Thus, Romano's emphasis on post-crisis review as a means of incorporating new information would appear to be based on a logic that would also favour the crisis legislation to the pre-crisis status quo, at least from an information perspective. Of course, from a Bayesian perspective it would be optimal, relative to a single post-crisis legislative review, to have constant review and upgrading of the regulatory framework in light of the greater information obtained with time. But if that is difficult to achieve because of legislative stickiness, the crisis legislation would be better informed than pre-crisis legislation, and sunsetting is not obviously desirable.

[6] Jacob Gersen, 'Temporary Legislation' (2006) John M Olin Program in Law and Economics Working Paper No 296.

[7] Sofia Ranchordas, 'Innovation-Friendly Regulation: The Sunset of Regulation, the Sunrise of Innovation' (2015) 55 Jurimetrics J 201.

4. Political Overshooting

There is more to the debate on sunset clauses than just information. Romano suggests that there are additional potential benefits from sunsetting because of political overshooting. She argues that in times of crisis politicians prefer to be seen as 'doing something' rather than nothing, even if it would be wise to wait for additional information before acting. There is thus a perceived political urgency to action, and Romano describes how policy entrepreneurs may seize the moment to advocate 'off-the-rack' reforms that only relate to the crisis tangentially at best, or overreact to factors that did cause the crisis. These political concerns serve as counterpoints to the idea that crisis legislation ought to be preferred to the pre-crisis status quo because of information from the crisis itself. Politics are likely to undermine the rational influence of the new information. On this thinking, there is no reason to presumptively favour the crisis legislation if it does not relate to the new information gleaned from the crisis. The express authorization of the Securities and Exchange Commission's (SEC) proxy access rule, which the SEC had been working on for over a decade, by Dodd-Frank, is a clear example of such legislation. As Romano highlights, the Volcker rule and the creation of the Consumer Financial Protection Bureau also fit this narrative.

But the fact that there may be a tendency to overreach in the midst of a crisis does not necessarily support sunsetting. As Berman, Finn, and Mooney have argued in the counterterrorism context, the inclusion of a sunset provision may act as a 'spoonful of sugar' to help controversial legislation win the necessary votes to become law.[8] In the near term, it is plausible that such provisions actually exacerbate the problem of overreach rather than rein it in, because legislators may feel less need to debate the crisis legislation in the present, comforted by the automatic termination provisions.

In addition, suppose that an approach were adopted today under which there is a presumption of sunsetting any legislation adopted in a future crisis. This would imply that past legislation that emerged from financial crises (eg, Sarbanes-Oxley and Dodd-Frank) would now be presumptively favoured relative to any new crisis legislation. This outcome may well be appropriate on Romano's view: if legislation is truly a one-way ratchet, then favouring

[8] Emily Berman, 'The Paradox of Counterterrorism Sunset Provisions' (2013) 81 Fordham Law Review 1777; Finn (n 5); and Chris Mooney, 'A Short History of Sunsets' (2004) Legal Affairs 67. See also Frank Fagan and Firat Bilgel, 'Sunsets and Federal Lawmaking: Evidence from the 110th Congress' (2015) 41 International Review of Law and Economics 1, arguing that the inclusion of a sunset clause increases the likelihood that a bill will be passed.

currently misguided legislation is better than allowing even more misguided legislation going forward. However, as this example illustrates, there is often no magic to the status quo, and thus it is not immediately clear that it should be favoured. To be sure, in the steady state, such a problem may recede in importance, but there would be transition issues with Romano's suggestion, including debates about what legislation precisely qualifies as 'crisis legislation'.

Finally, it is abundantly clear that passing legislation in the US has become increasingly difficult in recent years. Indeed, stickiness is part of Romano's justification for sunsetting. Where legislation is very difficult to change, the fact that crisis-precipitated legislation may not be rationally connected to the crisis is not *necessarily* a bad thing.[9] For example, there could be an inventory of 'good' legislative reforms that would otherwise not see the light of day. In a period of political urgency, such reforms may plausibly be attached to crisis legislation. This would be a reason *not* to sunset the crisis legislation, since by the time the sunset deadline is reached the political will to reform may have dissipated and the default, pre-crisis status quo will prevail without the continued enactment of the 'good' legislative reforms. If legislative stickiness were simply an exogenous fact of life, as it appears to be under the US system of checks and balances, then taking advantage of a crisis to pass other legislation may be a welcome legislative tool that sunsetting would undermine.

In short, while political urgency may lead to overreaching on the part of legislators, there are nonetheless reasons why a tendency to overreach does not necessarily support the sunsetting of crisis legislation.

5. The Costs of Temporary Legislation

Suppose that the norm of sunsetting takes hold, and future crisis legislation contains such provisions. Temporary legislation raises certain costs that are also important to consider. For example, one argument against temporary legislation is that decreasing regulatory certainty through the use of sunset clauses imposes costs on firms and individuals.[10] Romano disputes this, arguing that the multiyear period before a sunset is long enough for the completion of business planning regarding the regulation. According to her, the business planning affected by financial regulation does not typically consist of projects with a long development lead and as a result firms should be

[9] Coffee (n 3).

[10] For an empirical analysis of renewal uncertainty, see Jason S Oh, 'The Pivotal Politics of Temporary Legislation' (2015) 100 Iowa Law Review 1055.

well positioned at the time of sunset. However, Romano overlooks a different implementation cost that may be imposed. Legislation that authorizes implementation through administrative action might, as the Dodd-Frank experience illustrates, take some time to become operational.[11] If business does not want the law *ever* to become operational, sunsetting makes delay especially valuable. Businesses may work to bog down the implementation of the prescribed legislation in the hopes that the political will to impose the costs of reform on businesses will have dissipated by the time the legislation is due to expire. In other words, the presence of a sunset clause might motivate obstructionism more than permanent legislation would.

In both temporary and permanent legislation, interest group lobbying imposes a cost upon adoption. Romano contends that the inclusion of a sunset clause would lower the stakes for the initial vote on crisis legislation. This would have the effect of making interest group lobbying at adoption less intense and prolonged, because these groups would have a second chance to make their arguments during the sunset review. McKinley provides a counterpoint to this argument, however, suggesting that the lead time before a sunset review provides interest groups with a fixed-time target in advance of which they can coordinate their resources.[12] Ultimately, this may make lobbying at the sunset review stage even more intense than it otherwise would have been at the time of initial adoption. This consideration, in combination with the unusual political popularity of regulation following a crisis, suggest that sunsetting crisis legislation may aggravate the advantages of narrow, business interest groups in the political process.

In addition, Kysar contends that over the long run, temporary legislation increases rents from interest groups relative to permanent legislation.[13] The ongoing threat of expiration allows law-makers to extract rents from interest groups on a continuous basis, as these groups are repeatedly required to lobby legislators to achieve their goals.[14] This is in contrast to permanent legislation, where interest groups are protected by legislative stickiness from re-visiting

[11] As Romano highlights, four years after enactment 45 per cent of Dodd-Frank's 280 specified rule-making deadlines had been missed, and of its 398 rulemaking requirements 24 per cent had not yet even been proposed.

[12] McKinley (n 5).

[13] Rebecca M Kysar, 'The Sun Also Rises: The Political Economy of Sunset Provisions in the Tax Code' (2006) 40:2 Georgia Law Review 335. Making a related argument, Opheim, Curry, and Shields conducted a study of sunset review in Texas, concluding that automatic termination encourages political 'games', ie, the use of sunset review to promote unrelated agendas. See Cynthia Opheim, Landon Curry, and Patricia M Shields, 'Sunset as Oversight: Establishing Realistic Objectives' (1994) 24:3 American Review of Public Administration 253.

[14] See, also, Manoj Viswanathan, 'Sunset Provisions in the Tax Code: A Critical Evaluation and Prescriptions for the Future' (2007) 82:2 New York University Law Review 656.

already fought-over issues on an ongoing basis. Providing a narrow example, Kysar argues that sunset provisions threaten the continuance of tax benefits and thus allow legislators more possibilities to extract financial and electoral contributions from the recipients of those benefits.[15]

Also undermining the advantages of sunsetting, there will often be significant switching costs associated with changing the regulatory framework. In July 2015, the Volcker rule took effect, imposing considerable costs on banking entities that were required to adopt an organizational structure consistent with the rule.[16] Suppose that the Volcker rule contained a sunset clause, and that the sunset review were as dispassionate and analytic as one would hope. A review of the legislation post-implementation may generate a different cost-benefit result from that pre-implementation. The reason is that once the costs of the reform have been largely incurred (in the case of the Volcker rule, in excess of $4 billion), it could well be that the preferred course of action is to retain the newly adopted rule in place. Even if the overall costs of the Volcker rule exceed its benefits, once the considerable adoption costs are sunk, going forward it may well make economic sense to retain the rule that was a bad idea ex ante. This conclusion would be reinforced if changing the rule back to the pre-crisis status quo would generate further switching costs.

In short, there are a number of costs associated with temporary legislation that must be taken into account in assessing sunsetting and weighing its benefits.

6. A Speculative Alternative

It is undoubtedly the case that neither the pre-crisis status quo nor the crisis legislation is optimal. Rather, with time and better information, it is probable that an alternative will emerge as better than either of the existing options. However, legislative inertia would imply that we are likely to end up with the default legislation, whatever that may be.

There is an alternative approach to sunsetting that takes a more radical step in addressing legislative inertia. Recognizing the potential for a third, better alternative to emerge, the goal should be to encourage informed consideration of this third alternative. One way to do so is to make the default legislation unattractive to all parties, not because it would be adopted, but because it would motivate adoption of an alternative. For example, in the US, if an

[15] Kysar (n 13).

[16] The Office of the Comptroller of the Currency estimated in March 2014 that the rule would cost supervised banking entities $4 billion. This was challenged by the SEC as being far too low.

agreement on the debt ceiling cannot be reached at the same time that borrowing needs would exceed the limit, the options include default on debt or shutting down the federal government. The absence of an agreement would generate an outcome, default or shut-down, that would be disfavoured by both political parties. This makes agreement on the debt ceiling more likely.

Consider the following variation on sunsetting in the financial crisis setting. An expert panel is constituted to review the crisis legislation, and to make suggestions for revisions. If there is no legislative consensus on a new option that incorporates the proposed revisions by the sunset, another piece of reform legislation kicks in, but no one favours this version of reform. The idea is that the disfavoured default will force negotiation and compromise, nudging the parties towards the third, better alternative.[17]

This approach captures the possibility of improved law-making in light of better information, while also creating a strong counterweight to legislative inertia. A risk is created in that there is the possibility of the unattractive default prevailing (just as there is a risk of a government shutdown in the debt ceiling context), but the upside is the greater probability that the default will not obtain, and that new information will actually matter in crafting the regulatory framework. This avoids the problem with plain vanilla sunsetting: that the pre-crisis status quo is likely not optimal, yet is nonetheless the likely outcome.

Of course, if the pre-crisis legislation is clearly disfavoured by all parties as obviously misguided, then sunsetting would have the effect described in this section. I doubt, however, that this would often be the case in the context of financial regulation. Consider the Volcker rule. While there is a plausible case for it, and political support for it, there would be a plausible case against it, and political opposition to it, as well. It is plausible that the threat of its expiry by sunset would not invite bipartisan efforts to ensure that this did not occur.

[17] The suggestion is related to 'penalty defaults' in the contracts literature: contract law should sometimes supply disfavoured default rules to encourage parties to share information and contract around the unattractive default. See, eg, Ian Ayres and Robert Gertner, 'Filling Gaps in Incomplete Contracts: An Economic Theory of Default Rules' (1989) 99:1 Yale Law Journal 87; Charles Goetz and Robert Scott, 'Enforcing Promises: An Examination of the Basis of Contract' (1980) 89 Yale Law Journal 1261.

7. Conclusion

To counteract the legislative inertia that keeps misguided crisis legislation operative, Romano suggests the inclusion of sunset provisions as a best practice. When framed as a choice between the pre-crisis status quo and the crisis legislation, however, it is not clear why this is the case. From an information perspective, while crisis legislation may not be based on the best information, it is based on better information than existed pre-crisis. If the concern is political overreach in the time of crisis, sunsetting does not necessarily alleviate the problem and may, in fact, even exacerbate it or lead to other negative consequences. Supporting these critiques are cost arguments that favour permanent legislation as opposed to temporary. Finally, a variation on the sunset clause whereby a third piece of legislation, undesirable to all parties, becomes the default legislation, may do the best job of both incorporating enhanced information and countering legislative inertia. This final variation obtains if the pre-crisis legislation is clearly disfavoured by all parties, but this will often not be true.

6

China's Long March to Dismantling the Financial Great Wall

RMB Internationalization and Macroprudential Policy

*Weitseng Chen**

1. Introduction

In the summer of 2015, China saw its biggest financial crisis within the past two decades. First came the popping of its stock market bubble in mid-June. Within the following month, the Shanghai Composite Index and the China Securities Index 300 fell sharply, losing almost 40 per cent of their value.[1] Soon, investors were desperately begging the government to save their life-long savings to be used for their retirement and their children's education while heartbreaking stories, including the committing of suicide, spread through the mass media and Internet like wildfire. In response, Chinese regulators forked out almost $235 billion renminbi (RMB) to buy shares and to bolster prices and imposed draconian restrictions on the sale of stocks so as to slow the crash.[2] At the same time, police officers dropped in on investment firms and downloaded their transaction records in a bid to take to task

* The author has benefited from comments by Dan Awrey, Michael Bridge, Christopher Bruner, Jedidiah Kroncke, Curtis Milhaupt, Wei Shen, Michael J Trebilcock, and Hans Tjio, and from the financial assistance of NUS research fund (R-241-000-122-112).

[1] Samuel Shen and Pete Sweeney, 'China Stocks Slide as Crackdown on Speculators Spreads, Lose 11 Percent in August' *Reuters* (31 August 2015) <http://www.reuters.com/article/2015/08/31/us-markets-hongkong-china-stocks-open-idUSKCN0R003F20150831> accessed 15 November 2015.

[2] Edward Wong, Neil Gough, and Alexandra Stevenson, 'China's Response to Stock Plunge Rattles Traders' *NY Times* (9 September 2015) <http://www.nytimes.com/2015/09/10/world/asia/in-china-a-forceful-crackdown-in-response-to-stock-market-crisis.html?_r=0> accessed 10 October 2015.

China's Long March to Dismantling the Financial Great Wall: Renminbi Internationalization and Macroprudential Policy. First Edition. Weitseng Chen. Published 2016 by Oxford University Press.

those the Chinese government considered responsible for the state of affairs. Senior executives of several of China's biggest investment banks were arrested on suspicion of illegal trading, and a business journalist, who was arrested, was even shown apologizing on national television for writing an article that could have possibly caused investors to panic.[3] In short, China's stock markets were on fire.

The chaos wrought on China's stock markets might be unthinkable for someone who has focused only on China's ambitious plan to internationalize the RMB and project its global influence. For a start, the internationalization of the RMB seems to have gone smoothly; even after the stock market crash, it remains resilient and continues to make great progress. Not only has the International Monetary Fund (IMF) included the RMB into its basket of Special Drawing Rights (SDR) in November 2015, global financial centres have also been competing to be RMB offshore settlement centres. This has been achieved by not just market forces, but also strategic actions carried out by the party-state. Chinese leaders perceive the global financial crisis as an opportunity to end the dominance of the US dollar (USD) and reach the pinnacle of the RMB's international status, a strategy that they claimed to have learned from the US, which took advantage of Britain's war-torn economy after World War II to end the dominance of the British pound. Furthermore, market pundits continue to be positive about the RMB's future and foresee that offshore RMB may eventually exert a market force that is as strong and as powerful as the Eurodollar, which drove the development of global capital markets from the 1970s onwards. That said, one cannot help but wonder how the world can reconcile the two contrasting images of a traumatic stock market at home and a seemingly successful expansion of the RMB's influence overseas.

This chapter suggests that this contrast between the financial turmoil at home and the RMB's success overseas is fully explainable through the lens of macroprudential policies. To put this thesis into perspective, China's approach to the internationalization of the RMB is much like a bullet train driver who is only concerned with maximizing the speed of the train while ignoring dangers and warnings. In internationalizing the RMB, China focused on pro-cyclical policies aimed at spurring economic growth. But macroprudential

[3] Gabriel Wildau, 'China Probes Top Citic Securities Executives Over Insider Trading' *Financial Times* (16 September 2015) <http://www.ft.com/intl/cms/s/0/1ae0b140-5bc6-11e5-97e9-7f0bf5e7177b.html#axzz3nfHVN2Yk> accessed 15 October 2015; Shannon Tiezzi, 'Is This Man Responsible for China's Stock Market Crash?' *The Diplomat* (1 September 2015) <http://thediplomat.com/2015/09/is-this-man-responsible-for-chinas-stock-market-crash/> accessed 10 October 2015.

policies, which are aimed at mitigating systemic risk, are counter-cyclical by nature. In internationalizing the RMB without adopting due macroprudential policies, China underestimated the dangers posed by systemic risk.

In China, systemic risk is interwoven into the fabric of shadow banking, local governmental debts, capital flight, and non-performing loans, all of which are domestic issues that seem remote from China's global agenda for the RMB. Yet, in China's haste to internationalize the RMB by rapidly liberalizing its RMB-related financial sectors so as to manage her RMB portfolio in a way that connects with global markets, China may have unwittingly unleashed this risk. While liberalization per se is not the root of the 2015 stock market crisis, systemic risk may have been triggered by prematurely liberalizing financial markets and by distorting the sequencing of financial reforms that should have been issued in accordance with macroprudential guidelines. For instance, commentators have partly blamed the quick lifting of capital controls under the RMB internationalization scheme, without putting in ancillary regulation, for the speculative attacks suffered by China's fragile stock markets.[4] To put it glibly, an unbalanced focus on the internationalization of the RMB has backfired on China, and some prudential reforms have been neglected by the RMB scheme.

The balance of this chapter will proceed as follows. Section 2 examines China's strategy to internationalize the RMB, while Section 3 discusses how and to what extent the internationalization of the RMB concerns both microprudential as well as macroprudential policies of China. Section 4 elaborates on the concerns surrounding the systemic risk faced by China by looking at China's shadow banking industry. Section 5 revisits macroprudential policies in the context of developing economies. Section 6 concludes the chapter.

2. Liberalization by RMB Internationalization

China's goals in internationalizing the RMB are both economic and political. On the economic front, China's concern with the current dollar-dominant reserve system, like other major economies such as India, stemmed from the frustration with its dependence on US Treasury bonds as a means to store massive amounts of foreign reserve—that is, China's economy is subjected

[4] See, eg, Yu Yongding (余永定), 'Qita gaige wei wancheng zhiqian juedui buneng fangqi ziben guanzhi' [China should not give up capital controls before the completion of all other reforms] (27 January 2016) <http://www.21ccom.net/html/2016/zjds_0127/1232.html> accessed 18 February 2016.

to the negative externalities generated by US domestic monetary policy.[5] On the political front, China will be able to exert more influence over the world economy, and therefore global politics, if the RMB becomes the major reserve currency. One example is the Asian Infrastructure Investment Bank (AIIB), the China-led development bank that provides a potential platform to plough the region with RMB and RMB-denominated loans in the future.[6] In 2015, the successful launch of AIIB embarrassed the US after its key allies—the UK, Germany, Australia, and South Korea—applied to join the bank as founding members.[7] This undid the boycott that the US had imposed on the AIIB.

November 2015 was a milestone for RMB internationalization as the IMF announced that the RMB was to be included as the fifth currency in the SDR basket, together with the dollar, pound, yen, and euro. This represented a victory for China, and an important step in the ascendance of the RMB to the status of a global reserve currency. Christine Lagarde, the IMF's managing director, announced that the RMB met the fund's two main criteria for inclusion—that is, it is 'widely used' and 'freely usable'.[8] Considering that China launched its RMB internationalization scheme just two years ago, this development is striking, especially when the general public's impression of the RMB remains as a currency under the control of the Chinese Communist Party.[9] The following section conducts a brief review of what China has done to internationalize the RMB.

(a) Liberalization of Capital Controls

No currency can become an international reserve currency without being fully convertible. While the IMF has recognized the RMB as 'freely usable', 'freely usable' is not 'fully convertible', and the RMB is still a long way from attaining the status of a 'freely convertible' currency. To attain this status,

[5] Emily Merki, 'Why the Dollar Should No Longer be the World Reserve Currency: Solving Global Account Imbalances Through Structural Reform' (2015) 46 Georgetown Journal of International Law 1245.

[6] It should be noted that, while it had been widely speculated that the AIIB would use the RMB as its currency, it has decided in January 2016 to lend in USD at the moment.

[7] Shawn Donnan, 'White House Declares Truce with China over AIIB' *Financial Times* (27 September 2015) <http://www.ft.com/intl/cms/s/0/23c51438-64ca-11e5-a28b-50226830d644.html#axzz42BmkvekN> accessed 10 January 2016.

[8] Shawn Donnan, 'IMF Staff Say Renminbi Should Join Elite SDR Basket of Currencies' *Financial Times* (13 November 2015) <http://www.ft.com/intl/cms/s/0/f3c0948e-8a57-11e5-9f8c-a8d619fa707c.html#axzz3rk9JtcSe> accessed 10 October 2015.

[9] Many commentators nonetheless disagree with the IMF's view that the RMB is 'freely usable' and subject to limited manipulation. See, eg, Dean Baker, 'The Price of China's Yuan Manipulation: American Jobs' *The Guardian* (5 June 2015) <http://www.theguardian.com/world/2015/jun/06/china-yuan-us-economy-trade-deficit> accessed 20 November 2015.

China needs to lift capital controls. As a matter of fact, Chinese regulators have announced their plan to make the RMB fully convertible by 2020.[10] But the premature lifting of capital controls may give rise to various risks, as 'fully convertible' means that foreign capital can flow freely into a country while domestic capital can flow out. Sudden increases in capital inflow may create investment bubbles in the absence of deep capital markets while capital flight may lead to domestic credit crunches. As a matter of fact, massive capital flight occurred amid China's stock market crash, and it hit a record high in August 2015.[11]

Making the best use of its advantage as a large-scale economy, China's solution is to maintain the financial firewall of capital control while drilling holes into the firewall such that enough foreign capital may flow in to make a significant change. The recently adopted systems of the Qualified Foreign Institutional Investors (QFII) and the Renminbi Qualified Foreign Institutional Investors (RQFII) are two cases in point. Both grant direct access to China's domestic capital markets to selected foreign institutional investors. In particular, the RQFII acts as a bridge to repatriate offshore RMB back to China so as to fuel the development of the domestic capital market—a function similar to that of various mechanisms in the context of the USD-centred investment channels and offshore markets.[12] For China, the capital flowing in through these tiny holes in its financial firewall is sufficient to make a change but is still manageable.

Other restrictions on foreign exchange have been partially lifted too. This is done through measures such as removing the quota limit on the foreign exchange account, lifting the ceiling on foreign exchange purchases for overseas investments, and the system of Qualified Domestic Institutional Investors (QDII) that allows Chinese investors to invest outside of China.[13] This wave of liberalization has led to a rapid increase in international merger

[10] Enda Curran, 'For China, the End of the Beginning on Road to a Global Currency' *Bloomberg* (4 December 2015) <http://www.bloomberg.com/news/articles/2015-12-03/for-china-the-end-of-the-beginning-on-road-to-a-global-currency> accessed 4 December 2015.

[11] Official data indicates that more than $150 billion RMB left China in August 2015. 'Flow Dynamics: Capital Flight from China' *The Economist* (19 September 2015) <http://www.economist.com/news/finance-and-economics/21665042-lots-money-escaping-chinas-porous-capital-controls-flow-dynamics> accessed 20 November 2015.

[12] QFII and RQFII are mechanisms to recycle offshore RMB back to domestic markets so that offshore RMB can substantively contribute to the Chinese economy. Such recycling is also prominent and crucial for offshore USD and the US economy. For example, the US's oil purchases bring large amounts of USD into the Middle East but these petrodollars can be recycled back to the US market through the sovereign wealth funds of Middle Eastern countries.

[13] Ellen Kelleher, 'Demand for QDII Funds "Feeble"' *Financial Times* (17 June 2014) <http://www.ft.com/intl/cms/s/0/b8d73e6e-2644-11e3-aee8-00144feab7de.html#axzz34rjrYFgv> accessed 15 March 2015.

and acquisition transactions conducted by Chinese investors, some of which have caused political controversies and raised national security concerns in foreign countries.[14] Overall, the pace of liberalization is fast.

(b) Facilitation of RMB Circulation Worldwide

China has also been facilitating the RMB's circulation and trading worldwide through financial diplomacy as well as by establishing the relevant institutional infrastructure. For example, since the late 2000s, China has been promoting RMB-denominated bonds (commonly known as 'dim sum' bonds) that are traded outside China. And with further deregulation of these dim sum bonds in 2010, the market has taken off significantly. This boom of dim sum bonds has reconfigured the institutional settings of capital markets in the region in terms of market players (eg, increased involvement of Chinese lawyers and accountants), settlement institutions (eg, a switch from mechanisms controlled by American banks to those by Chinese banks), and deal structures (eg, the arrangement of a security package for bond offerings has to take into account considerable considerations about compliance with Chinese law that governs assets in China).[15] In short, it is a game-changer in Asian capital markets, affecting not only banking but also professional industries.

In addition, China has applied an institutional bridging strategy to connect fragmented markets at home and to link onshore with offshore markets. One recent example is the linking of the Shanghai and Hong Kong stock exchanges with the rationale that the larger the market is, the more liquidity the market possesses, thereby creating better economies of scale.[16] If successful, the next steps are probably to link these markets to Singapore, and thereby to the ASEAN markets in the south, as well as to the Taiwan Stock

[14] For a detailed discussion, see Weitseng Chen, 'From the Middle East to the Far West: What Can Chinese Overseas Investments Tell Us About Law and Development and Global Regulatory Regimes?' in Charlotte Schriwer and Nele Lenze (eds), *Converging Regions: Global Perspectives on Asia and the Middle East* (Ashgate 2014); Weitseng Chen, 'Screening the Dragon's Gift: National Security Review of China's Outbound Invesment' in John Garrick and Yan Bennett (eds), *China's Socialist Rule of Law: Deepening Reform and International Implications* (Routledge 2016).

[15] Weitseng Chen, 'Institutional Arbitrage: China's Economic Power Projection and International Capital Markets' (2013) 26:2 Columbia Journal of Asian Law 347.

[16] In theory, China has a number of models to choose from for bridging domestic and foreign stock exchanges, including secondary listing, cross listing, and a national security market model used by US regulators to link the European and the US markets. China's regulators chose the most aggressive model: a direct link between China and offshore markets. David Donald, 'Beyond Fragmentation: Building a Unified Securities Market in China (and Asia)' in Jiaxiang Hu, Matthias Vanhullebusch, and Andrew Harding (eds), *Finance, Rule of Law and Development in Asia: Perspectives From Hong Kong, Singapore and Shanghai* (Brill 2016).

Exchange in the east.[17] This bridging strategy is the revised version of the institutional bridging approach that China adopts at home to deal with fragmented regulations and variations in local economies so as to harness large-scale market advantages.[18]

Financial diplomacy is also manifested by the rapidly increasing number of bilateral currency swap agreements between China and foreign jurisdictions. As at the end of 2015, thirty-two countries had reached an agreement with the People's Bank of China (PBoC). Functionally, swap agreements serve as a vital mechanism for providing RMB liquidity outside of China and for laying the foundation of offshore RMB settlement.[19] Nonetheless, these agreements, together with negotiations and subsequent collaboration, have gone beyond a mere technical arrangement and have instead fuelled the competition between global and regional financial centres (eg, London, Luxemburg, Hong Kong, or Singapore), as well as between rising RMB-centred markets and incumbent USD-centred markets.

(c) Institutional Experimentation

To establish the necessary institutional setting for its RMB internationalization scheme, China, as usual, has introduced bold banking and financial reforms. One high-profile initiative is the Shanghai Free Trade Zone (SFTZ) established in 2013 together with unprecedented deregulation of the banking sector and foreign exchange markets within designated areas. Private banks, for example, have been allowed to incorporate and foreign banks are permitted to provide full services within these designated zones (subject to limited capital control).[20]

[17] Singapore and China also began integrating their securities markets in 2013. See 'SGX and China Securities Regulatory Commission Establish Direct Listing Framework' (Wong Partnership Briefing November 2013) <http://www.wongpartnership.com/index.php/files/download/1134> accessed 10 October 2015.

[18] For a discussion about institutional bridging in terms of the ways China organizes its legal system and SOEs, see Curtis J Milhaupt and Katharina Pistor, *Law & Capitalism: What Corporate Crises Reveal About Legal Systems and Economic Development around the World* (University of Chicago Press 2008); Li-Wen Lin and Curtis J Milhaupt, 'We are the (National) Champions: Understanding the Mechanisms of State Capitalism in China' (2013) 65 The Stanford Law Review 697.

[19] Ulrich Volz, 'RMB Internationalisation and Currency Cooperation in East Asia' in Frank Rövekamp and Hanns Günther Hilpert (eds), *Currency Cooperation in East Asia* (Springer 2014).

[20] For example, Cathay United Bank, a foreign bank, was established in the SFTZ in July 2014 and is not subjected to any limits on foreign exchange or the uses of the capital it lends for cross-border trading purposes within the zone. Tsu-Pei Chen and Hui-Te Yeh, 'Cathay United is First Taiwanese Bank in Shanghai FTZ' *Want China Times* (26 July 2014) <http://www.wantchinatimes.com/news-subclasscnt.aspx?id=20140726000084&cid=1102&MainCatID=11> accessed 15 March 2015.

The SFTZ, among several other zones created subsequently, has moved beyond the reconfiguration of China's banking system to experiment with the privatization of state-owned enterprises (SOEs) and the liberalization of capital account controls.[21] Perhaps more importantly, the SFTZ and other similar zones allow the potential risks of these experiments to be contained within that zone. As a result, private banks, which generally have more competitive lending and savings rates than the state-owned banks against which they compete, are not able to draw clients and drain away cheap capital from the state banking system outside of these zones.[22] The past two years have seen experiments with initial success being expanded by Chinese regulators to the rest of China quickly.[23]

Thus far, the outcomes of reforms seem promising. However, the stock market plunge in summer 2015 revealed the flip side of rapid RMB internationalization—that is, a lack of sufficient microprudential and macroprudential policies to address various risks deeply embedded into China's banking and financial sectors. While these policies seem relatively remote when viewed from the perspective of RMB internationalization, internationalization seems to have unleashed systemic risk, as exemplified by the free fall of the Chinese stock markets regardless of an individual firm's financial standing (a typical symptom of systemic risk). In response, Chinese regulators had to suspend trading on dozens of securities accounts for months.[24] PBoC also caught the global investors off guard by depreciating the value of the RMB several times in just a few months in order to stabilize China's

[21] For example, the opening of free trade accounts has also been allowed within the zone not only for banks but also for non-bank financial institutions. Residents, individuals, and corporate entities alike can apply for resident accounts that allow them to freely wire capital in and out without approval in advance. Accordingly, enforcement of anti-money-laundering regulations has been strengthened within the zone to prevent speculators from abusing the free movement of capital.

[22] Mengzhen Wang, 'China Authorizes Free Trade Account Opening in Shanghai' (CRI English 19 June 2014) <http://english.cri.cn/12394/2014/06/19/3684s832358.htm> accessed 15 March 2015; Dexing Qin, 'FTZ Expands Free Trade Accounts' *China Daily* (4 September 2014) <http://www.ecns.cn/business/2014/09-04/132995.shtml> accessed 15 March 2015.

[23] Reforms adopted for the SFTZ are starting to find their way into the rest of China. China has been expanding its experiments nationwide rapidly: an additional thirty-plus special economic zones have been designated to follow SFTZ and carry out the RMB liberalization scheme. Betty Tam and Frank Qi, 'SAFE Circular 36: Liberalising Capital Account Settlement for FIEs' *Mondaq* (8 August 2014) <http://www.mondaq.com/x/333560/Financial+Services/SAFE+Circular+36+Liberalising+Capital+Account+Settlement+for+FIEs> accessed 15 March 2015.

[24] The China Securities Regulatory Commission (CSRC) also launched a probe into a wide range of brokerage firms, investment companies, foreign-invested companies trading in PRC securities, as well as its own CSRC regulators. See Kit Tan, 'CSRC Official the Latest Target of Beijing's Stock Probe' *CNBC* (16 September 2015) <http://www.cnbc.com/2015/09/16/csrc-official-zhang-yujun-the-latest-target-of-beijings-stock-probe.html> accessed 10 November 2015.

economy. This volatility has caused great concern,[25] and has contradicted the ethos of the RMB internationalization scheme, which is to 'let the market play a decisive role'.

3. Achilles Heel: Systemic Risk and RMB Internationalization

China's RMB internationalization scheme has geo-political underpinnings, and the timing is strategically chosen. The RMB scheme was launched at a time when the US and European economies were badly hit by a series of financial crises which China's economy survived well and continued to grow rapidly. As widely perceived by Chinese leaders, the driver of the USD's dominance can primarily be attributed to the US government's strategic actions to end the dominance of the British pound. As World War II took its toll on the British economy, the US seized this long-awaited opportunity to finally make the USD the international reserve currency, decades after the US had actually replaced the UK as the world's superpower. Likewise, the Governor of PBoC manifested a similar rationale in his public speech: 'The internationalization of the RMB requires luck and opportunity, and the global financial crisis is just that.'[26]

Thanks to this political nature of China's RMB internationalization scheme, China has no qualms about instituting the unprecedented liberal reforms necessary to achieve its goal. On the one hand, these reforms are unprecedented because many of them would change the core structure of China's state-controlled economy, such as lifting capital controls, loosening exchange rate manipulation, liberalizing interest rates, and privatizing state-owned banks. On the other hand, they are not as unprecedented as they may seem, since these reforms are merely experiments implemented only within designated areas such as the SFTZ. This experimental approach has been adopted by China throughout its economic transition in the past three decades. All in all, the PBoC successfully geared the course of reforms towards its favoured direction, until the stock market crashed. The question is, besides the RMB's

[25] Tiecheng Yang, Francis Edwards, Robert Lee, and Yin Ge, 'Will China Tighten Its Grip on the Market Following the Stock Market Crash?' (Clifford Chance 3 September 2015) <http://www.metrocorpcounsel.com/articles/32912/will-china-tighten-its-grip-market-following-stock-market-crash-prc-sending-mixed-mes> accessed 10 October 2015.

[26] Renminbi guojihua bu shixian anpai sudu jiezou shidian' [Timing and Pace of RMB Internationalization Was Not Manually Set] *Caixin* (11 March 2014) <http://finance.caixin.com/2014-03-11/100649710.html> accessed 1 November 2015.

international achievement, what other metrics should one apply to evaluate the RMB scheme and assess the prospect of its internationalization?

To assess the progress of China's RMB internationalization scheme, we may apply two sets of metrics—that is, microprudential and macroprudential policy standards. Traditionally, microprudential policies focus on regulations and institutional design that prevent endogenous risks within individual financial institutions, such as banking regulations that prevent maturity mismatch between short-term liability and long-term obligations. Macroprudential policies, on the other hand, focus on both endogenous risks as well as exogenous risks that lead to systemic risk.

(a) Microprudential Assessment

Microprudential regulations range from specific managerial measures to broad institutional reforms. Examples of the former include imposing restrictions on a bank's leverage to prevent excessive risk-taking and introducing loss-absorbing instruments that strengthen the resiliency of banks, while examples of the latter include introducing good corporate governance into banks and a disclosure system that helps market participants identify risks and internalize both the premium of higher returns and any costs associated with increases in risk exposure.[27]

In order to apply these benchmarks, we need to focus on China's domestic institutions that are expected to support the RMB's internationalization. Three sets of institutions, which are often raised by academics as prerequisites for any currency to attain international reserve currency status, will be looked at. One involves market institutions, while the other two focus on the domestic political system and global financial networks respectively.

The first and oft-discussed prerequisite is a basket of market mechanisms that usually exists in advanced banking and capital markets. These mechanisms are related to the first and foremost requirement for any currency that aims to reach the status of international reserve currency—full convertibility. The flip side of full convertibility is lax capital control and free cross-border

[27] Robert Hockett, 'Macroprudential Turn: From Institutional Safety and Soundness to Systematic Financial Stability in Financial Supervision' (2014) 9 Virginia Law & Business Review 201; Rolf Weber, Douglas W Arner, Evan C Gibson, and Simone Baumann, 'Addressing Systemic Risk: Financial Regulatory Design' (2014) 49 Texas International Law Journal 149, 153; Kristin N Johnson, 'A Sustainable Approach to Regulating Financial Markets' (2013) 3 University of Illinois Law Review 881, 887; William W Bratton and Michael L Wachter, 'The Case Against Shareholder Empowerment' (2010) 158 University of Pennsylvania Law Review 653, 659; Rolf Weber and Douglas Arner, 'Toward a New Design for International Financial Regulation' (2007) 29 University of Pennsylvania Journal of International Economic Law 391.

capital flow, which usually bring in large increases in capital. As such, deep domestic capital markets are necessary and relevant financial institutions need to have the capacity to accommodate large increases in capital flow. If capital markets are shallow, capital would instead flood into speculative markets (eg, real estate markets), thereby causing investment bubbles. In a similar vein, a competitive banking system is equally important. Banking is about risk management. Exposed to more dynamic market conditions brought by increasing capital movement, banks need to estimate their risk portfolio diligently and independently and possess wide latitude in pricing such risks through setting various interest rates. A failure is likely to happen if the management tools of banks are restricted by the state or if the capacity of banks is weakened by government bailouts and resultant moral hazards.[28]

The second prerequisite is political stability. This is an indicator of the country's monetary system, its fiscal and budgetary regulations, the relationship between the state and private sectors, and overall political economy. International investors would not pour their assets into a currency whose value is vulnerable to political turbulence and financial manipulation, especially during periods of economic downturn that may prompt an insecure state to rescue its economy at the expense of foreign investors. Therefore, the focus of this prerequisite is on whether a state's political system has the capacity to self-correct and stabilize its financial system. One oft-mentioned example is the Swiss franc, a major international reserve currency issued by a small economy with less than half of Shanghai's population.[29] Despite its relatively small population, the political stability of Switzerland accounts for the wide acceptance of the Swiss franc by international investors and central banks. The opposite example is Greece. Investors' assets were trapped in a problematic economy and currency when Greece unexpectedly banned the remittance of the euro overseas amid its debt default crisis in 2015.

The last necessary prerequisite relates to sizable onshore and offshore markets as well as a wide circulation of the currency. Whether markets are sizeable and whether a currency is widely circulated are determined by not only economic fundamentals but also the availability of institutional support. This support includes efficient settlement mechanisms, active trading markets and market regulations, and professional services (eg, accountants, lawyers, and

[28] See generally, Emmanuel Farhi and Jean Tirole, 'Collective Moral Hazard, Maturity Mismatch, and Systemic Bailouts' (2012) 102 American Economic Review 60; Sara Hsu and Jianjun Li, 'The Rise and Fall of Shadow Banking in China' (2015) Political Economy Research Institute, University of Massachusetts Amherst, Working Paper No 375.

[29] The Swiss franc is legal tender only in Switzerland, the tiny principality of Liechtenstein, the Italian enclave of Campione d'Italia, and the German town Büsingen with a population of less than 2,000 residents.

bank analysts). The USD is often mentioned as a typical example. For one, its wide circulation is determined by the US's extraordinarily large economy. What is equally crucial is the wide offshore use of the USD as supported by international trade and securities regulations. For example, the 'petrodollar' deal struck between the US, Saudi Arabia, and other OPEC countries ensures the USD as the currency of choice for oil transactions, and this also recycles offshore USD back to onshore markets for investment purposes.[30] Another example is the creation of trading markets and regulatory changes for facilitating the circulation of 'Eurodollars', which greatly contributed to the trans-atlantic capital markets development. [31]

China ostensibly fulfils this final prerequisite. Wide circulation and sizable markets for the RMB are manifest in quick international acceptance of the RMB indicating China's achievements on the global stage. However, China underperforms on the first two prerequisites. For one, several vital market mechanisms, such as exchange rate and bank interest rates, are still subjected to the government's political will. As observed in the recent stock market plunge, China still resorts to manipulating the RMB exchange rate to maintain its market competitiveness. Global stock market panic occurred when the PBoC orchestrated a sudden depreciation of the RMB in August 2015, followed by another depreciation in October.[32] In between, markets also saw the PBoC trying to counteract excessive depreciation.[33] Such fluctuations, if they occur constantly, will make the RMB an international currency for speculation rather than reserve.

Furthermore, China's capital markets and state-controlled banking system have so far not proven effective in either providing efficient corporate

[30] For a discussion about the recycling of the USD through sovereign wealth funds, see Kyle Hatton and Katharina Pistor, 'Maximizing Autonomy in the Shadow of Great Powers: The Political Economy of Sovereign Wealth Funds' (2011–12) 50 Columbia Journal of Transnational Law 1.

[31] For example, Rule 144A of the US Securities Act of 1933 15 USC § 77a et seq. has created a favourable regulatory environment for the circulation of Eurodollars through unregistered securities offerings. The adoption of Rule144A manifested a fundamental change in the securities regulation regime (ie, issuer-choice model), which was a product of a fierce academic debate for cross-border securities transaction. See Roberta Romano, 'Empowering Investors: A Market Approach to Securities Regulation' (1998) 107 Yale Law Journal 2359; Stephen J Choi and Andrew T Guzman, 'Portable Reciprocity: Rethinking the International Reach of Securities Regulations' (1998) 71 Southern California Law Review 903; Howell E Jackson and Eric J Pan, 'Regulatory Competition in International Securities Markets: Evidence from Europe in 1999—Part I' (2000–01) 56 Business Lawyer 653, 655, 684–85.

[32] Neil Gough, 'Discordant Financial Messages From China Spur Global Unease' *NY Times* (19 October 2015) <http://www.nytimes.com/2015/10/20/business/international/discordant-financial-messages-from-china-spur-global-unease.html?hp&action=click&pgtype=Homepage&module=first-column-region&region=top-news&WT.nav=top-news&_r=0> accessed 10 October 2015.

[33] Usually this would be reflected by a strong rebound of the value of RMB, such as the one in September 2015.

financing or in disciplining the management of listed companies. The problems of false financial disclosure, insider trading, and corporate governance of both SOEs and private firms have all been well-documented.[34] As such, large-scale capital flow brought in by the internationalization of the RMB may raise new concerns. In particular, shallow capital markets do not seem to be able to accommodate large amounts of increased capital inflow. Foreign capital may therefore flow into overheating real estate markets and informal banking sectors, which provide more lucrative returns than typical securities investments. Similarly, capital flight is likely to increase owing to the RMB's full convertibility. This may cause some banks in the state-controlled banking system, which is highly protected by a fixed interest rate system promising cheap capital, to fail. Lacking the opportunity to estimate their risk portfolio independently, Chinese banks may not be able to develop timely business models that appeal to customers in order to prevent the risk of capital flights.

Having said all that, China's large-scale economy is probably the largest asset that bestows upon Chinese regulators not only bargaining power but also leeway in conducting institutional experiments for the benefit of the RMB internationalization scheme. Can an authoritarian state, short in political accountability and sophisticated market mechanisms in its financial system, successfully make its currency an international reserve currency primarily based on the magnetic force of its large-scale economy? It is too early to say. Indeed, some institutional designs are only made possible in a large-scale economy. For example, as I have argued elsewhere, China's experiments with its capital markets can be categorized as 'pluralist capitalism', with the SFTZ modelled after Singapore (ie, a typical state capitalism) and the Qinhai pilot zone modelled after Hong Kong (ie, a classical laissez-faire capitalist system).[35] Nonetheless, it remains to be observed whether China's extraordinary large-scale economy may compensate for its deficiencies in these two microprudential prerequisites.

All in all, unlike what the label 'internationalization' conveys, the internationalization of the RMB is more of a domestic than an international project.

[34] See, eg, Donald C Clarke, 'Law Without Order in Chinese Corporate Governance Institutions' (2010) 30 Northwestern Journal of International Law & Business 131; Yong Kang, Lu Shi, and Elizabeth D Brown, *Chinese Corporate Governance: History and Institutional Framework* (The Rand Corporation 2008) <http://www.rand.org/pubs/technical_reports/TR618.html>; Lay-Hong Tan and Jiangyu Wang, 'Modeling an Effective Corporate Governance System for China's Listed State-Owned Enterprises: Issues and Challenges in a Transitional Economy' (2007) 7:1 Journal of Corporate Law Studies 143; SJ Gabriel, *Chinese Capitalism and the Modernist Vision* (Psychology Press 2006) 147.

[35] See Weitseng Chen, 'Size Matters? RMB Internationalization and the Beijing Consensus' in Weitseng Chen (ed), *The Beijing Consensus? How China Has Changed the Western Ideas of Law and Economic Development* (CUP 2016).

Major challenges come from within the country rather than from abroad, and these challenges concern capital markets regulation, the capacity of China's state-owned banking system, and capital account liberalization. As such, this chapter now turns to an assessment of the RMB internationalization scheme from a macroprudential perspective, which is primarily concerned with systemic risk. Briefly, system risk exists in China's financial sector, and this chapter contends that systemic risk could be triggered by the rapid pace of the RMB's internationalization. The next two sections elaborate this view in a general manner as well as in the context of China's shadow banking industry specifically.

(b) Macroprudential Assessment

Macroprudential policies focus not only on the risk that individual financial institutions may fail but the systemic risk that may bring down an entire financial system.[36] Systemic risk often catches regulators off guard because the contemporary banking industry is inextricably interconnected. Default of Bank A on loans borrowed from Bank B can affect Bank C that holds debts issued by Bank B, regardless of Bank C's actual performance. Such contagion may be amplified by increasing numbers of unregulated financial institutions that operate as a substitute for formal banks and which therefore give rise to similar risks.

The interconnectedness between multiple financial markets also generates systemic risk. One such way is the capital flow between interconnected institutions within a financial web composed of formal and informal banks, financial and non-financial institutions, and onshore and offshore capital markets. For example, controlling one type of capital flow (eg, restricting the flow of foreign capital into the domestic stock market) may lead to increases in capital flow through other channels (eg, the flow of foreign capital into domestic real estate markets). Similarly, the liberalization of capital accounts may increase capital flow into not only the destination that regulators intend (eg, securities markets), but also into other destinations that provide higher returns for speculators (eg, shadow banks). In this regard, the RMB internationalization, which concerns both capital controls as well as liberalization of capital controls, needs to deal with systemic risk embedded in this complex financial web. Regulators have to consider factors that affect not only currency exchange but also the overall health of various financial sectors, including the depth of capital markets, the capacity of domestic banks, the impact

[36] See also Anita Anand, Michael Trebilcock, and Michael Rosenstock, Chapter 1 in this volume.

of industrial policy, and even the state of the political climate.[37] The current RMB internationalization scheme does not appear to take into account this wide variety of factors with necessary macroprudential policies.

The other issue with China's RMB internationalization scheme is that it is *pro-cyclical* in nature. The main difference between microprudential and macroprudential thinking is that the former is *pro-cyclical* while the latter is *counter-cyclical. Procyclicity* refers to the availability of cheap capital and collateral in a booming economy, which encourages borrowers to borrow more from financial institutions, which in turn rely on credit default swap to hedge against increases in risks of default. As a result, financial institutions assume it is safe to lend more and this fuels the economy. However, this sort of financial engineering engenders nothing more than a 'false sense of security',[38] and this feedback loop continues until the bubble bursts, triggering systemic risk. Critically, the traditional regulatory regime facilitates this spiral circle and whatever systemic risk present is directly amplified by the holding of high yield but risky assets that result from pro-cyclical build-ups.[39] As commentators have noted, 'the [US] Federal Deposit Insurance premiums [prior to 2005] have either been risk-insensitive or relied only on individual bank failure risk and never on systemic risk'.[40] In other words, this programme was functionally pro-cyclical.[41]

The successful internationalization of the RMB is a product of China's booming economy, and China's goal is to continue this trend, and therefore, to act pro-cyclically. To encourage the use of RMB, among other reasons, the PBoC has been increasing the money supply. Commonly noted in academic discussions in China, the internationalization of the RMB is expected to bring in more foreign capital through the lifting of capital controls so as to defuse the risks potentially to be brought by slowing growth, weakening consumer markets, and massive capital flight.[42] Therefore, for China, the

[37] ibid. As Anand et al. argue, these factors also affect the approach to regulating financial markets in that the institutional design for the financial regulatory model is highly path-dependent.

[38] Jeffery Atik, 'Basel II: A Post-crisis Post-mortem' (2011) 19 Transnational Law & Contemporary Problems 731, 749.

[39] Daniel Schwarcz and Steven L Schwarcz, 'Regulating Systemic Risk in Insurance' (2014) 81 University of Chicago Law Review 1569, 1599.

[40] Viral V Acharya, João A. C. Santos, and Tanju Yorulmazer, 'Systemic Risk and Deposit Insurance Premiums' (2010) Federal Reserve Bank of New York Economic Policy Review 89, 91 <http://www.newyorkfed.org/research/epr/10v16n1/1008yoru.pdf> accessed 10 November 2015.

[41] Hockett, 'Macroprudential Turn: From Institutional Safety and Soundness to Systematic Financial Stability in Financial Supervision' (n 27) 226.

[42] It has been reported that Beijing carried out policies to boost the stock market with the aim of reducing the reliance of local companies on government subsidies and to incentivize Chinese companies to borrow more from the market. Sun Tao (孫濤) and Pu Shi (朴實), 'Gushi yuanhe

paramount objective is to maintain its high growth rate so that any economic slowdown would not cause a liquidity crisis as indicated by the governmental slogan 'bao qi' or 'to protect 7% of growth rate by using all possible means' (it used to be 'bao ba' or 'to protect 8%' prior to 2013[43]).

Other institutional reforms promulgated by China for its financial sector also mainly follow microprudential thinking rather than macroprudential policy. For example, microprudential regulations, such as Basel I and Basel II, generally rely on market forces and a bottom-up process to detect risks and to allow banks to internalize such risks, presuming that banks know their risks and know how to manage their risk exposures better than regulators.[44] This market-oriented mindset resulted in a disclosure-based regime as the overarching regulatory structure.[45] Similarly, legal scholars in China have been advocating a disclosure-based regime for China's securities regulation, with the view that the present merit-based regime is a major obstacle that slows the pace of capital market transactions.[46] In short, the RMB internalization scheme aims to boost the market in a pro-cyclical manner and related initiatives are also pro-cyclical in nature.

While the RMB internationalization scheme's pro-cyclical nature gives regulators a strong mandate to pursue visible success, especially at the international level, it may distract regulators from more pressing and fundamental issues at home. As a matter of fact, the rapid progress of the scheme overseas partially reflects the shared frustration of central bankers worldwide about the USD's dominance. However, this frustration alone cannot bolster the RMB to the status of an international reserve currency.[47] To the contrary, institutional deficits at home appear to be the biggest challenge for the RMB scheme.

kuangbiao' [What has Accounted for China's Stock Market Boom] China Reform (中國改革) *Caixin* (June 2015).

[43] See, eg, Jamil Anderlini, 'China's Growth Model Running Out of Steam' *Financial Times* (5 March 2012) <http://www.ft.com/intl/cms/s/0/3467d94c-66d1-11e1-863c-00144feabdc0.html#axzz42BmkvekN> accessed 30 January 2016.

[44] Behzad Gohari and Karen E Woody, 'New Global Financial Regulatory Order: Can Macroprudential Regulation Prevent Another Global Financial Disaster' (2014) 40 Journal of Corporation Law 403, 419–20.

[45] ibid.

[46] Yingmao Tang, 'The Chinese Model for Securities Law' in Chen (ed) (n 35).

[47] In the wake of the dominant USD, central banks worldwide generally welcome any alternative reserve currency. 'Dollar trap', a concept used by Eswar Prasad to describe the frustration of private and central bankers around the world who have no better option but to increase holding of USD-denominated assets so as to hedge against currency risk. This frustration largely accounts for the quick progress of the RMB scheme overseas. Eswar Prasad, *The Dollar Trap: How the US Dollar Tightened Its Grip on Global Finance* (Princeton University Press 2014). Also see, Merki, 'Why the Dollar Should No Longer be the World Reserve Currency' (n 5).

By macroprudential standards, China seems to be trapped in its own success with the RMB overseas. First, its unbalanced focus on the internationalization of the RMB may distort the sequence of necessary reforms at home. For example, some commentators have blamed the once-lauded Shanghai-Hong Kong Stock Connect under the RMB scheme for creating a channel of speculative capital and therefore contributing to the stock market crash in summer 2015.[48] The heart of the issue concerning the RMB scheme implementation lies in the sequencing of domestic reforms and China's burning desire to project the RMB internationally. China focused on the latter but domestic institutional reforms have proven to be more crucial.

Second, even if China shifts to a macroprudential focus, the pro-cyclical nature of the RMB internationalization scheme is likely to offset the effects of any macroprudential policy. Recent empirical research shows that macroprudential regulations are not particularly effective when they lean in the opposite direction of expansionary monetary policy.[49] This is because

> macroprudential policy works by restraining borrowing, [and,] naturally, [the] most successful instances of macroprudential policies are those where macroprudential policies and monetary policy are pulling in the same direction ... When monetary policy and macroprudential policies are pulling in opposite directions, they should be far less effective since economic agents are being told simultaneously to borrow more and borrow less.[50]

In other words, macroprudential policies are more likely to succeed when introduced during periods of tightened interest rates and contractionary monetary policy. To the contrary, China's most frequent approach to defusing systemic risk is to cut interest rates and to use expansionary monetary policy, which may undermine macroprudential policies.

Last but not least, the role that politics plays has to be taken into account when any government implements macroprudential policies. The RMB internationalization scheme has given rise to an internal power struggle between governmental agencies that may or may not benefit from the implementation of macroprudential policies. Like other policies, macroprudential policies

48 'Agu baofa guzai: chao 32 yi zijin jing hugangtong chaodi' [A-Share Market Crash: More Than 3.2 Billion of Bottom-Fishing Investment Through Shanghai-Hong Kong Stock Connect] *Phoenix Finance* (凤凰财经) (26 June 2015) <http://finance.ifeng.com/a/20150626/13800886_0.shtml> accessed 30 January 2016.

49 Valentina Bruno, Shim I, and Hyun Song Shin, 'Comparative Assessment of Macroprudential Policies' (2015) BIS Working Paper No 502 <http://ssrn.com/abstract=2617286> accessed 1 November 2015.

50 Matthew C Klein, 'When "Macroprudential" Policy Works—and Doesn't' *Financial Times* (15 June 2015) <http://ftalphaville.ft.com/2015/06/15/2131746/when-macroprudential-policy-works-and-doesnt/> accessed 1 November 2015.

create winners and losers in a bureaucratic system. China's central bank, the PBoC, would arguably be the biggest winner whereas agencies whose institutional power is tied to state-owned banks and SOEs would be the losers. In addition, big banks and big SOEs would be winners because they have better capacity to compete in a relatively free market, whereas regional financial institutions and small SOEs would be worse off because their reliance on governmental subsidies and protection would be cut off. As a result, the RMB scheme has reportedly ignited factional politics within the Chinese Communist Party.[51] As far as macroprudential policy is concerned, such political struggle would affect regulatory coordination, which is essential to the success of the policies. [52]

In fact, a large part of macroprudential thinking deals with the regulatory fragmentation inherent in a conventional microprudential regulatory regime. Macroprudential policy does not function in isolation but interacts with other policies that bear on systemic risk. For example, one of biggest failures of Basel II, which sought to address systemic risk, was caused by its delegation of the monitoring of financial institutions to private rating agencies, which have appeared to provide a skewed assessment of systemic risk.[53] Therefore, regulatory fragmentation can be dealt with but this requires not only the realignment of polices but also strong coordination between micro- and macroprudential agencies, which is crucial for mega-data collection and cross-sector and cross-institutional monitoring.[54] Unfortunately, regulatory fragmentation is a serious problem in China and would be worsened by the political struggles caused by the implementation of the RMB scheme.[55]

[51] See, eg, Injoo Sohn, 'Five Political Challenges in China's Monetary Ambition' Brookings East Asia Commentary No 86 (March 2015) <http://www.brookings.edu/research/opinions/2015/03/09-china-monetary-ambition-sohn> accessed 30 January 2016.

[52] Coordination is needed not only at the domestic level but also at the international level. Financial diplomacy is particularly detrimental as macroprudential policies concern monetary policies. See Daniel Heath, 'International Coordination of Macroprudential and Monetary Policy' (2013) 45 Georgetown Journal of International Law 1093; Douglas W Arner, Michael A Panton, and Paul Lejot, 'Central Banks and Central Bank Cooperation in the Global Financial System' (2010) 23 Pacific McGeorge Global Business & Development Law Journal 1.

[53] Gohari and Woody, 'New Global Financial Regulatory Order: Can Macroprudential Regulation Prevent Another Global Financial Disaster' (n 44) 416.

[54] ibid 428, 436.

[55] The Federal Stability Board (FSB) completed a peer review of China on her macroprudential management framework and non-bank credit intermediation on 14 August 2015. The FSB report generally endorses the PBoC's efforts to enforce macroprudential policies. However, it urged for better inter-agency coordination and the major area to be improved is that of non-bank credit. FSB, 'Report: Peer Review of China' (13 August 2015) <http://www.financialstabilityboard.org/2015/08/peer-review-of-china/> accessed 1 November 2015.

In short, the pro-cyclical nature of the RMB internationalization scheme is at odds with macroprudential policies. From the perspective of macroprudential policy, the RMB scheme is more of a domestic than an international project. Notwithstanding an explainable and effective international strategy, China's plan to internationalize the RMB has not been accompanied by the domestic macroprudential policies necessary to mitigate or account for systemic risk. Until the domestic banking and financial industries are overhauled, systemic risk will continue to grow unchecked in China. In the next section, this chapter elaborates on the macroprudential concerns in the context of China's shadow banking industry, which is a major source of systemic risk in China.

4. Shadow Banking and RMB Internationalization

Alibaba.com, the largest Chinese online retailer, made financial history in 2014 as the company to launch the biggest initial public offering in history. Alipay, the payment and financial service arm of Alibaba.com, provides users with a money-managing account that allows them to invest earnings or the balance left over from a transaction, and this account, called YuE' Bao or 'leftover treasure', earns them interest. However, unlike a traditional bank, YuE' Bao requires no minimum deposit, eliminates all transaction fees, and, most importantly, provides depositors with a better return that is approximately double the average 3 per cent return that state banks provide. Moreover, its services are mobile friendly and users, even those living abroad, can deposit and withdraw money instantly by touching the screen of their smartphones. Within one year, it attracted more than 100 million investors, exceeding the 77 million active stock-trading accounts that China has.[56] With some 574 billion yuan (or $93 billion USD) under its management as at June 2014, Alipay is the biggest money-market fund in China, and one of the biggest in the world.[57] Although YuE' Bao's business model is creative and praised as probably the greatest financial innovation in China's banking industry,[58] the fact remains that it is a shadow bank.

[56] Sheng Songcheng (盛松成) and Zhai Chun (翟春), 'Jinrong chuangxin yu huobi gongji' [Financial Innovation and Money Supply] China Reform (中國改革) *Caixin* (June 2015).

[57] 'Alibaba's Maturity Mismatch' *The Economist* (24 June 2014) <http://www.economist.com/blogs/freeexchange/2014/07/chinese-finance> accessed 10 October 2015.

[58] See generally, Takeshi Jingu, 'Internet Finance Growing Rapidly in China' Nomura Research Institute, lakyara vol 189 (10 March 2014).

The shadow banking system is broadly defined by the Financial Stability Board (FSB), the shadow banking monitoring agency, as 'credit intermediation involving entities and activities outside the regular banking system'.[59] In the face of YuE' Bao's quick success, Chinese regulators are confronted with a dilemma: on the one hand, they do not want to stop a seemingly successful financial innovation that has not just brought this Chinese retailer to the global stage but also made it one of the world's largest financial institutions. On the other hand, any potential failure of a financial institution of this scale, operating outside the realm of banking regulations, would undoubtedly give rise to a tremendous crisis, economically as well as politically. It may create a typical 'too-big-to-fail' scenario in which the government has to bear the final liability. YuE' Bao's impressive business sheds light onto the nature of shadow banking in China.

(a) Systemic Risk: A Move from Back Alleys to Main Streets

Shadow banking entities conduct maturity, credit, and liquidity transformation without explicit access to central bank liquidity or the public sector's credit guarantees. In theory, intermediating credit through non-banking channels has important advantages and contributes to the financing of the real economy. While the formal banking system enjoys privileges such as the central bank's support and the availability of deposit insurance, these privileges reflect the fragility of the formal banking system in that it is vulnerable to systemic risk. This is where the shadow banking system comes in. One way to manage systemic risk, among others, is to distribute risks to non-bank intermediaries that are usually small in scale and hence lack the capacity of producing complex financial products (eg, asset-backed securities) to reach a large pool of investors. Therefore, compared to formal banks, the business model of shadow banking entities is less likely to contain large-scale systemic risk. Also, shadow banking entities offer alternative lending channels for borrowers that are not the targeted customers of formal banks, especially at a time when regulators tighten up the leverage requirements on formal banks.[60] Against this backdrop, shadow banking has been quickly expanding

[59] FSB, 'Global Shadow Banking Monitoring Report 2014' (4 November 2014) <http://www.financialstabilityboard.org/2014/11/global-shadow-banking-monitoring-report-2014/> accessed 15 November 2015.

[60] Nicola Gennaioli, Andrei Shleifer, and Robert W Vishny, 'A Model of Shadow Banking' (2013) 68 The Journal of Finance 1331; Shen Wei, 'Shadow Banking System in China: Origin, Uniqueness, and Governmental Responses' (2013) 1 Journal of International Banking Law and Regulations 20; Gary Gorton and Andrew Metrick, 'Regulating the Shadow Banking System' (2010) Brookings Papers on Economic Activity 261.

in the wake of the credit crunch that has followed the financial crisis. As Jamie Dimon, JP Morgan's CEO put it, 'one of the main sources of competition [to formal banks] would be shadow banks'.[61] As such, the shadow banking system can supplement the formal banking system.

Indeed, China's shadow banking industry plays a vital role in promoting development like that of other non-bank financial institutions in other high-growth jurisdictions such as India, South Korea, and Hong Kong.[62] The Chinese government has been practising what economists call 'financial repression' for years, extracting savings from households and the private sector through state-controlled banks in order to allocate cheap capital to SOEs and other strategic industries.[63] Shadow banks, therefore, not only channel much-needed capital to a private sector starved of debt financing but also grant savers higher returns.[64] In effect, the shadow banking system liberalizes China's financial sector.[65]

Nevertheless, shadow banking entities raise serious concerns with respect to systemic risk when they offer complex products and services and when their connections to the formal banking system strengthen. In China, thanks to peer-to-peer (P2P) lending made possible by the Internet, the shadow banking industry has crossed the traditional firewall that had historically isolated shadow banks from large-scale systemic risk. As exemplified by Alipay, shadow banks in China have obtained logistic capacity and professional expertise to reach once-unthinkable numbers of customers in a short period of time. What is praised as 'financial innovation', such as P2P lending and microfinance, has now become the driver of this booming industry. Taking advantage of information technology, China's shadow banking entities quickly fill the gap between monopolistic state-owned banks and back-alley lending entities such as pawn shops and tight-knit community units.[66] Estimates of the size of shadow banking in China vary, but an average of estimates, according to a report issued by the Brookings Institution, is approximately RMB 25

[61] 'Do It Right: Reshaping the Financial Sector' *The Economist* (10 May 2014) 15.

[62] Ross Buckley, Douglas W Arner, and Michael Panton, 'Financial Innovation in East Asia' (2014) 37 Seattle University Law Review 307.

[63] See generally, Nicholas Lardy, 'Financial Repression in China' (2008) Peterson Institute Policy Brief 08-8.

[64] Shen, 'Shadow Banking System in China: Origin, Uniqueness, and Governmental Responses' (n 60) 24.

[65] Kelley Tsai, *Back-alley Banking: Private Entrepreneurs in China* (Cornell University Press 2002); Yasheng Huang and Wenhua Di, 'A Tale of Two Provinces: The Institutional Environment and Foreign Ownership in China' William Davidson Institute Working Paper No 667 (2004).

[66] Tsai (n 65).

trillion as of the end of 2013, or about 43 per cent of China's GDP.[67] As such, systemic risk within the shadow banking industry is a major concern.

The lending structure of China's shadowing banking industry used to be far less complex, but that is not exactly the case anymore. Indeed, a substantial number of shadow banking entities engage in straightforward lending structures with a limited number of parties rather than in asset-backed securitization,[68] while some have been able to develop complex products and reach a large number of customers by applying securitization and by using a cross-regional underwriting process. Thus, it is premature to assume that China's shadow banking is less likely to exacerbate negative externalities of banking failure. On the contrary, it is usual for local Chinese governments and formal banks to be involved in this securitization process as a guarantor, lender, facilitator, or underwriter. In this way, securitization and the use of cross-guarantees strengthen the interconnectedness between the shadow banking and the formal banking systems. As a result, systemic risk that arises from cross-institutional linkages and creates contagion by diffusing risks from one crashing market to another is of great concern to China's shadow banks.

A brief description of the lending structure used by Chinese shadow banks may help illustrate how systemic risk arises. Most Chinese shadow banks that garner a large number of customers are incorporated as trust companies, a type of asset-management company allowed under the Chinese Company Law. A trust company would first collaborate with a loan borrower, usually a large company that has secured loans from a state-owned bank. The trust company, which usually has close ties with a state-owned bank of this kind, then securitizes the loan credits and sells the securities underlying the credits and interest payments to investors who hope to receive a higher return than they would normally receive from a formal bank. Under this entrusted loan structure, no security is usually offered on the issued securities.[69] Nor is there any formal guarantee that the investment would provide the advertised

[67] Douglas Elliott, Arthur Kroeber, and Yu Qiao, 'Shadow Banking in China: A Primer' Brookings Institution (March 2015) <http://www.ccdigs.com/wp-content/uploads/2015/08/shadow_banking_china_elliott_kroeber_yu.pdf> accessed 1 November 2015.

[68] The FSB, for example, primarily focuses on the shadow banking entities involved in asset-backed securitization, rather than those that engage in straightforward lending structure with limited number of parties involved. Suleika Reiners, 'Strengthening Oversight and Regulation of Shadow Banking' (14 January 2013) <http://www.worldfuturecouncil.org/fileadmin/user_upload/Future_Finance/Shadow_Banking_FSB_Suleika_Reiners_WFC_140112.pdf> accessed 1 October 2015.

[69] 'A Question of Trust: China' *The Economist* (10 May 2014) 13. From a macroprudential perspective, where securitization vehicles are used as funding channels, there should be restrictions on maturity/liquidity transformation as well as liquidity requirements between the securities issued and the underlying pool of assets.

return, or even that the principal would be repaid.[70] If the borrower fails to repay either the principal or the interest, investors will be the ultimate losers while the trust company bears little liability.

Compared to this peculiar, simple structure of securitization that offers no proper security package, the underwriting process is much more complex. In particular, state-owned banks may be involved so that a wide pool of investors can be reached. For example, the Industrial and Commercial Bank of China, the country's largest bank, underwrote the bonds of a solar-panel manufacturer named Chaori, and the company eventually defaulted on its debt payment in March 2014. Investors, many of whom purchased the bonds mainly because they were sold by the reputable bank, protested and called for a state bailout. Eventually, China's Premier Li Keqiang was compelled to intervene.

Notwithstanding the otherwise simple structure of the shadow banking sector set out above, it can become more complicated if local governments and SOEs are involved. Unfortunately, this is nearly always the case. It has been reported that 90 per cent of lenders in this shadow industry are cash-rich SOEs, many of which have finance arms in the form of finance and trust companies.[71] Their ties to local governments grant them better access to excessive credits in the formal banking system and also enable them to circumvent existing regulations. Large SOEs, such as China Mobile, PetroChina, China Railway Group, Cofco, and Yangzijiang Shipbuilding Holdings, have been directly involved in the lending business with their excess cash through their shadow banking units.[72] Moreover, the blurry boundary between SOEs and government means that local governments, using off-balance sheet practices, can act as lenders too.[73] In this way, local governments can make better use of massive subsidies given by the central government, while, most likely, siphoning a part of it as well.

Consequently, the complex networks consisting of local governments, SOEs, local banks, and trust companies become a source of systemic risk. This is different from the shadow banking of China's past. Risks of shadow banking to date have been complicated by the cross-sector networks and amplified by securitization, the use of cross-guarantees among SOEs and

[70] 'Battling the Darkness: Shadow Banking in China' *The Economist* (10 May 2014) 71; 'A Question of Trust: China' (n 69).

[71] Brooke Masters, Henny Sender, and Dan McCrum, 'Shadow Banks Move in Amid Regulatory Push' *Financial Times* (9 September 2011) 15; Henny Sender, 'China Groups Fuel Shadow Banking' *Financial Times* (7 September 2011) 18; Shen, 'Shadow Banking System in China: Origin, Uniqueness, and Governmental Responses' (n 60) 22.

[72] Shen, 'Shadow Banking System in China: Origin, Uniqueness, and Governmental Responses' (n 60) 22.

[73] ibid.

local governments, and widespread underwriting. At present, various financial institutions are increasingly offering inter-substitutable products and services, and this convergence further extends the domino effect of a financial crash.[74]

Another trait of China's shadow banking is its pro-cyclical feedback loop that may lead to systemic risk. In China's booming economy, borrowers have tremendous collateral available for borrowing more, and, in response, both formal and shadow banks are willing to lend more. Investors are also willing to participate in this business by purchasing securities underlying the credits and interest payments in loan transactions of this kind, and this in turn encourages lenders to lend more and borrowers to borrow more. Furthermore, securitization increases pro-cyclicality. Such a vicious cycle leads to a bubble—exactly what macroprudential policies try to counteract.

Despite this systemic risk, it is difficult for Chinese regulators to act counter-cyclically. In the US, regulation of shadow banking has been fraught with difficulty, and opponents cite a potential reduction of economic growth as one of the reasons to maintain the status quo.[75] Similar opposition exists in China as shadow banking is now entrenched in China's development, particularly at the regional level. A run on shadow banks may be accidentally precipitated if regulators move too forcefully to control informal lending. To act counter-cyclically is practically difficult and politically risky.

(b) Shadow Banking and RMB Internationalization

Shadow banks in China can create bank-like systemic risk, considering their massive scale, the involvement of both state and private actors, and securitization. Cross-institutional and cross-sector links exist, and feedback loops underlie every aspect of systemic risk.[76] It makes sense to *de-risk* shadow banking before lifting capital controls and introducing full convertibility of the RMB, a necessary step to make the RMB a genuine international reserve currency. Any sudden increase of capital flow owing to the liberalization of capital controls may exacerbate systemic risk in the shadow banking industry. Capital flight for better or more secure returns available overseas may destabilize the liquidity of the shadow banking industry, whereas capital inflow may increase speculative activities in the informal sector if the formal sector

[74] Hockett, 'Macroprudential Turn: From Institutional Safety and Soundness to Systematic Financial Stability in Financial Supervision' (n 27) 210.

[75] Gohari and Woody, 'New Global Financial Regulatory Order: Can Macroprudential Regulation Prevent Another Global Financial Disaster' (n 44) 426.

[76] Hockett, 'Macroprudential Turn: From Institutional Safety and Soundness to Systematic Financial Stability in Financial Supervision' (n 27).

lacks sufficient investment channels. Therefore, to reform the shadow banking industry, a gradual approach is required to avoid any liquidity crunch and maturity mismatch. This is particularly crucial for emerging economies where shadow banks serve a key role in facilitating credit allocation.

Indeed, the regulation of shadow banks may pose greater challenges for developing economies than mature economies. Formal banks in mature economies operate in competitive markets and thus offer services and investment opportunities that may attract most customers, whereas shadow banks naturally have less leverage to engage in any large-scale, complex financial services. In other words, shadow banks generally supplement formal banks even though there may be competition between the two. In comparison, shadow banks play a larger role in developing economies that are financially repressed. Besides China, developing states, such as South Korea, Taiwan, and Japan, have applied a similar approach in the early years of their respective economic developments to extract cheap capital from the general public for their strategic industries or SOEs. As a result, in developing economies, shadow banks usually substitute formal banks, offering credit for borrowers normally excluded by formal banking, which is usually stated-controlled. Market players in emerging economies also appear to be less risk-averse and more willing to participate in shadow banking given limited information and investment opportunities for them in the formal banking industry. As such, reforms of shadow banking in emerging markets appear to be more challenging than in developed economies, and this complication needs to be taken into account when China carries out its RMB internationalization scheme.

Experiences of other developing states may shed light onto shadow banking reform for China. In particular, Taiwan's reforms of shadow banking are illuminating because these reforms were conducted for similar reasons—to liberalize capital accounts and currency regulation and to alter the direction of manipulative policies to those that are more market-oriented and free of capital control and financial repression. In fact, both countries share similar banking structures and pressures for change. Like China, Taiwan's state-owned banks dominated the financial markets prior to the reforms promulgated in the late 1980s. Taiwanese banks provided cheap capital for SOEs as well as government-linked private enterprises, while ordinary households and firms had difficulty obtaining sufficient loans from the state banking system.[77] Also, prior to the reforms, the Taiwanese government controlled twenty-one of the country's twenty-four banks, which in turn held 90 per cent of all deposits.[78]

[77] Andrew Wedeman, *Double Paradox: Rapid Growth and Rising Corruption in China* (Cornell University Press 2012) 43.

[78] Karl Fields, *Enterprise and the State in Korea and Taiwan* (Cornell University Press 1995) 149.

Consequently, financial repression abounded with large amounts of bad loans and rampant corruption in the banking system. The informal banking system naturally played a vital role in the private sector by filling in the gaps in supply created by the formal banking system, even though it was also associated with political scandals, Ponzi schemes, and white-collar crime.

Taiwan eventually carried out banking reforms in the late 1980s under political and economic pressure. The policy considerations were similar to those of underpinning the internationalization of the RMB. First, Taiwan's successful export industry led to immense foreign reserve (ranked as world number one in 1991 when banking reforms began), which led to the appreciation of its currency vis-à-vis the USD and in turn harmed the export industry. Second, the government's attempt to manipulate the exchange rate compromised the effectiveness of its interest rates and monetary policies. Third, large amounts of domestic savings needed to be channelled into better investment vehicles, domestically and internationally, but stringent capital controls made it difficult for this to happen. Fourth, financial repression also resulted in political pressure on the government from the disgruntled middle class.

However, unlike China, Taiwan's regulators decided to first address its domestic problems, especially the systemic risk associated with shadow banking. The Taiwanese government gradually overhauled the banking sector in the late 1980s with measures that include the privatization of state-owned banks, the institutionalization of non-bank financial institutions, the opening of financial markets for foreign banks, the liberalization of interest rates, the granting of foreign investors with more room to invest in the domestic securities market and, eventually, the lifting of restrictions on the convertibility of currency.[79] This process, which was accompanied with bank failures, political backlash, and stock market crashes, took approximately fifteen years, if not more.[80]

Compared to the Taiwanese sector, China's shadow banking is more complex and larger in scale, with local governments and state-owned banks

[79] Take an example of the liberalization of exchange rate policy in Taiwan: Five selected banks were allowed to create a foreign exchange market among banks and established a joint committee to decide their own exchange rates. Four years later the central bank expanded this institutional experiment by setting the once centralized exchange rate based on the rates determined by the five selected banks. Finally in 1989, Taiwan's central bank abolished entirely the controls on foreign exchange rates in the belief that the banks had obtained the ability and necessary skills to fully decide foreign exchange rates. Cheng-Ming Hsu (許振明), 'You jinrong ziyouhua yu guojihua de guocheng tan jinrong jianli' [Financial Liberalization, Internationalization and Supervision] (2001) National Policy Foundation Policy Report No 090-039 <http://old.npf.org.tw/PUBLICATION/FM/090/FM-R-090-039.htm> accessed 1 October 2015.

[80] Similarly, Japan took decades to liberalize its capital account.

involved through cross-guarantees, underwriting, securitization, or direct lending. Unlike China, smartphones played little role in Taiwan's shadow banking sector and Internet banking was also unheard of. If Taiwan, given its much smaller economic scale and the lending structure of its shadow banks, spent more than a decade to complete gradual reforms of its shadow banking industry, interest rate liberalization, and overhaul of state-owned banks, it may well indicate that Chinese regulators face a more difficult task which may take a longer time to complete. If China pushes for the internationalization of RMB at a rate that is too fast, the sequence of reforms will be distorted and systemic risk may not be managed well.

At the end of day, regulating shadow banking is a matter of reconfiguring a country's banking sector. Historically, non-bank finance has played a vital role in facilitating credit intermediation and thus promoting growth in many Asian jurisdictions, including Japan, Hong Kong, Taiwan, Singapore, and South Korea, in addition to China. In light of the many financial crises and stringent regulations being advocated thereafter, regulators in Asia are understandably inclined to rely on minimizing risks rather than capturing the development potential of non-bank finance as they have always done.[81] In this regard, two contrasting models have manifested in Asian jurisdictions recently. For one, Indonesian regulators adopted an approach that emphasized risk minimization at the expense of potential economic development. In comparison, Indian regulators started to amend highly restrictive regulations with a view towards developing a wider range of credit markets.[82] In China's case, however, its current regulatory strategy is unclear if not incoherent. Multiple approaches exist in different regions: some are excessively restrictive while others are extremely lax. Once an internationalized RMB brings in immense capital inflow, a coherent policy is needed as capital is mobile and incoherent policies will eventually lead to regulatory arbitrage.

[81] Buckley et al., 'Financial Innovation in East Asia' (2014) 37 Seattle University Law Review 307 (n 62); Rolf Weber et al., 'Addressing Systemic Risk: Financial Regulatory Design' (2014) 49 Texas International Law Journal 149 (n 27) 175–76.

[82] In comparison, the FSB has adopted a functionalist approach that is activities-based to govern all non-banking financial entities regardless of their legal form. This approach applies policy tools, such as capital requirements and liquidity buffers, that are analogous to those imposed on formal banks. See Weber et al., 'Addressing Systemic Risk: Financial Regulatory Design' (n 27) 173–74.

5. Revisiting Macroprudential Thinking in Developing Economies

'Systemic risk' is a context-dependent concept. What European economies view as 'systemic risk' may be different from that viewed by, say, Canada or Japan, in that EU member states share a notion of 'community risk' that is to be borne by all countries within the EU.[83] In a similar vein, 'systemic risk' in developed economies may be different from that in developing economies, because institutional configurations of banking and financial industries of the former are less sophisticated even though they may not be less complicated. Likewise, the systemic risk of Islamic banking in Malaysia could well be very different from that of non-Islamic banking in her ASEAN neighbour Singapore. Such contexutal variations in systemic risk give rise to varying versions of macroprudential thinking.

Despite systemic risk being context-dependent, there is the expectation that macroprudential policy will provide a formulaic remedy capable of limiting systemic vulnerabilities. Experts have also created various 'toolkits' even as our understanding of financial stability and regulatory tools hurries to catch up with the ever-evolving financial industry.[84] Furthermore, the premature implementation of any remedy may limit the capacity of the sector it targets. For example, Ross Buckley et al. argue that some macroprudential measures of Basel III will significantly limit the ability of banks in developing countries to provide affordable financing to small and mid-sized businesses because these regulations are based on banking structures found in developed Western economies.[85] As such, pluralist macroprudential policies should exist to conform to different contexts. The focus of a macroprudential policy should vary depending on the nature of a given economy and the status of its development as well as the nature and extent of its systemic risk.

In the US, for example, one macroprudential policy in early years was the requirement of the separation of investment banking from depository banking, and this was hailed as the saviour of the financial industry considering

[83] In Europe, risk management requires financial institutes to account for the interests of citizens in other EU member states even if measures implemented dilute the institute's existing commitments to citizens within its national territory. Such a narrative reconfigures sovereignty and citizenship and is unique to the EU.

[84] Daniel Heath, 'International Coordination of Macroprudential and Monetary Policy' (2013) 45 Georgetown Journal of International Law 1093, 1102.

[85] For example, empirically, default rates of trade finance are different from those of mortgage-backed finance. Depending on the respective structures of their finance sectors, countries should

the absence of financial crises between 1940 and 1970.[86] Developmental economists, who have studied developing economies in Asia and Latin America, have also proposed for developing economies various policies to ensure a smooth economic transition. Briefly, a key focus of these proposals is the proper sequence and means of liberalizing various economic sectors, including banking, capital markets, and currency regulations. Of note, developmental economists are less critical of developmental states and mercantilism, and their approach combines the prevention of systemic risk with the goals of what modern thinkers now consider as 'macroprudential policy'. Their proposals therefore offer useful insights on mitigating systemic risk in developing economies.

For example, in light of the failures of financial reforms in Chile, Argentina, and Uruguay in the 1980s, Ronald McKinnon suggests a system of priorities for the liberalization of a state-controlled economy. The presumption is that, in developing economies, premature liberalization before the establishment of a prudential regulatory structure can lead to destabilized markets and financial crisis.[87] As such, for example, prudent fiscal controls should be implemented first to prevent the need for the government to cover deficits by increasing money supply. What then follows is domestic financial liberalization, which needs to begin with the liberalization of interest rates and end with the privatization of state-owned banks.[88] The privatization of banks comes later because market mechanisms should be introduced incrementally as state-owned banks have become used to protective policies and thus need time to adjust to a competitive market.

After privatization, the next step is to liberalize regulations targeting external sectors. Examples include the lifting of foreign exchange controls and import or export restrictions. Finally, capital accounts should be made fully convertible; particularly, the order of capital account liberalization should be set as follows: capital inflow prior to capital outflow; long-term capital prior to short-term capital; direct investment prior to indirect investment;

adopt different, rather than uniform, rules to limit financial vulnerabilities. See Buckley et al., 'Financial Innovation in East Asia' (n 62).

[86] Gohari and Woody, 'New Global Financial Regulatory Order: Can Macroprudential Regulation Prevent Another Global Financial Disaster' (n 44) 436. The Glass-Steagall Act of 1933 separated investment and commercial banking activities until 1999.

[87] Philip Arestis and Murray Glickman, 'Financial Crisis in Southeast Asia: Dispelling Illusion the Minskyan Way' (2002) 26 Cambridge Journal of Economics 237; Ross Buckley, 'Tale of Two Crises: The Search for the Enduring Reforms of the International Financial System' (2001) 6 UCLA Journal of International Law and Foreign Affairs 1.

[88] Ronald McKinnon, *The Order of Economic Liberalization: Financial Control in the Transition to a Market Economy* (Johns Hopkins University Press 1993).

and capital of institutional investors prior to that of individuals.[89] At the same time, the state needs to use capital controls wisely and cannot depend on capital controls to compensate for poor economic management.[90] Generally, Taiwan's liberalization of its financial sectors fits into this sequencing model almost perfectly and is therefore often cited by developmental economists.

Apart from China's RMB internationalization scheme, other Asian countries that have experienced drastic economic growth after World War II have gone through a similar process of liberalizing their capital accounts and introducing full convertibility of their currencies. Singapore and Taiwan are two cases in point. Capital account liberalization is not only necessary for any genuine international reserve currency but also a significant indicator of the health of capital markets and banking systems in an economy. As such, the macroprudential policies suggested by developmental economists posit that the sequence of reforms is crucial. Prior to lifting capital controls, market manipulation largely needs to be removed from financial sectors so that financial institutions can operate competitively and thus be gradually equipped with the necessary expertise. With diverse and competitive investment opportunities and institutional environments, capital inflow could be well accommodated while irregular capital flight could be prevented. This is particularly important for the RMB internationalization scheme. In China, massive capital flight has been a serious issue for years,[91] while speculative capital inflow, as evidenced by the stock market crash, has raised great concerns. Both may give rise to systemic risk either in the form of a liquidity crunch or economic bubbles.

In this regard, China's RMB internationalization scheme, if properly designed, has the ability to liberalize China's banking system in a stable and measured manner through the introduction of ideal macroprudential policies. Similar to China's strategy to reform its economy in 2000 when it joined the WTO, the RMB scheme can benefit China so long as it strikes a balance between its international agenda and domestic institutional reforms. In this way, the progression and progress of the scheme could also indicate the improved capacity of domestic financial institutions and capital markets. However, the current RMB internationalization scheme appears to

[89] ibid.

[90] Capital control, if introduced, works best when a country has strong macroeconomic fundamentals, which require good economic management. Jonathan D Ostry et al., 'Capital Inflows: The Role of Controls' (IMF 2010) 5 <https://www.imf.org/external/pubs/ft/spn/2010/spn1004.pdf> accessed 1 November 2015; Philip J MacFarlane, 'The IMF's Reassessment of Capital Controls after the 2008 Financial Crisis: Heresy or Orthodoxy?' (2015) 19 UCLA Journal of International Law and Foreign Affairs 167, 209.

[91] Tsai (n 65).

favour global progress rather than address domestic obstacles and distorts the sequencing of reforms due to its pro-cyclical design.

What is more debatable is whether capital account liberalization is a desirable policy for developing countries. After the 2008 global financial crisis, debates arose and eventually led to the IMF changing its position on capital account liberalization, which was long viewed as an uncompromising mandate of the IMF. In fact, the liberalization of capital accounts was excluded in the IMF's original mandate under the Bretton Woods system but was incorporated into the IMF's agenda at a much later date,[92] and the recent change in the IMF's position resonates with recent empirical findings on capital accounts. For example, Kang-kook Lee and Arjun Jayadev found a persistent negative correlation between capital account liberalization and labour's share in national income.[93] Seeraj Mohammed and Kade Finnoff also discovered that, in South Africa, the loosening of capital controls has given wealth holders more opportunities for flight.[94] Similar correlations were found in Chile, Turkey, Brazil, and Thailand.[95] Turning to China, capital flight is closely associated with the shadow banking industry as well as the overall health of its financial system. Against this backdrop, the IMF finally changed its position on the liberalization of capital accounts and began to support the use of capital controls for countries that are vulnerable to volatile capital movements.[96] All in all, these recent developments also raise flags for the Chinese government which aims to make the RMB full convertible by 2020.[97]

6. Conclusion

Macroprudential policy is a regulatory response to the conundrum associated with institutions that are 'too-big-to-fail.' China's financial industry as a

[92] In fact, in the face of strong opposition, the IMF had to drop the proposal to amend its charter to officially include the liberalization of capital accounts as part of its mandate. Rawi Abdelal, *Capital Rules: The Construction of Global Finance* (Harvard University Press 2007) 121–61.

[93] Kang-kook Lee and Arjun Jayadev, 'Capital Account Liberalization, Growth and the Labor Share of Income: Reviewing and Extending the Cross-country Evidence' in Gerald Epstein (ed), *Capital Flight and Capital Controls in Developing Countries* (Edward Elgar 2005).

[94] Seeraj Mohammed and Kade Finnoff, 'Capital Flight from South Africa: 1980–2000' in Epstein (n 93) 85.

[95] Gerald Epstein, 'Introduction' in Epstein (n 93) 3–15.

[96] Naoyuki Yoshino, Sahoko Kaji, and Tamon Asonuma, 'Dynamic Transition of Exchange Rate Regime in China' (2014) 22 China and World Economy 36; Jonathan D Ostry et al., 'Managing Capital Inflows: What Tools to Use?' Staff Discussion Note No 11/06 (International Monetary Fund, 2011); Volz, 'RMB Internationalization and Currency Cooperation in East Asia' (n 19) 369.

[97] Curran, 'For China, the End of the Beginning on Road to a Global Currency' (n 10); Ronald McKinnon and Gunther Schnabl, 'China's Exchange Rate and Financial Repression: The Conflicted Emergence of the RMB as an International Currency' (2014) 22 China World Economy 1.

whole has become 'too-big-to-fail', and this is not only a problem for Chinese regulators but also its trading partners around the world. Moving ahead, the internationalization of the RMB will further strengthen the interconnectedness of China's economy and international trade and finance, and therefore complicate matters: failure may trigger financial contagion. As such, the approach taken under the RMB internationalization scheme requires some rethinking. In particular macroprudential policy should be incorporated, as stabilizing the global financial system will be an inevitable responsibility of China as the issuer of a major international reserve currency.

At the moment, the RMB internationalization scheme has primarily pitched itself as an international project rather than a domestic one. This chapter suggests otherwise. The RMB scheme will not succeed without improving the capacity of various domestic financial institutions. Overemphasis on its global outcomes distorts the sequence of reforms necessary for a successful scheme and is likely to destabilize China's domestic banking and financial sectors—that is, the areas where systemic risk exists. That said, with a realigned focus, the RMB scheme could serve to inject fresh dynamics into ongoing reforms by introducing a host of macroprudential policies.

Serious challenges and obstacles lie ahead, including the problem of regulatory fragmentation, deep involvement of state actors in the shadow banking industry, and the trade-off between the liberalization of capital accounts and the stability of China's domestic economy. Perhaps the most challenging obstacle is that of changing the regulators' mindset—to switch from a pro-cyclical approach to a counter-cyclical approach—given that China's success is largely attributable to an essentially pro-cyclical approach. This tendency towards pro-cyclical practices is further exacerbated by China's fear of economic slowdown, which, if materialized, would trigger not only economic but also political crisis. The RMB will sooner or later achieve global status, reflecting China's crucial role in the global economy. Before then, macroprudential thinking deserves more focus in China's RMB internationalization scheme in its long march to dismantling the financial great wall.

7

Emergency Liquidity Assistance and Systemic Risk

Rosa María Lastra[*]

> The object is to stay calm and nothing therefore should be done to cause alarm. But the way to cause alarm is to refuse someone who has good security to offer. The news of this will spread in an instant through all the money market at a moment of terror.
>
> Walter Bagehot, Lombard Street (1873)

1. Introduction

Responses to the global financial crisis that commenced in 2007 and reached its zenith in 2008 included unprecedented central bank emergency liquidity assistance (ELA) and a myriad of bailout programmes (comprising guarantees, recapitalization, other forms of government support, and even nationalization) that compromised the fiscal position of some countries, notably Eurozone member states, leading in some cases to a sovereign debt crisis (the doom loop or vicious link between bank debt and sovereign debt).

The expansive use of lender of last resort (LOLR) has been a defining and evolving feature of the responses to the crisis. Central banks around the world operated as lenders of last resort, market makers of last resort and, at times, lenders of primary resort or lenders of only resort. This extraordinary provision of liquidity assistance was done by central banks working under their own statutory requirements (that is domestic law, with the exception of the

[*] Professor in International Financial and Monetary Law, Centre for Commercial Law Studies, Queen Mary University of London. E-mail: r.lastra@qmul.ac.uk. My thanks to Thomas Baxter, Charles Goodhart, and Hal Scott for helpful comments. Errors are mine alone.

European Central Bank (ECB), whose primary law is a treaty), thus highlighting the dichotomy between national law and global markets.

Financial history must be rewritten following the experience of the last nine years. Notwithstanding the recurrent nature of financial crises, and the presence of some elements that are common in previous episodes (such as the boom and bust of housing finance), a novel characteristic of the recent crisis is the new understanding of systemic risk (no longer confined to banking with the advent of systemically important financial institutions (SIFIs)) and the use of macroprudential tools to combat it. The magnitude of the responses by the public authorities to tackle systemic risk also raises issues about their ability to confront future crises.

This chapter provides a revisionist account of liquidity support, leaving aside solvency support, in the aftermath of the crisis. It is not so much what we know about the various tools used so far, but what we do not know about the reverberations of central bank policies concerning ELA and quantitative easing (QE) that poses significant economic, legal, and political challenges. The chapter adopts a comparative perspective[1] in the analysis of ELA/LOLR and discusses the effectiveness of this instrument[2] in the prevention and containment of systemic risk.[3] The challenge remains to design adequate

[1] For a recent comparative study on the subject see Hal Scott, 'The Federal Reserve: The Weakest Lender of Last Resort Among Its Peers' (2015) 18:3 International Finance 321. Scott's study is the first research piece that provides a current comparative assessment of the law in the UK, US, Japan, and the Eurozone/EU, and as such a seminal study. I am grateful to him for inviting me to contribute to a high level meeting he organized in Washington DC on 10 February 2016 to discuss the lender of last resort from an international perspective. Though the session was conducted under Chatham House rules, the speech by Stanley Fischer with regard to the US is available at: Stanley Fischer, 'The Role of the Lender of Last Resort Function in the United States' ('The Lender of Last Resort: An International Perspective' conference, Washington, 10 February 2016) <http://www.federalreserve.gov/newsevents/speech/fischer20160210a.htm> accessed 10 February 2016; the comments by Peter Praet with regard to the ECB are available at: Peter Praet, 'The ECB and Its Role as Lender of Last Resort During the Crisis' ('The Lender of Last Resort: An International Perspective' conference, Washington, 10 February 2016) <https://www.ecb.europa.eu/press/key/date/2016/html/sp160210.en.html> accessed 10 February 2016; and the speech by Andrew Hauser with regard to the Bank of England is available at: Andrew Hauser, 'Between Feast and Famine: Transparency, Accountability and the Lender of Last Resort' ('The Lender of Last Resort: An International Perspective' conference, Washington, 10 February 2016) <https://www.bis.org/review/r160211h.htm> accessed 10 February 2016.

[2] The Bank of International Settlements (BIS) published a collection of papers on LOLR in 'Re-Thinking the Lender of Last Resort' (2014) BIS Working Paper No 79 <http://www.bis.org/publ/bppdf/bispap79.pdf> accessed 25 January 2016. Notable amongst the contributions in this collection is the paper written by Paul Tucker, 'The Lender of Last Resort and Modern Central Banking: Principles and Reconstruction'.

[3] Drawing on my earlier writings on the subject, in particular: Rosa M Lastra, 'Lender of Last Resort and Banking Union' in Juan E Castañeda, David G Mayes, and Geoffrey Wood (eds), *European Banking Union: Prospects and Challenges* (Routledge 2015); Rosa M Lastra, 'Reflections on Banking Union, Lender of Last Resort and Supervisory Discretion' in ECB Legal Conference 2015, 'From Monetary Union to Banking Union, On the Way to Capital Markets Union—New Opportunities for European Integration' <http://www.ecb.europa.eu/pub/pdf/other/

regulatory structures that transcend the domain of domestic jurisdictions in order to regulate such risk adequately.

Following this introduction the chapter is divided into four sections. Section 2 deals with some definitional issues concerning LOLR, systemic risk, and financial stability. Section 3 considers the multi-dimensional nature of LOLR, as a crisis management instrument, a macroprudential tool in the pursuit of financial stability, a monetary policy instrument, and the classic exercise of the central bank's role as bankers' bank. Section 4 examines critically the notion of constructive ambiguity, and the need for a clear legal framework that permits ample discretion and flexibility, balanced by adequate mechanisms of accountability. Section 5 presents a comparative analysis[4] of recent developments in the UK, US, and Eurozone/banking union, looking both at individual liquidity assistance and market liquidity assistance. As regards the Eurozone, the EU rules on state aid and the interaction between monetary policy, macroprudential supervision and liquidity assistance are also considered. The chapter finishes with some concluding observations.

2. Definitional Issues

(a) Lender of Last Resort

Lender of last resort (LOLR) is the name given to the central bank function of providing liquidity to banks (and other financial institutions) when other credit sources are unavailable. Paul Davies refers to this function as an insurance strategy which gives 'the bank the right to exchange illiquid assets for liquid assets at the central bank in times of financial stress'.[5] Though the terms LOLR and ELA are often used indistinctly, under UK law the term ELA is now confined to the liquidity facilities outside the Bank of England's published facilities as discussed below.

The decision to serve as LOLR can be taken either to support a single institution suffering from a liquidity crisis (individual bank liquidity, the classic

frommonetaryuniontobankingunion201512.en.pdf>; and Rosa M Lastra, *International Financial and Monetary Law* (OUP 2015) Chapters 2 and 4; and Rosa M Lastra, 'Lender of Last Resort, an International Perspective' (1999) 48 International and Comparative Law Quarterly 340.

[4] Drawing on the methodology developed in the seminal article by Scott (n 1).

[5] Paul Davies refers to this function as an insurance strategy which gives 'the bank the right to exchange illiquid assets for liquid assets at the central bank in times of financial stress'. See Paul Davies, 'Liquidity Safety Nets for Banks' (2013) 13:2 Journal of Corporate Law Studies 287, 296. Davies reminds us that the liquidity risk for banks is that of unanticipated large-scale withdrawals of short-term funds (bank run), since banks can cope with anticipated fluctuations in the levels of short-term funding: at 291.

'discount window' or bilateral assistance) or to preserve the stability of the banking system as a whole, by supplying extra reserves to all banks suffering from large cash withdrawals (market liquidity assistance).

LOLR thus comes in two forms. The first form is the traditional 'Thornton-Bagehot' model of last resort lending, which is based upon four principles: [6] (1) the central bank should prevent temporarily illiquid but solvent[7] banks from failing—this type of lending is by nature short-term; (2) the central bank should be able to lend as much as is necessary, but charge a high rate of interest (a penalty rate as interpreted by some commentators);[8] (3) the central bank should accommodate anyone with good collateral, valued at pre-panic prices; (4) the central bank should make its readiness to lend clear in advance. The second form is the provision of 'market liquidity assistance' via ordinary open market operations and via extraordinary or unconventional measures.[9]

The praxis of central banking teaches us a few other things about the *modus operandi* of LOLR. First, this role is discretionary, not mandatory, which constitutes a safeguard against moral hazard incentives. Secondly, since the immediacy of the assistance is the key to its effectiveness, time constraints are always present. Often operating under significant information limitations,

[6] These are doctrinal principles, not necessarily legal principles. See Henry Thornton, *An Enquiry into the Nature and Effects of the Paper Credit of Great Britain* (first published in 1802, AM Kelley 1991); Walter Bagehot, *Lombard Street: A Description of the Money Market* (first published in 1873, Wiley 1999). Studies of the work of Thornton and Bagehot on the LOLR are found in Thomas M Humphrey, 'The Classical Concept of the Lender of Last Resort' (1975) 61:1 Federal Reserve Bank of Richmond Economic Review 2; Michael D Bordo, 'Alternative Views and Historical Experience' (1990) 76:1 Federal Reserve Bank of Richmond Economic Review 18.

[7] See also Geoffrey Wood, 'The Lender of Last Resort Reconsidered' (2000) 18:2 Journal of Financial Services Research 203.

[8] Charles Goodhart contends that Bagehot's proposal that LOLR lending be at 'high' rates is incorrectly translated into 'penalty' rates. See Charles Goodhart, 'Myths about the Lender of Last Resort' (1999) 2:3 International Finance 339. Several authors have suggested a rate lower than the market rate. Goodhart argues that the cost of the initial [borrowing] tranche should be kept very low to avoid the stigma problem associated with borrowing from the central bank. See Charles Goodhart, *The Regulatory Response to the Financial Crisis* (Edward Elgar 2009) 71. See also Rafael Repullo, 'Who Should Act as a Lender of Last Resort? An Incomplete Contract Model' (2000) 32:3 Journal of Money, Credit and Banking 580 and JC Rochet, *Why Are There So Many Banking Crises?* (Princeton University Press 2008) 89.

[9] There is a school of thought supported by some in the US that suggests that LOLR should only take place via open market operations and that the discount window ought to be abolished. Tucker (n 2) 16 refers to this view as the Richmond Fed school of thought on LOLR (based on the seminal article, Marvin Goodfriend and Robert G King, 'Financial Deregulation, Monetary Policy, and Central Banking' (1988) 74:3 Federal Reserve Bank of Richmond Economic Review 3): 'Bilateral lending … takes the monetary authority into distributional issues, which is the proper preserve of the fiscal authority': ibid 18. Charles Goodhart in a paper presented at Gerhard Illing's Festschrift in Munich on 4 March 2016 suggests this view ignores the dynamics of contagion: Charles Goodhart, 'Balancing Lender of Last Resort Assistance with Avoidance of Moral Hazard' (Gerhard Illing's Festschrift, Munich, March 2016).

the central bank assesses not only whether the situation is of illiquidity or insolvency but also whether the failure of an institution can trigger by contagion the collapse of other institutions. It is difficult to calculate *ex ante* how far a crisis can extend. Market sentiment is often hard to predict and, sometimes, irrational (as Minsky[10] and Kindleberger[11] remind us), which renders any rational prediction meaningless. The dynamic of a panic is self-fulfilling. Indeed, it is this consideration that prompted Thornton and Bagehot to suggest that providing liquidity (lending freely and early on security) was the best way of containing a panic.

(b) Systemic Risk and Financial Stability

Though the very definition of financial stability remains a matter of controversy, it is generally accepted that systemic risks pose a threat to financial stability and, that as part of its financial stability mandate, the central bank needs to prevent and contain systemic risk.

Hal Scott defines systemic risk as 'the risk that a national, or the global, financial system will break down'.[12] Systemic risk refers to the risk or probability of breakdowns in an entire system, as opposed to breakdowns in individual parts or components.[13] While for some authors this risk can be identified with default or credit risk, in my opinion, any risk (liquidity risk, legal risk, interest rate risk, exchange rate risk, etc.) can grow into systemic proportions when its negative impact extends beyond an individual institution and affects or threatens to affect other institutions, often creating a disruption in the monetary and payments systems within a country or across different jurisdictions. Systemic risk can thus be defined as the risk that financial difficulties at

[10] See Hyman P Minsky, *John Maynard Keynes* (Columbia University Press 1975) and Hyman P Minsky, 'The Financial Stability Hypothesis: Capitalistic Processes and Behaviour of the Economy' in Charles Kindleberger and Jean Pierre Laffargue (eds), *Financial Crises: Theory, History and Policy* (CUP 1982) 13–29. Goodhart (n 9) argues that the definition of solvency is 'fuzzy': 'We think that we know what it means, ie, that the value of assets is greater than the valuation of the liabilities. But in practice we do not, because it all depends on how the assets (and liabilities) are valued, and that depends on the viewpoint of the valuer, and also on the (changing) conventions and practices of the accountant.'

[11] See Charles P Kindleberger, *Manias, Panics and Crashes. A History of Financial Crises* (first published 1978, 3rd edn, John Wiley & Sons 1996).

[12] Hal Scott, 'Reducing Systemic Risk Through the Reform of Capital Regulation' (2010) 13:3 Journal of International Economic Law 763, 763.

[13] See inter alia Steven L Schwarcz, 'Systemic Risk' (2008) 97 Georgetown Law Journal 193; Anna Gelpern, 'Financial Crisis Containment' (2009) 41 Connecticut Law Review 1051; John Coffee, 'Systemic Risk after Dodd-Frank: Contingent Capital and the Need for Regulatory Strategies Beyond Oversight' (2011) 111 Columbia Law Review 795, 816; and Rosa M Lastra, *International Financial and Monetary Law* (2nd edn, OUP 2015) Chapter 4.

one or more financial institutions could spill over to a large number of other financial institutions or the financial system as a whole.

What makes a crisis of a systemic nature is not so much the trigger event (*causa proxima*) but the transmission mechanisms, domestically and internationally. If the linkages are strong, the potential for systemic instability increases. If the connections are weak, there is less of a threat of systemic risk. It is the understanding of the interconnections of the system that requires much greater research and analysis in the aftermath of the global financial crisis.

Financial stability is often more identifiable in its negative definition, namely what instability is, than in its positive definition. Yet it is a most important policy objective that transcends institutional mandates and geographic boundaries. Episodes of instability—like a Tsunami—do not respect physical borders. The interconnectedness of financial markets has rendered financial stability as a 'national, regional and international goal'.[14] This makes it a global public good[15] that 'does not stop at national borders'.[16]

Acknowledging the lack of a clearly established analytical and operational framework for the understanding of financial stability, the late Tommaso Padoa-Schioppa referred to it as a 'land in between' monetary policy and supervision.[17] Financial stability, systemic risk/contagion control and sound banking and finance are 'close cousins'.

The renewed interest in systemic risk has underlined the importance of Frank Knight's classic distinction between risk and uncertainty[18] in relation to the information asymmetries faced by market participants and regulatory authorities.[19] The contemporary definitions of systemic risk might conflate quantifiable contingencies and immeasurable ones.

In terms of institutional mandates, the relative simplicity that characterized the pre-1999 'Bundesbank model' of central banking (one goal—price stability; one instrument—monetary policy; one authority—the central bank),

[14] Rosa M Lastra, 'Systemic Risk, SIFIs and Financial Stability' (2011) 6:2 Capital Markets Law Journal 198, 207.

[15] Joel P Trachtman, 'The International Law of Financial Crisis: Spillovers, Subsidiarity, Fragmentation and Cooperation' (2010) 13:3 Journal of International Economic Law 721.

[16] Dirk Schoenmaker, 'A New Financial Stability Framework for Europe' (2008) 13:3 The Financial Regulator, 7.

[17] See Tommasso Padoa-Schioppa, 'Central Banks and Financial Stability. Exploring a Land in Between' (ECB's Second Central Banking Conference, The Transformation of the European Financial System, Frankfurt, 24–25 October 2002) <http://www.ecb.int/home/conf/cbc2/tps.pdf> accessed 26 April 2016.

[18] Frank H Knight, *Risk, Uncertainty and Profit* (1st edn, Hart, Schaffner & Marx 1921).

[19] See Emilios Avgouleas, *Governance of Global Financial Markets: The Law, the Economics and the Politics* (CUP 2012) 104.

in line with the Tinbergen rule,[20] which states that for each and every policy target there must be at least one policy tool, contrasts with the multiplicity and complexity that characterize the pursuit of financial stability in the aftermath of the global financial crisis. Financial stability co-exists with other goals (price stability, growth, employment, consumer protection), and there are multiple instruments deployed in its pursuit (supervision, regulation, LOLR/ELA, resolution and crisis management, monetary policy, fiscal policy, etc.) and the central bank shares responsibility for maintaining financial stability with other authorities at different levels of governance (national, regional, and international).[21] At the national level financial stability is also a goal for other supervisory agencies and for the Treasury/Minister of Finance. At the regional level in Europe, the different jurisdictional domains of the EU/single market and the Eurozone/banking union present additional challenges. And internationally, several international financial institutions and standard setters are also involved (IMF, BIS, FSB, etc.).

The Dodd-Frank Act 2010 in the US reinforced the financial stability mandate of the Federal Reserve System and the law governing the Bank of England in the UK has also been revised to reflect the twin mandate of monetary stability and financial stability. At the EU level, while the hierarchy of objectives remains (price stability reigns supreme in the Treaty), the mandate of the ECB has been substantially expanded via secondary legislation (the SSM regulation and ensuing normative) into the field of prudential supervision.

3. The Multi-Dimensional Nature of LOLR

The lender of last resort function can only be undertaken by a central bank. The involvement of central banks in financial stability originates in their role as monopolist suppliers of fiat money and in their role as bankers' bank. Only the ultimate supplier of money can provide the necessary stabilizing function in a nationwide scramble for liquidity, as the financial crisis has amply evidenced, with conventional and

[20] Jan Tinbergen, *On the Theory of Economic Policy* (North Holland Pub Co 1952).

[21] The Financial Stability Oversight Council (FSOC) in the US is a good example of the multiple authorities involved in the pursuit of financial stability. The FSOC is made up of ten voting members under the chairmanship of the Secretary of the Treasury (the other nine members are the Chairman of the Board of Governors of the Federal Reserve System, the Comptroller of the Currency, the Director of the Bureau of Consumer Financial Protection, the Chair of the SEC, the Chair of the Commodity Future Trading Commission, the Chair of FDIC, the Chair of the Federal Housing Finance Agency, the Chair of the National Credit Union Administration, and an independent member with insurance expertise) and five non-voting members.

> non-conventional monetary policy operations (quantitative easing and others). This is a clear lesson of the crisis in the UK, where the problems of Northern Rock caught the Bank of England by surprise: having timely information is particularly crucial during financial crises and the best way to ensure access is to have daily supervision by the central bank, as the literature has noted.[22]

This quote from an article I wrote with Luis Garicano conveys the unique nature of the LOLR role of the central bank, which involves different aspects and links several central banking functions:

(a) MONETARY POLICY—The discount rate at which the central bank lends to authorized institutions, acting in its capacity as LOLR, is an instrument of monetary policy. The central bank can and does provide market liquidity via open market operations and via other non-conventional instruments. The crisis has changed the traditional understanding of monetary policy. The resort to unconventional measures such as QE provide further evidence of the intersection and interaction between these two central banking functions. Indeed it was the central bankers' 'obsession' with a narrow dimension of a price stability oriented monetary policy that led them to ignore the 'elephant in the room', namely the financial instability that was building up in the system.[23]

(b) FINANCIAL STABILITY AND MACROPRUDENTIAL SUPERVISION—The LOLR is part of the financial stability function of the central bank and an instrument in its macroprudential toolkit.[24]

(c) CRISIS MANAGEMENT INSTRUMENT—The immediacy of the availability of central bank assistance makes the LOLR a particularly suitable first line of defence in a crisis. This 'immediacy' contrasts with the 'time framework' of some other crisis management instruments. Neither deposit insurance nor resolution and bank insolvency proceedings can achieve this. By their very nature they tend to be more lengthy processes

[22] Luis Garicano and Rosa M Lastra, 'Towards a New Architecture for Financial Stability: Seven Principles' (2010) 13:3 Journal of International Economic Law 597.

[23] ibid 610: 'Monetary policy not only affects inflation rates, but the price (and thus the amount) of risk taking. An excessively accommodating Federal Reserve convinced actors that they would be saved from their folly (the famous "Greenspan put") and led to excessive risk taking. Thus, those in charge of monetary policy need to know the amount of risk and instability in the system. Moreover, the absence of stable prices harms the stability of the financial system, while financial fragility in turn, negatively affects monetary stability … Of course, extracting synergies never comes without organizational costs. One key problem with combining tasks has to do with the difficulty in providing adequate incentives and measurement on the stability task.'

[24] See Rosa M Lastra, 'Systemic Risk and Macro-prudential Supervision' in Ferrán Eilis, Jennifer Hill, and Niamh Moloney (eds), *Oxford Handbook of Financial Regulation* (OUP 2015).

which take into account the interests of many stakeholders and are subject to greater legal constraints.

(d) BANKER'S BANK—The LOLR is a service provided by the central bank in its capacity as bankers' bank, since it centralizes the reserves of the commercial banks. During the crisis the central bank became the financiers' bank and not simply the bankers' bank. This authority to lend to non-banks is now being restricted in the US as we discuss below.

The problem is that what constitutes 'ordinary' liquidity assistance as opposed to 'emergency'/LOLR liquidity assistance becomes blurred during a crisis, since the drying of the inter-bank market gives the central bank a primary role in the provision of liquidity.

The expansion of central bank liquidity operations during the crisis turned what ought to be extraordinary into 'ordinary', ordinary in the sense that with the crisis central banks often became the lender of primary or only resort, and at times market makers of last resort. Rather than discouraging its use, the central bank was keen to encourage various types of LOLR operations, whatever qualification one wishes to attribute to them: ordinary or extraordinary, in order also to prevent the stigma problem (that only the desperate go to the central bank, undermining confidence when credibility is most needed).[25]

Interestingly, while the Fed and the Bank of England have emphasized the complementarity[26] between monetary policy, macroprudential policy, LOLR, and microprudential supervision, the ECB on the other hand has highlighted the separation between monetary policy and banking supervision in a Decision of 17 September 2014, in accordance with Article 25(2) of the SSM Regulation.[27] The German government has recently advocated a complete separation of the ECB's supervisory function from its monetary policy role.[28]

[25] In principle, programmes of broad eligibility—like the Term Auction Facility in the US—tend to have no stigma.

[26] The Fed conceives of its monetary policy as having been largely grafted onto its stabilization and supervisory functions, and regards such functions as a prerequisite and complement of its monetary policy responsibilities. In the UK, the Bank of England launched its One Bank—One Mission strategic plan in March 2015 stressing the links between the 3Ms: Monetary policy, macroprudential and microprudential supervision.

[27] Council Regulation (EU) No 1024/2013 of 15 September 2013 conferring specific tasks on the European Central Bank (ECB) [2013] OJ L287/63 (SSM Regulation), Art 25(2): 'The ECB shall carry out the tasks conferred on it by this Regulation without prejudice to and separately from its tasks relating to monetary policy and any other tasks. The tasks conferred on the ECB by this Regulation shall neither interfere with, nor be determined by, its tasks relating to monetary policy. The tasks conferred on the ECB by this Regulation shall moreover not interfere with its tasks in relation to the ESRB or any other tasks.'

[28] See Rainer Buergin, 'Merkel Coalition Backs Resolution Urging Split of ECB Duties' *Bloomberg* (18 February 2016) <http://www.bloomberg.com/news/articles/2016-02-18/

However, the reality of central banking is one of complementarity of functions, which explains why they are placed under the same roof; if one wants to have the functions truly separate, then assign them to different entities.[29] Conflicts of interest between monetary policy and banking supervision are of course possible, but there are ways to solve or mitigate them. The SSM Regulation establishes a mediation panel to deal with such conflicts.[30]

4. Constructive Ambiguity and Discretion

Ambiguity and uncertainty about the procedures and loci of power are never constructive. In a crisis, the procedures to follow should be crystal clear, even though the assistance should remain discretionary.[31] It is this discretionary element—this uncertainty about whether or not the emergency liquidity assistance will be provided—that reduces the moral hazard incentives inherent in any support operation. But there should not be any doubt about who is in charge and how the assistance will be provided. The law ought to be clear

merkel-s-coalition-backs-resolution-urging-split-of-ecb-duties> accessed 26 April 2016 and, 'Koalition Gegen Zu Viel EU-Regulierung' *Deutscher Bundestag* (17 February 2016) <https://www.bundestag.de/presse/hib/201602/-/408330> accessed 26 April 2016.

[29] On the subject of separation between monetary policy and supervision the seminal article by Charles Goodhart and Dirk Schoenmaker, 'Should the Functions of Monetary Policy and Banking Supervision be Separated?' (1995) 47:4 Oxford University Papers 539, which summarizes the pros and cons. I contend that supervision and crisis management are part of a seamless process, which requires timely communication and coordination between the competent authorities, as well as judgment in the exercise of discretion. Assistance on a rainy day, as the central bank provides, requires either supervision on a sunny day or close cooperation with the supervisory authorities in order to gather the information required to assess whether or not to provide ELA/LOLR. For example the Bank of Japan (as noted by Scott (n 1) 333–334) has the statutory right to examine any institution (bank or non-bank) to which it lends.

[30] SSM Regulation, Art 25(5): 'With a view to ensuring separation between monetary policy and supervisory tasks, the ECB shall create a mediation panel. This panel shall resolve differences of views expressed by the competent authorities of participating Member States concerned regarding an objection of the Governing Council to a draft decision by the Supervisory Board.' According to SSM Regulation, Art 32(1), the European Commission is due to evaluate by the end of 2015 the effectiveness of the separation between supervisory and monetary policy functions within the ECB.

[31] As stated in the article I wrote with Andrew Campbell, 'Revisiting the Lender of Last Resort' (2009) 24:3 Banking and Finance Law Review 453: 'The assumed benefits of "constructive ambiguity" do not actually exist. Ambiguity and uncertainty as to the procedures and loci of power are not constructive. In the event of a crisis, the procedures to follow should be crystal clear ex ante for the institution affected, other market participants and the public at large The only "ambiguity" that can be constructive in LOLR is the discretionary component in the provision of such assistance, in the sense that there is no obligation for the central bank to provide LOLR loans. It is this discretionary nature that reduces the moral hazard incentives inherent in any support operation, together with the fact that once an institution's collateral has run out it gets no further assistance. Bagehot and Thornton contended that the LOLR's responsibility is to the market, to the entire financial system and not to specific institutions.'

about these issues. I quite like the term 'constructive certainty' coined by Tom Huertas in the context of resolution.[32]

What we need is a clear legal framework that sets out procedures, criteria and requirements *ex ante*, leaving ample discretion to act and establishing adequate accountability *ex post*. In the UK, as discussed below, after the Winters report and the Plenderleith review, the publication of a comprehensive list of liquidity facilities (Sterling Monetary Framework) sets out such a framework.

Before exercising its discretion to act or not as LOLR the central bank should conduct a cost-benefit analysis (under pressure with limited information and with the need to reach a prompt decision). The costs are the risk of loss to the central bank (to the public) and moral hazard. The benefits are the speed, flexibility, and decisiveness to avert contagion. The central bank should be held accountable for the use of its discretionary powers.

To minimize the risk of moral hazard, it is therefore important to demarcate *ex ante* clearly what the central bank can do and what the central bank cannot do—or should not do—through its LOLR. The central bank can provide emergency liquidity—quick cash upfront—over a short period of time, when no other sources of funding are readily available. What the central bank should not do is to lend over an extended period of time, committing taxpayers' money, without the explicit approval of the fiscal authority. Goodhart points out, 'a central bank can create liquidity, but it cannot provide for new injections of equity capital. Only the fiscal authority can do that'.[33] The central bank should not lend to insolvent institutions[34] though, of course, it is difficult to define insolvency. In a crisis the difference between illiquidity and insolvency is a time line and concerns about liquidity can be an indication of insolvency.[35] Any prohibition in this regard (not to lend to insolvent institutions) may have little 'bite' if the central bank retains the discretion to

[32] See Thomas Huertas. 'A Resolvable Bank' (Managing and Financing European Bank Resolution Conference, London, 24 March 2014). On constructive ambiguity see inter alia, Xavier Freixas, 'Optimal Bail Out Policy, Conditionality and Constructive Ambiguity' (1999) Working Paper No 400 <http://ssrn.com/abstract=199054> accessed 25 January 2015; Vinogradov Dmitri, 'Deconstructive Effects of Constructive Ambiguity in Risky Times' (2010) ECB <http://www.ecb.int> accessed 25 January 2015; and Sylvester Eijffinger and Rob Nijskens, 'A Dynamic Analysis of Bail Outs and Constructive Ambiguity' (2012) Paolo Baffi Centre Research Paper No 2012-119 <http://papers.ssrn.com/sol3/papers.cfm?abstract_id=2118439> accessed 25 January 2015.

[33] See Charles Goodhart, 'Foreword' in Tommasso Padoa-Schioppa (ed), *Regulating Finance* (OUP 2004).

[34] However, Charles Goodhart in a recent paper (n 9) argues that 'if an agent is certain to repay her debts, on time and meeting all the required terms and covenants, she can always borrow at current riskless market interest rates. So a liquidity problem almost always indicates deeper-lying solvency concerns.'

[35] Goodhart, ibid, argues that the definition of solvency is 'fuzzy'. 'We think that we know what it means, ie, that the value of assets is greater than the valuation of the liabilities. But in practice we

determine whether or not to lend. One way of dealing with this is to establish mechanisms of accountability like the amendment to Section 10(b) of the Federal Reserve Act by FDICIA,[36] requiring that Federal Reserve banks should lend only to *viable* institutions, with penalties imposed in the case of extended lending to under-capitalized institutions, thus shifting the financial burden from the Federal Deposit Insurance Corporation to the Federal Reserve System if the latter chose to lend via its Discount Window Lending to insolvent or critically under-capitalized institutions.

Bagehot and Thornton wrote in 1873 and 1802 respectively, when banks were the key transmitters of contagion. As the global financial system has changed profoundly since the LOLR theory was first presented, we must adapt it to the situation today with interconnected markets and instruments. Notwithstanding the key role that banks still play other institutions and markets can also be a source of systemic risk. The concept of SIFI tries to address this new reality.

This posits the question of the extent to which a central bank should lend to non-banks, considering the nature of financial markets today. Interconnectedness today is far more complex than it was in the nineteenth century. Hal Scott contends that the 'the US financial system has approximately \$7.4 to \$8.2 trillion in runnable short-term liabilities. Non-banks have issued approximately 60% of this total'.[37]

The advent of resolution tools and strategies—as one of the great regulatory developments in response to the global financial crisis—does not diminish the importance of liquidity assistance. Rather the opposite, for resolution to be effective and credible, liquidity provision remains essential.

In the ensuing section, we examine the changes in the law in the UK, US, and Eurozone/EU.

5. Recent Legal Developments

(a) Developments in the UK

Before the crisis the UK framework for LOLR was characterized by a lack of published rules on LOLR. In 2007 the provision of emergency liquidity

do not, because it all depends on how the assets (and liabilities) are valued, and that depends on the viewpoint of the valuer, and also on the (changing) conventions and practices of the accountant.'

[36] The Federal Deposit Insurance Corporation Improvement Act of 1991, Pub L No 102-242, 105 Stat. 2236 (1991) (FDICIA).

[37] Scott (n 1) 337. He concludes in his study that the US is the weakest of the four after a thorough analysis of the law in the jurisdictions he considers.

assistance to Northern Rock failed to restore public confidence (the stigma effect was clearly present) and indeed it was only the announcement by the Chancellor of the Exchequer that all deposits in Northern Rock would be guaranteed that put an end to the bank run.[38]

In April 2008 the Bank of England launched the Special Liquidity Scheme (SLS)[39] to inject liquidity to the banks in the UK on a temporary basis in response to the failure of the inter-bank market. This was followed by a substantive review of the procedures available that led to the introduction of a comprehensive framework of published facilities, both on a bilateral basis and on a market-wide basis.

In May 2012, the Court of the Bank of England commissioned a review of the Bank's framework for providing liquidity to the banking system as a whole, the so called Winters review,[40] and a review of how the Bank discharged its responsibilities as LOLR in 2008–09, the so-called Plenderleith review.[41]

When explaining the UK framework, it is helpful to draw a distinction between published and unpublished liquidity facilities, but some other jurisdictions do not make such a distinction.

The Bank's *published facilities* under the Sterling Monetary Framework (SMF) are outlined in the so-called 'Red Book'.[42] The SMF was introduced in 2013 and comprises: (1) the discount window facility (DWF), which is bilateral on demand and firm specific; (2) the indexed long-term repo (ILTR), which is market-wide and aimed at regular and predictable needs for liquid assets (allowing participants to bid for reserves against a full range of eligible and published collateral); and (3) the contingent term repo facility (CTRF), which is also market-wide but aimed at actual or prospective market-wide

[38] See Rosa M Lastra, 'Northern Rock and Banking Law Reform in the UK' in Franco Bruni and David Llewellyn (eds), *The Failure of Northern Rock: a Multi-Dimensional Study* (SUERF 2009).

[39] Bank of England, 'Special Liquidity Scheme: Information' (21 April 2008) <http://www.bankofengland.co.uk/markets/Documents/sls/sls-information.pdf> accessed 25 January 2016.

[40] Bill Winters, 'Review of the Bank of England's Framework for Providing Liquidity to the Banking System' (October 2012) <http://www.bankofengland.co.uk/publications/Documents/news/2012/cr2winters.pdf> accessed 25 January 2016.

[41] Ian Plenderleith, 'Review of the Bank of England's Provision of Emergency Liquidity Assistance in 2008–2009' (October 2012) <http://www.bankofengland.co.uk/publications/Documents/news/2012/cr1plenderleith.pdf> accessed 25 January 2016. A number of recommendations were made and the Bank's response to these reviews can be found at Bank of England, 'Response of the Bank of England to the Three Court-Commissions Reviews' (March 2013) <http://www.bankofengland.co.uk/publications/Documents/news/2013/nr051_courtreviews.pdf> accessed January 2016.

[42] See Bank of England, 'Sterling Monetary Framework' (June 2015) <http://www.bankofengland.co.uk/markets/Pages/sterlingoperations/redbook.aspx> accessed 25 January 2016. The SMF legal documentation (including the eligibility criteria) can be found at Bank of England, 'Terms and Conditions for Participation in the Bank of England's Operations Under the Sterling Monetary

stress of exceptional nature against the full range of eligible collateral (prior to January 2014 the CTRF was called the extended collateral term repo facility).

The first facility (DWF) is therefore for individual assistance while ILTR and CTRF are for market liquidity assistance. Other traditional open market operations (OMOs), such as weekly short-term OMOs, fine tune OMOs, and gilt purchase OMOs[43] are now suspended.[44]

If a bank did not meet the conditions for borrowing under the SMF, but the Bank of England nevertheless decided to lend outside those published facilities, such bespoke liquidity provision is generally referred to as Emergency Liquidity Assistance (ELA). *ELA therefore sits outside the Bank's published facilities.*

In a speech made in October 2013,[45] Governor Mark Carney spoke about the circumstances in which banks would be able to access the Bank of England's facilities, noting that those facilities

> are there to be used by banks to access money and high-quality collateral. We are offering money and collateral for <u>longer</u> terms. The range of assets we will accept in exchange will be <u>wider</u>, extending to raw loans and, in fact, any asset of which we are capable of assessing the risks.

The Governor went on to say:

> Banks can be confident that, when they want to use our facilities, they will be allowed to access them. Because we are both the supervisor and the central bank, the strong presumption is now that, if a bank meets the supervisory threshold conditions to operate and has signed up to our framework, it will be able to use our facilities.

On 12 June 2014 the Governor announced that non-banks should have access to the Bank of England's facilities.[46] The changes introduced in November

Framework' (5 November 2014) <http://www.bankofengland.co.uk/markets/Pages/money/documentation.aspx> accessed 25 January 2016.

[43] These are different from the Asset Purchase Facility Gilt Purchase undertaken by the Bank as part of QE.

[44] See Bank of England, 'SMF Operating Procedures' (2 November 2015) 10, table 2 <http://www.bankofengland.co.uk/markets/Documents/money/documentation/smfopprocs.pdf> accessed 25 January 2016.

[45] Mark Carney, 'The UK at the Heart of Renewed Globalisation' (An Event to Celebrate the 125th Anniversary of the Financial Times, London, 24 October 2013) <http://www.bankofengland.co.uk/publications/Documents/speeches/2013/speech690.pdf> accessed 25 January 2016.

[46] Mark Carney, 'Speech' (At the Lord Mayor's Banquet for Bankers and Merchants of the City of London at the Mansion House, London, 12 June 2014) <http://www.bankofengland.co.uk/publications/Documents/speeches/2014/speech736.pdf> accessed 25 January 2016.

2014 extended SMF membership to broker-dealers and central counterparties (CCPs) and expanded collateral eligibility criteria.[47]

As stated in the SMF annual report,[48] though the facilities provided by the Bank were used extensively during the financial crisis, lending in these facilities has been lower in recent years, given also the greater liquidity provided by the Bank via QE and the Funding for Lending Scheme (FLS), which was launched in July 2012 to boost lending to the UK real economy. While the FLS sits outside the SMF, there are important inter-linkages.[49]

The Financial Services Act 2012 sets out (in Part 4) how the UK authorities must collaborate during a crisis. Section 65 of the Act requires the Treasury (HMT) and the Bank (including the Prudential Regulation Authority) to maintain a memorandum of understanding (MoU)[50] outlining how they will coordinate to discharge their respective functions so far as they relate to the stability of the UK financial system and affect the public interest.

The MoU seeks to describe (amongst other things): (a) the responsibilities of HMT and the Bank in relation to financial crisis management; (b) the Bank's obligation to notify HMT of a risk to public funds; and (c) the Chancellor's power of direction over the Bank.

The Bank's obligation to notify HMT of a possible need for public funds (in certain specified circumstances) is set out in Section 58 of the Financial Services Act 2012. This is done by way of the Bank serving a public funds notice on HMT. Sections 60–62 the Financial Services Act 2012 set out the circumstances in which the Chancellor may exercise a power of direction over the Bank. Paragraphs 25–33 of the MoU set out more details regarding the circumstances in which such a power of direction may be exercised.

The Bank of England has also been willing to act as market maker of last resort by buying and selling capital market assets against central bank money.[51]

[47] These changes were also in response to the Winters review, which had proposed the extension of the SMF to non-banks financial institutions given their potential severe impact on the financial system (systemic importance), and the interconnectedness of markets.

[48] Bank of England, 'Sterling Monetary Framework: Annual Report 2014–15' (June 2015) <http://www.bankofengland.co.uk/markets/Documents/smf/annualreport15.pdf> accessed 25 January 2016.

[49] ibid.

[50] HMT, 'Memorandum of Understanding on Financial Crisis Management' (19 December 2012) <https://www.gov.uk/government/uploads/system/uploads/attachment_data/file/210018/Memorandum_of_Understanding_on_Financial_Crisis_Management.pdf> accessed 25 January 2016.

[51] See Hauser (n 1).

With the SMF the UK has now moved beyond 'constructive ambiguity' (a term I never liked) into the realm of constructive certainty.[52]

(b) Developments in the US

The Federal Reserve Act and its implementing Regulation A[53] (the first regulation adopted by the Federal Reserve Board at its creation, and a Regulation that has been periodically revised over time) provide a framework for the granting of both bilateral liquidity assistance (DWL) and market liquidity assistance (open market operations).[54]

During the financial crisis, the Fed embarked on a massive programme of emergency liquidity assistance, with a range of new facilities and programmes.[55] For example, in October 2008, the Fed opened the commercial paper funding facility; in November 2008 the Fed announced the Term Asset-Backed Securities Lending Facility (TALF), with a longer duration than any previous facility, at least one year and available to all US persons. Funding was also offered on a longer-term basis in the US via the TAF (Term Auction Facility).[56] The expanding list of facilities was characterized by the widening range of acceptable collateral, the lengthening of the term of the loan, and the ability to reach to specific non-depository financial institutions[57] (such as Bear Stearns, the investment bank, and AIG, the insurance company).

[52] Minouche Shafik, 'Goodbye Ambiguity, Hello Clarity: The Bank of England's Relationship with Financial Markets' (University of Warwick, Warwick, 26 February 2015) <http://www.bankofengland.co.uk/publications/Pages/speeches/2015/801.aspx#6)> accessed 25 January 2016.

[53] Federal Reserve Act (12 USC 221 et seq.). Congress has assigned to the Federal Reserve Board responsibility for implementing certain laws pertaining to a wide range of banking and financial activities. The Board implements those laws in part through its regulations, which are codified in title 12, chapter II, of the Code of Federal Regulations (CFR). See Board of Governors of the Federal Reserve System, 'Regulations' (21 April 2016) <http://www.federalreserve.gov/bankinforeg/reglisting.htm> accessed 26 April 2016. In the US, DWL operates according to rules set up in Sections 10a and 10b of the Federal Reserve Act and in the implementing Regulation A. See 12 CFR Chapter II, Part 201, 'Extension of Credit by Federal Reserve Banks' (Regulation A), <http://www.gpo.gov/fdsys/pkg/CFR-2011-title12-vol2/pdf/CFR-2011-title12-vol2-part201.pdf>. There are rules that specify inter alia the short-term nature of the lending (60 days, 120 days …) as well as the penalty rate applicable and the type of instruments that can be used as collateral.

[54] My thanks to Tom Baxter for sharing with me his presentation on LOLR at the Bank of England on 11 March 2016.

[55] The Board of Governors of The Federal Reserve System, 'Term Auction Facility' (12 February 2016) <http://www.federalreserve.gov/newsevents/reform_taf.htm> accessed 10 February 2016.

[56] See Federal Reserve Bank of New York, 'Forms of Fed Lending' (July 2009) <https://www.newyorkfed.org/medialibrary/media/markets/Forms_of_Fed_Lending.pdf> accessed 20 October 2009.

[57] It is also worth recalling that in September 2008 following the collapse of Lehman Brothers some US financial firms such as Goldman Sachs and Morgan Stanley became bank holding companies in order to benefit from the Fed's liquidity facilities.

The Emergency and Economic Stabilization Act (EESA) enacted in 2008 highlighted some systemic risk situations where LOLR assistance was justified.[58] (While the Federal Reserve System provided ample liquidity assistance, during the crisis the Treasury provided the necessary capital with the Troubled Asset Relief Programme, TARP.)

The main statutory provisions that deal with LOLR under the Federal Reserve Act are: Section 10(b) for lending to banks ('depository institutions' in the language of the Statute); Sections 13(3) and 13(13) for lending to non-bank institutions; and Sections 12(a) and 14 for open market operations.

Regulation A deals in some detail (including time periods) with the implementation of the lending powers of the Fed. As stated in the Regulation, except as otherwise provided, the regulation applies to US branches and agencies of foreign banks that are subject to reserve requirements under the applicable Federal Reserve Regulation.[59]

Section 10(b) of the Federal Reserve Act[60] governs access to the 'discount window' by individual member banks, that is the extension of credit—through

[58] Emergency Economic Stabilization Act of 2008, Pub L No 110-343, 122 Stat 3765 (2008).

[59] I am grateful to Tom Baxter for sharing with me the presentation on LOLR he gave at the Bank of England on 11 March 2016 where he clarified a number of points concerning the law applicable in the US under Section 10(b) of the FRA and implementing Regulation A:

- Under Regulation A, the financial condition of the depository institution generally determines whether it is eligible for *primary credit* (in generally sound financial condition) *or secondary credit.* Depository institutions with regular needs for funding arising from expected patterns of loan and deposit movements may be eligible for *seasonal credit.*
- Maturity: Primary and secondary credits are generally extended on a short-term basis (usually overnight) as a backup source of funding (seasonal credit may be extended for longer periods). The statute imposes a limit on maturity of not more than 4 months except for credit secured by one-to-four family mortgages, which maturity may be as prescribed by the Federal Reserve Board.
- Interest rate: Credits extended under the primary, secondary or seasonable program incur interest at the primary credit rate, secondary credit rate or seasonal credit rate, as applicable. These rates are generally set above the FOMC's target federal funds rate.
- Secured to the satisfaction of the lending Federal Reserve Bank: For discount window lending to depository institutions, obtaining a first priority perfected security interest in eligible collateral with a lendable value which exceeds the amount of credit extended is the traditional approach to being 'secured to the satisfaction' of the lending bank. (Compare to specifications under §13(3) of the FRA)
- No obligation to lend: Irrespective of the security available, a Federal Reserve Bank has no obligation to make, increase, renew or extend a discount window loan to a depository institution.

[60] Federal Reserve Act (12 USC 221 et seq.) Section 10(b) had been amended by FDICIA, linking the intensity of supervision to the level of capitalization, with severe treatment for 'critically undercapitalized' depository institutions. Under FDICIA, Federal Reserve banks should lend only to viable institutions, with penalties imposed in the case of extended lending to undercapitalized institutions, thus shifting the financial burden from the Federal Deposit Insurance Corporation to

advances or discounts—in both ordinary and extraordinary circumstances. The authority under this section was extended to designated financial market utilities (FMUs) by Section 806 of the Dodd-Frank Act.[61,62]

The Fed can also agree to supply emergency liquidity to foreign institutions operating in the country in accordance with Section 13(14) of the Federal Reserve Act.[63]

the Federal Reserve System if the latter chose to lend via its DWL to insolvent or critically under-capitalized institutions.

[61] Section 806 of the Dodd-Frank Wall Street Reform and Consumer Protection Act, Pub L No 111–203 (2010) (commonly referred to as the Dodd-Frank Act 2010 or simply Dodd-Frank) allows the Fed to lend to designated financial market utilities: The Board of Governors may authorize a Federal Reserve bank under Section 10(b) of the Federal Reserve Act (12 USC 347b) to provide to a designated financial market utility discount and borrowing privileges only in unusual or exigent circumstances, upon the affirmative vote of a majority of the Board of Governors then serving (or such other number in accordance with the provisions of Section 11(r)(2) of the Federal Reserve Act (12 USC 248(r)(2)) [1] after consultation with the Secretary, and upon a showing by the designated financial market utility that it is unable to secure adequate credit accommodations from other banking institutions. All such discounts and borrowing privileges shall be subject to such other limitations, restrictions, and regulations as the Board of Governors may prescribe. Access to discount and borrowing privileges under Section 10(b) of the Federal Reserve Act as authorized in this section does not require a designated financial market utility to be or become a bank or bank holding company.

While it is true that Dodd-Frank opened Section 10(b) to FMUs, some of the statutory requirements in Section 806 of Dodd-Frank are borrowed from Section 13(3). Eg, 'unusual or exigent' circumstances must exist, and the putative borrower must be 'unable to secure credit' from other banking institutions. So, it is more of blend of authorities. I thank Tom Baxter for observations on this point.

[62] US Department of the Treasury, 'Federal Stability Oversight Council' (27 July 2015) <https://www.treasury.gov/initiatives/fsoc/designations/Pages/default.aspx#FMU> accessed January 2016. The designated FMUs are

- The Clearing House Payments Company LLC on the basis of its role as operator of the Clearing House Interbank Payments System
- CLS Bank International
- Chicago Mercantile Exchange, Inc.
- The Depository Trust Company
- Fixed Income Clearing Corporation
- ICE Clear Credit LLC
- National Securities Clearing Corporation
- The Options Clearing Corporation

[63] Section 13.14 of the Federal Reserve Act allows the Federal Reserve Banks to lend to a branch or agency of a foreign bank; it reads as follows:

Subject to such restrictions, limitations, and regulations as may be imposed by the Board of Governors of the Federal Reserve System, each Federal Reserve bank may receive deposits from, discount paper endorsed by, and make advances to any branch or agency of a foreign bank in the same manner and to the same extent that it may exercise such powers with respect to a member bank if such branch or agency is maintaining reserves with such Reserve bank pursuant to section 7 of the International Banking Act of 1978. In exercising any such powers with respect to any such branch or agency, each Federal Reserve bank shall give due regard to account balances being maintained by such branch or agency with such Reserve bank and the proportion of the assets of such branch

Sections 12(a) and 14 of the Federal Reserve Act provide authority to the Fed to conduct open market operations; these sections were not amended by the Dodd-Frank Act.[64]

Authority under Section 14 of the Federal Reserve Act permits dollar liquidity swaps with foreign central banks such as the standing swap lines that exist between the Fed and the Bank of Canada, Fed and Bank of England, Fed and Bank of Japan, Fed and ECB, and Fed and Swiss National Bank. These swap lines are the responsibility of the Federal Open Market Committee (FOMC) and require an annual re-authorization.[65]

Lending to non-banks under US law is governed by Section 13(3) and Section 13(13)[66] of the Federal Reserve Act, ('Discounts for individuals, partnerships and corporations'). The authority under Section 13(3) has been restricted by the Dodd-Frank Wall Street Reform and Consumer Protection Act[67] which now requires that any emergency lending programmes and facilities authorized by the Federal Reserve under Section 13(3) of the Federal Reserve Act must have 'broad-based eligibility' and must be approved by the Secretary of the Treasury.[68] Thus, the Fed cannot engage in rescues of

or agency being held as reserves under section 7 of the International Banking Act of 1978. For the purposes of this paragraph, the terms 'branch', 'agency', and 'foreign bank' shall have the same meanings assigned to them in section 1 of the International Banking Act of 1978.

[64] See Thomas C Baxter Jr. and M Benjamin Snodgrass, 'The Role of the Lender of Last Resort: A Response to Professors Gortsos and Scott' in ECB, ECB Legal Conference 2015: 'From Monetary Union to Banking Union, On the Way to Capital Markets Union—New Opportunities for European Integration' <http://www.ecb.europa.eu/pub/pdf/other/frommonetaryuniontobankingunion201512.en.pdf>.

[65] See Stephen G Cecchetti, 'Towards an International Lender of Last Resort' (2014) BIS Papers No 79, 136 <http://www.bis.org/publ/bppdf/bispap79l_rh.pdf> accessed January 2016.

[66] Section 13(13) permits borrowing by individuals, partnerships, or corporations if the borrowing is secured by government or agency securities. It was not limited by Dodd-Frank like Section 13(3), but is of limited utility because of the collateral class it requires.

[67] Dodd-Frank Wall Street Reform and Consumer Protection Act, Pub L No 111–203 (2010) (commonly referred to as the Dodd-Frank Act 2010 or simply Dodd-Frank).

[68] See Board of Governors of the Federal Reserve System, 'Federal Reserve Act: Section 13: Powers of Federal Reserve Banks' (23 May 2013) <http://www.federalreserve.gov/aboutthefed/section13.htm> accessed January 2016. A programme or facility that is structured to remove assets from the balance sheet of a single/specific company or that is established to assist a single/specific company avoid bankruptcy, resolution, or insolvency proceeding will not be considered a programme or facility with broad-based eligibility. The Dodd-Frank Act 2010 requests the Federal Reserve to give immediate notice and periodic reports to Congress regarding any Section 13(3) facility and also to disclose information concerning the participants and the amount of individual transactions in all credit facilities under Section 13(3) and borrowers or counterparties in discount window and open market transactions.

See BIS, 'Central Bank Governance and Financial Stability: Report by a Study Group' (2011) <http://www.bis.org/publ/othp14.pdf> accessed January 2016. See also Board of Governors of the Federal Reserve System, 'Monthly Report on Credit and Liquidity Programs and the Balance

individual firms (ie, cannot use this authority for the 'purpose' of assisting a 'single and specific company' like it did in the case of Bear Stearns or AIG).[69]

The Fed implemented the revised Section 13.3 in a Regulation published in 2015,[70] which sets out in rather restrictive terms what constitutes a programme or facility of 'broad-based' eligibility, specifying inter alia that no fewer than five persons or entities must be eligible to participate in such a facility (Section 201.4 paragraph d).

During the crisis Section 13(3) of the Federal Reserve Act had permitted the Fed to lend to financial institutions other than a regulated depository institution due to 'unusual and exigent circumstances'.[71] This was the first

Sheet: March 2012' (2 August 2013) <http://www.federalreserve.gov/monetarypolicy/clbs-appendix-c-201203.htm> accessed January 2016 and Dodd-Frank.

[69] As explained by Tom Baxter in his presentation at the Bank of England on 11 March 2016 the key terms for lending under Section 13(3) after Dodd-Frank are as follows:

- Maturity: A §13(3) program or facility will cease extending new credit no later than one year after the date of the first extension of credit thereunder or the date of any extension of the program or facility by the Federal Reserve Board.
  - The Federal Reserve Board may terminate a Section 13(3) program or facility at any time.
  - It will periodically review the existence of unusual or exigent circumstances, program or facility usage and extent the continuing authorization thereof facilitates restoring or sustaining confidence in identified financial markets, ongoing need for the liquidity, and other appropriate factors.
  - Lending under a program or facility will be terminated promptly upon finding that conditions no longer warrant continuation of the program or facility or that it is no longer appropriate.
- Interest rate: The Federal Reserve Board will determine the penalty interest rate to be charged on any §13(3) credit and may do so through auction or other method as appropriate. The penalty rate will be set at a level that is (i) a premium to market rate in normal circumstances, (ii) affords liquidity in unusual and exigent circumstances, and (iii) encourages repayment and discourages use as economic conditions normalize.
- Secured to the satisfaction of the lending Federal Reserve Bank: All §13(3) credit must be indorsed or secured to the satisfaction of the lending Federal Reserve Bank.
- In determining whether an extension of §13(3) credit is secured to its satisfaction, prior to the time credit is initially extended, a Federal Reserve Bank must assign a lendable value to all collateral for the program or facility, consistent with sound risk management practices and to ensure the protection for the taxpayer.
- No obligation to extend credit: No person or entity is entitled to obtain any §13(3) credit or any increase, renewal or extension of any such credit.
- Other consideration: In addition to penalty interest rate, the Federal Reserve Board may require the payment of fees, penalties, charges or other consideration (such as equity) it determines to be appropriate to protect and appropriately compensate the taxpayer for the risks associated with such credit.

[70] Board of Governors of the Federal Reserve System, 'Press Release' (30 November 2015) <http://www.federalreserve.gov/newsevents/press/bcreg/20151130a.htm> accessed 25 January 2016.

[71] <https://www.newyorkfed.org/medialibrary/media/markets/Forms_of_Fed_Lending.pdf> accessed 25 January 2016.

time since the 1930s that such provision had been used. Before the Dodd-Frank Act amendment, Section 13(3), 'Discounts for individuals, partnerships, and corporations', read as follows

In unusual and exigent circumstances, the Board of Governors of the Federal Reserve System, by the affirmative vote of not less than five members, may authorize any Federal reserve bank, during such periods as the said board may determine, at rates established in accordance with the provisions of section 14, subdivision (d), of this Act ', to discount for any individual, partnership, or corporation, notes, drafts, and bills of exchange when such notes, drafts, and bills of exchange are indorsed or otherwise secured to the satisfaction of the Federal Reserve bank: Provided, That before discounting any such note, draft, or bill of exchange for an individual, partnership, or corporation the Federal reserve bank shall obtain evidence that such individual, partnership, or corporation is unable to secure adequate credit accommodations from other banking institutions. All such discounts for individuals, partnerships, or corporations shall be subject to such limitations, restrictions, and regulations as the Board of Governors of the Federal Reserve System may prescribe.[72]

Restricting the authority to provide lender of last resort assistance under Section 13(3) of the Federal Reserve Act after Dodd-Frank is considered by many to be unwise.[73] However, this restriction, of course, is part of a broader legislative package, since Dodd-Frank (Title II) establishes a clear resolution framework under the Orderly Liquidation Authority. It can also be argued that the incidental powers provision under Section 4 of the Federal Reserve Act can be effectively used in a crisis, since it reinforces the Federal Reserve Banks' capacity to act in ways that are not expressly prohibited by the Statute and thus give them a degree of flexibility.[74]

(c) Developments in the Eurozone/Banking Union[75]

The ECB has clear competence to provide market liquidity, according to Article 18 of the ESCB Statute and Article 127(2) in the Treaty on the Functioning of

[72] Christian Johnson has conducted an analysis of the extensive use of this provision during the crisis: Christian Johnson, 'Exigent and Unusual Circumstances: The Federal Reserve and the US Financial Crisis' in Kern Alexander and Niamh Moloney (eds), *Law Reform and Financial Markets* (Edward Elgar 2011).

[73] Scott (n 1).

[74] This point was made by Tom Baxter in a presentation in London on 11 March 2016.

[75] This section of the chapter draws on Rosa M Lastra, *International Financial and Monetary Law* (OUP 2015) Chapter 10. See also Chapter 7 therein for the non-conventional responses by the ECB to the crisis and Rosa M Lastra, 'Banking Union and Single Market: Conflict or Companionship?' (2013) 36:5 Fordham International Law Journal 1189 for a consideration of how banking union fits

the European Union.[76] The ECB did indeed provide hugely expanded liquidity operations during the crisis and made ample use of the considerable set of operational tools at its disposal to handle a liquidity crisis.[77]

The ECB is also competent to act as LOLR if the crisis originates in the payments system, according to Article 127(2) TFEU, which states that the European System of Central Banks (ESCB) is entrusted with the 'smooth operation of payment systems'.

However, when it comes to individual bank assistance, though the ECB is competent to provide liquidity assistance to 'financially sound' banks,[78] the provision of secured loans to troubled illiquid but solvent banks is understood to remain a national competence because it has not been specifically transferred.[79] In 1998, the ESCB adopted a restrictive reading of the ECB competences, concluding that the provision of lender of last resort assistance to specific illiquid individual institutions was a national task of the national central banks (NCBs) in line with Article 14.4 of the ESCB Statute (a provision which allows NCBs to perform non-ESCB tasks on their own responsibility and liability).[80] Therefore the classic collateralized lines of credit to

within the single market in financial services. For a short account of banking union see Rosa M Lastra, Bernd Krauskopf, Christos Gortsos, and René Smits, 'European Banking Union' (International Law Association, International Monetary Law Conference, Washington 2014) <http://www.ila-hq.org/en/committees/index.cfm/cid/22> accessed 25 January 2015.

[76] Treaty on the Functioning of the European Union [2012] OJ C326/01 (TFEU).

[77] Though ELA is technically available to all financial institutions, in the light of the wording of Art 18 of the ESCB Statute (which refers to 'other market participants') and according to Chiara Zilioli, ECB General Counsel, no ELA has been granted yet by any of the Eurosystem central banks to non-banks. See Chiara Zilioli, 'Introduction' in ECB, ECB Legal Conference 2015: 'From Monetary Union to Banking Union, On the Way to Capital Markets Union—New Opportunities for European Integration' (1 September 2015) <http://www.ecb.europa.eu/pub/pdf/other/frommonetaryuniontobankingunion201512.en.pdf> accessed January 2016.

[78] ECB, 'The Implementation of Monetary Policy in the Euro Area' (2008) 11 <http://www.ecb.europa.eu/pub/pdf/other/gendoc2008en.pdf> accessed 25 January 2016.

[79] René Smits has always held a different opinion, regarding this LOLR responsibility as an exclusive EU competence. See René Smits, 'The Role of the ESCB in Banking Supervision' in ECB, 'Legal Aspects of the European System of Central Banks' (2005) <https://www.ecb.europa.eu/pub/pdf/other/legalaspectsescben.pdf?2836f971198cc2b573779f5185159749> accessed 25 January 2016.

[80] Art 14.4 reads as follows: 'National central banks may perform functions other than those specified in this Statute unless the Governing Council finds, by a majority of two thirds of the votes cast, that these interfere with the objectives and tasks of the ESCB. Such functions shall be performed on the responsibility and liability of national central banks and shall not be regarded as being part of the functions of the ESCB'. The ECB can assess whether a given LOLR operation by a NCB interferes with monetary policy and, if so, either prohibit it or subject it to conditions. To this effect, the ECB has some internal rules (MoU) requiring *ex ante* notification to the Governing Council of such LOLR operation (Art 14.4). I thank Antonio Sainz de Vicuña for observations on this point. The following is an excerpt from the ECB Annual Report 1999 (p 98): 'The institutional framework for financial stability in the EU and in the euro area is based on national competence and international cooperation … Co-ordination mechanisms are primarily called for within the

individual institutions remain the responsibility of the national central banks, at their own risk and cost, but with the fiat of the ECB. (Article 14.4 assigns the Governing Council of the ECB responsibility for restricting ELA operations if it considers that these operations interfere with the objectives and tasks of the Eurosystem. Such decisions are taken by the Governing Council with a majority of two-thirds of the votes cast.) This interpretation is somewhat awkward, though it has been reaffirmed in a resolution of the Governing Council of 17 October 2013.[81]

Granting the ECB a clear LOLR does not require a Treaty change. The ECB is already competent to provide liquidity assistance to 'financially sound' banks. ELA/LOLR links monetary policy and supervision (thus the complementarity between monetary policy, supervision and liquidity assistance). All is needed is a reinterpretation of Article 14.4 in the light of new circumstances brought about by the advent of banking union (centralization of supervision) and in accordance with Article 18 and the principle of subsidiarity. At the very least such an interpretation should be required for significant institutions.

When prudential supervision was at the national level, it was perhaps logical to assume that the national authorities had the adequate expertise and information to assess the problems of banks within their jurisdictions

Eurosystem. This is the case for emergency liquidity assistance (ELA), which embraces the support given by central banks in exceptional circumstances and on a case-by-case basis to temporarily illiquid institutions and markets … If and when appropriate, the necessary mechanisms to tackle a financial crisis are in place. The main guiding principle is that the competent NCB takes the decision concerning the provision of ELA to an institution operating in its jurisdiction. This would take place under the responsibility and at the cost of the NCB in question … The agreement on ELA is internal to the Eurosystem and does not affect the existing arrangements between central banks and supervisors at the national level or bilateral or multilateral co-operation among supervisors and between the latter and the Eurosystem'.

[81] See ECB, 'ELA Procedures' (18 October 2013) <http://www.ecb.europa.eu/pub/pdf/other/201402_elaprocedures.en.pdf> accessed January 2016.

ELA means the provision by a Eurosystem NCB of (a) central bank money and/or (b) any other assistance that may lead to an increase in central bank money to a solvent financial institution, or group of solvent financial institutions, that is facing temporary liquidity problems, without such operation being part of the single monetary policy. Responsibility for the provision of ELA lies with the NCB(s) concerned. This means that any costs and the risks arising from, the provision of ELA are incurred by the relevant NCB. NCBs must inform the ECB within two days of an ELA operation, with details of the counterparties involved, the value of the operation, the haircuts and collateral applied, and the rate of interest paid on the funds. A limit of €500 million in ELA assistance can be provided to a given financial institution or group of institutions before the NCB(s) involved must inform the ECB as early as possible prior to the extension of the intended assistance. If the overall volume of ELA operations passes €2 billion for a given central bank, the Governing Council considers whether there is a risk that the ELA involved may interfere with the objectives and tasks of the Eurosystem. Upon the request of the NCB(s) concerned, the Governing Council may then decide to set a threshold and not to object to intended ELA operations that are below that threshold and conducted within a pre-specified short period of time.

(assistance on a rainy day—supervision on a sunny day). But now that supervision is European, the ECB should be at all effects lender of last resort for all those institutions it now supervises. ELA in all forms should be an ECB competence, in accordance with Article and 18 of the ESCB Statute, Article 127 TFEU and the principle of subsidiarity. According to Article 5.3 of the Treaty on European Union (TEU) (principle of subsidiarity):

> In areas which do not fall within its exclusive competence, the Union shall act only if and insofar as the objectives of the proposed action cannot be sufficiently achieved by the Member States, either at central level or at regional and local level, but can rather, by reason of the scale or effects of the proposed action, be better achieved at Union level.

In a crisis, action by the ECB is more effective than action by a national central bank or national authority. National supervisory authorities do not have the ability, authority, or inclination to deal effectively with externalities with cross-border effects. The ECB is able to better judge the risk of contagion.

Since the SSM became operational on 4 November 2014, it is clear in my opinion that the ECB should formally be the ultimate provider of liquidity in the euro area, both in cases of market liquidity and in cases of individual liquidity assistance, is a necessary consequence of the transfer of supervisory powers from the national to the European level.[82] The national competent authority (NCA) is neither the monetary policy authority nor the supervisor. The only advantage of continuing with the current interpretation is that any eventual loss is not shared (but yet it would have an impact on the whole euro area).

The problem with having the ECB as LOLR in all cases is, of course, the 'fiscal backstop', when the institution receiving the assistance is no longer illiquid, but insolvent. Fiscal policy remains decentralized in the Eurozone,[83] albeit subject to increasing coordination, conditionality, and stringent rules. Thus, while the Bank of England is ultimately backed by the fiscal resources of the UK Treasury, and the Federal Reserve System is ultimately backed by the fiscal resources of the US Treasury, the ECB does not have a European-wide fiscal counterpart.

[82] Notwithstanding the ECB Decision of 18 October 2013 on ELA (n 80), which assigns 'responsibility for the provision of ELA' to the 'NCB(s) concerned', further specifying that 'This means that any cost of, and the risks arising from, the provision of ELA are incurred by the relevant NCB'.

[83] Alexandre Lamfalussy remarked in an interview with *The Guardian* on 16 August 2003 that 'the great weakness of EMU is the E. The M part is institutionally well organized. We have a solid framework. We don't have that for economic policy': Mark Milner, 'Europe's Financial Architect' *The Guardian* (16 August 2003) <http://www.theguardian.com/business/2003/aug/16/3> accessed January 2014.

A limited fiscal backstop in Europe is provided via the European Stability Mechanism (ESM),[84] modelled upon the IMF (but with more limited funding, since it has a lending capacity of €500 billion, backed up by an authorized capital of €700 billion[85]). The *Pringle* ruling confirmed the legality of the ESM in 2012.[86] On 10 June 2014, euro area member states reached a political understanding on the operational framework of the ESM direct recapitalization instrument.[87]

(i) State Aid and LOLR

In my opinion the EU rules on state aid can afford protection to the ECB by providing a demarcation into what constitutes solvency support under EU law, since an inherent subsidy exists whenever the central bank lends to an insolvent institution. The Luxembourg Court of Justice recognized in a ground-breaking decision, the *Züchner* case, that EU competition rules are also applicable to the banking sector.[88]

The rules on state aid to the banking sector have been rewritten in response to the crisis. On 5 December 2007, the EU Commission in its approval of the rescue aid package for Northern Rock concluded 'that the emergency liquidity assistance provided by the Bank of England on 14th September 2007, which was secured by sufficient collateral and was interest-bearing, did not

[84] The Treaty Establishing the European Stability Mechanism (Brussels, 2 February 2012) entered into force on 27 September 2012. The ESM was inaugurated on 8 October 2012 following the ratification by all the euro area members.

[85] The ESM raises funds by issuing money market instruments and medium and long-term debt with maturities of up to thirty years, which are backed by a paid-in capital of €80 billion and the irrevocable and unconditional obligation of ESM member states to provide their contribution to ESM's authorized capital stock.

[86] Case C-370/12 *Thomas Pringle v The Government of Ireland, Ireland and the Attorney General* [2012] I-000, nyr and *Thomas Pringle v The Government of Ireland, Ireland and the Attorney General* [2012] IESC 47, para 5 (SC Ir.).

[87] <http://www.esm.europa.eu/pdf/FAQPreliminaryDRIJune2014.pdf> accessed 25 January 2016. Following the relevant national procedures and the formal adoption by the ESM Board of Governors, the instrument is expected to be added to the toolkit of the ESM. Once operational, it is expected that the instrument may be activated in case a bank fails to attract sufficient capital from private sources and if the ESM member concerned is unable to recapitalize it, including through the instrument of indirect recapitalization of the ESM. For a transitional period until 31 December 2015, a bail-in of 8 per cent of all liabilities will be a precondition for using the instrument, as well as the use of the resources available in the ESM member's national resolution fund. From 1 January 2016, bail-in in line with the rules of the Bank Recovery and Resolution Directive will be required. The financial assistance will be provided in accordance with EU state aid rules and the ESM member will be asked to invest alongside the ESM.

[88] See Case 172/80 *Züchner v Bayerische Vereinsbank* [1981] ECR 2021.

constitute state aid'.[89] The Commission Communication of 13 October 2008 further reiterated this point:[90] In establishing a single market in financial services, it is important that the Treaty's state aid rules are applied consistently and equally to the banking sector, though with a regard to the peculiarities and sensitivities of the financial markets.[91]

In August 2013 the Commission published another Communication extending the 'crisis rules' for banks.[92] According to paragraph 53 of this August 2013 communication:

[89] European Commission, 'State Aid: Commission Approves UK Rescue Aid Package for Northern Rock' (5 December 2007) <http://europa.eu/rapid/press-release_IP-07-1859_en.htm?locale=en.> accessed January 2010: 'However, the guarantee on deposits granted by the Treasury on 17th September, as well as the measures granted on 9th October, which provided further liquidity and guarantees to Northern Rock and were secured by a Treasury indemnity, do constitute state aid.' On 17 March 2008, six months after the first state aid measures ('rescue aid') took place, the UK authorities submitted to the Commission a restructuring plan. The Commission then launched an in-depth investigation into this 'restructuring aid'. See European Commission, 'State Aid: Commission Launches In-Depth Investigation into UK Restructuring Aid Package for Northern Rock' <http://europa.eu/rapid/pressReleasesAction.do?reference=IP/08/489> accessed January 2010.

[90] European Commission Communication, 'The application of State aid rules to measures taken in relation to financial institutions in the context of the current global financial crisis' OJ C270, 25.10.2008, 8, paragraph 51: '[T]he Commission considers for instance that activities of central banks related to monetary policy, such as open market operations and standing facilities, are not caught by the State aid rules. Dedicated support to a specific financial institution may also be found not to constitute aid in specific circumstances. The Commission considers that the provision of central banks' funds to the financial institution in such a case may be found not to constitute aid when a number of conditions are met, such as: the financial institution is solvent at the moment of the liquidity provision and the latter is not part of a larger aid package; the facility is fully secured by collateral to which haircuts are applied, in function of its quality and market value; the central bank charges a penal interest rate to the beneficiary; the measure is taken at the central bank's own initiative, and in particular is not backed by any counter-guarantee of the State.'

[91] From the beginning of the global financial crisis in the autumn of 2008 to December 2010, the Commission issued four communications which provided detailed guidance on the criteria for the compatibility of state support to financial institutions with the requirements of Art 107(3)(b) of TFEU: (1) Communication on the application of State aid rules to measures taken in relation to financial institutions in the context of the current global financial crisis (Banking Communication); (2) Communication on the recapitalisation of financial institutions in the current financial crisis: limitation of aid to the minimum necessary and safeguards against undue distortions of competition (Recapitalisation Communication); (3) Communication from the Commission on the treatment of impaired assets in the Community banking sector (Impaired Assets Communication); and (4) Communication on the return to viability and the assessment of restructuring measures in the financial sector in the current crisis under the State aid rules (Restructuring Communication). European Commission, 'State Aid Temporary Rules Established in Response to the Economic and Financial Crisis' (30 July 2013) <http://ec.europa.eu/competition/state_aid/legislation/temporary.html> accessed January 2014.

[92] European Commission, 'Communication from the Commission on the Application, from 1 August 2013, of State Aid Rules to Support Measures in Favour of Banks in the Context of the Financial Crisis ("Banking Communication")' (30 July 2013) <http://eurlex.europa.eu/legalcontent/EN/ALL/?uri=CELEX:52013XC0730(01)> accessed January 2014.

Liquidity support and guarantees on liabilities temporarily stabilise the liability side of a bank's balance sheet. Therefore, unlike recapitalisation or impaired asset measures which in principle must be preceded by the notification of a restructuring plan by the Member State concerned and approval by the Commission before they can be granted, the Commission can accept that Member States notify guarantees and liquidity support to be granted after approval on a temporary basis as rescue aid before a restructuring plan is approved.

Paragraph 62 further clarifies:

The ordinary activities of central banks related to monetary policy, such as open market operations and standing facilities, do not fall within the scope of the State aid rules. Dedicated support to a specific credit institution (commonly referred to as 'emergency liquidity assistance') may constitute aid unless the following cumulative conditions are met:[93]

(a) the credit institutions is temporarily illiquid but solvent at the moment of the liquidity provision and is not part of a larger aid package;
(b) the facility is fully secured by collateral to which appropriate haircuts are applied, in function of its quality and market value;
(c) the central bank charges a penal interest rate to the beneficiary;
(d) the measure is taken at the central bank's own initiative, and in particular is not backed by any counter-guarantee of the State.

It is rather interesting that the Thornton-Bagehot doctrinal principles find their way into a legal text.

Paragraph 63 of this 2013 Communication further specifies that: 'interventions by deposit guarantee funds to reimburse depositors in accordance with Member States' obligations under Directive 94/19/EC on deposit-guarantee scheme do not constitute state aid'.

(ii) Monetary Policy, Macroprudential Supervision, and Liquidity Assistance

Some of the most controversial non-conventional measures the ECB adopted to combat the crisis remind us of the multipolar nature of LOLR. LOLR is the central banking function that links monetary policy and supervision (macro and micro).

In 2010 the ECB decided to help keep down borrowing costs of crisis-hit countries through the Securities Markets Programme or SMP (a

[93] See also recitals 2 and 41 and Art 32(4)(d) of the Bank Recovery and Resolution Directive at <http://eur-lex.europa.eu/legal-content/EN/TXT/?uri=celex%3A32014L0059>. The EU resolution framework clarifies that the need for emergency liquidity assistance from a central bank, per se, does not necessarily trigger the resolution of a bank, and it acknowledges the role of central banks in providing liquidity to the financial system in times of stress.

bond-purchasing programme) in order to 'restore an appropriate transmission mechanism of monetary policy'[94] and then announced in August 2012, the Outright Monetary Transactions or OMTs.[95] Mario Draghi, ECB president, publicly proclaimed that the central bank would do 'whatever it takes' to ensure the future stability of the euro.[96] The legality of OMT was then challenged in the German Constitutional Court (GCC). The GCC referred the case to Court of Justice of the European Union (CJEU) for preliminary ruling.[97]

In January 2015, Advocate General Cruz Villalón issued his opinion in the reference for a preliminary ruling on *Gauweiler et al. v Deutscher Bundestag* on the ECB's OMT.[98] The GCC had asked the CJEU to clarify whether the OMT programme was an economic rather than a monetary measure and whether the ECB had therefore exceeded its powers by establishing it. The GCC had also raised the question of whether the OMT programme was in contravention of the prohibition of monetary financing (Article 123 TFEU). According to Advocate General Cruz Villalón, the ECB's OMT programme is compatible in principle with the TFEU but if the programme is implemented, its compatibility will depend on certain conditions being met. Interestingly, the Advocate General pointed out (paragraph 6), addressing the question of admissibility, that 'a simple press release' (following the meeting of the ECB governing council on 5 and 6 September 2012) was fundamental, given the 'special role played by public communication in central bank activity'. The complainants had raised the substantial issue of whether the ECB is 'a lender of last resort for the States of the euro area' (paragraph 7). The CJEU made its final ruling of the OMT case in June 2015, declaring the conditional OMT programme to be legal, since it 'does not exceed the powers of the ECB in relation to monetary policy and does not contravene the prohibition of monetary financing of EU nations'.[99]

[94] Decision of the European Central Bank of 14 May 2010 establishing a securities markets programme [2010] L124/8.

[95] See ECB, 'Technical features of Outright Monetary Transactions' (6 September 2012) <http://www.ecb.int/press/pr/date/2012/html/pr120906_1.en.html> accessed January 2014.

[96] 'Within our mandate, the ECB is ready to do whatever it takes to preserve the euro. And believe me, it will be enough': Mario Draghi, 'Speech by Mario Draghi, President of the European Central Bank' (Global Investment Conference, London, 26 July 2012) <http://www.ecb.europa.eu/press/key/date/2012/html/sp120726.en.html> accessed January 2014.

[97] Case C-62/14 *Peter Gauweiler and Others* [2014] OJ C129/11.

[98] ibid.

[99] CJEU, 'Press Release No 70/2015: The OMT Programme Announced by the ECB in September 2012 Is Compatible with EU Law' (16 June 2015) <http://curia.europa.eu/jcms/upload/docs/application/pdf/2015-06/cp150070en.pdf> accessed January 2016.

The ECB must of course comply with the prohibition of monetary financing (Article 123 TFEU)[100] and with the so-called no bailout clause (Article 125 TFEU).

The ECB entered into unchartered territory with the approval by the ECB Governing Council of a large QE programme on 22 January 2015, with effective QE operations commencing on 9 March 2015.[101] The ECB started purchasing government and private sector bonds in June 2015 (€60 billion a month till September 2016, for a total of €1 trillion)[102] in order to revitalize the euro area economies and to counter deflation. Non-conventional measures of monetary policy—the latest being negative nominal interest rates—have become the new norm.

The interaction between macroprudential supervision[103] monetary policy and liquidity assistance is a challenge for the ECB in the discharge of its multiple functions, as Charles Goodhart and myself emphasized in a report to the European Parliament,[104] ahead of the Monetary Dialogue with President Draghi in September 2015:

> Monetary policy has entered uncharted territory following the great financial crisis. While prior to the crisis it had broadly converged toward one with a price stability (inflation) target and a short term interest rate as a policy tool, there is now a 2nd variant of monetary policy, which involves varying both the size, and perhaps, the composition of a central bank's balance sheet, with implications for monetary policy and also for financial stability.[105]

[100] Art 123 TFEU only forbids the ESCB from giving credit to or purchasing sovereign debt directly from EU member states but there is no ban on purchases of government bonds on the secondary markets, which the ECB has been doing since May 2010, when it began buying the government debt of Greece.

[101] Mario Draghi, 'Introductory Statement to the Press Conference' (Press Conference, Nicosia, 5 March 2015) <http://www.ecb.europa.eu/press/pressconf/2015/html/is150305.en.html> accessed January 2016. As noted by Catherine Lubochinsky in private correspondence, while the objective of SMP and OMT was to prevent the collapse of the euro, since 2014 the issue is inflation—which at the aggregate level is zero in the Eurozone (fight against deflation)—and the goal with QE is to flatten the yield curve and decrease credit spreads in countries like Italy.

[102] Mario Draghi, 'Introductory Statement to the Press Conference' (Press Conference, Frankfurt, 22 January 2015) <http://www.ecb.europa.eu/press/pressconf/2015/html/is150122.en.html> accessed January 2016.

[103] Responsibility for macroprudential supervision is shared between the ECB, national authorities/councils of financial stability, and the European Systemic Risk Board (though the latter's 'powers' are rather limited).

[104] The report is available in the dedicated section (Economic Policies, Monetary Dialogue) of the European Parliament ECON website: European Parliament Committees, 'Monetary Dialogue of 23 September 2015' (2 February 2016) <http://www.europarl.europa.eu/committees/en/econ/monetary-dialogue.html> accessed February 2016.

[105] ibid: 'There is a misleading, but commonly used, phrase about some Central Bank operations having "quasi-fiscal" effects. All Central Bank operations on their balance sheet, and to affect the level and pattern of interest rates, have fiscal implications, perhaps especially the most traditional open market operations in Treasury Bills to adjust the official short-term interest rate. But there is

Financial stability is—as stated earlier—a goal that transcends institutional and geographic boundaries. It also permeates through different markets beyond banking: 'The limits of the ECB's authority in the pursuit of financial stability remain open, considering also the interconnection between banking markets and other markets (sovereign debt, derivative, etc.) and the designation of systemically important financial institutions.'[106] The problem is further compounded by the fact that 'asset markets—especially the housing market—are not homogeneous throughout the eurozone. Thus, while the ECB can, and should, aim for a single euro-wide macro-prudential policy, for the foreseeable future macro-prudential policies should be heterogenous across markets and countries.'[107]

The experience in Greece[108] reminds us that there are limits as to how much central banks can do with the tools at their disposal—monetary policy and emergency liquidity assistance—to deal with the causes and effects of a crisis in the absence of fiscal and structural reforms.

6. Conclusions

The lender of last resort role of the central bank is unique as a crisis management tool because of the immediacy of the assistance. This feature is in contrast with other crisis management instruments, such as resolution tools or deposit insurance that by definition require a longer time framework.

The first line of defence against a banking crisis is liquidity support. Central banks provide liquidity when no other sources of liquidity are readily available (or at least are not available at 'reasonable market prices'). Then it is up to the government to provide capital (recapitalization of troubled entities—bailout programmes). Paul Tucker reminds us: 'Liquidity assistance to sound firms is not a bailout'.[109] This chapter discussed the two forms of central bank liquidity support: lending (targeted or micro support, the 'discount window')

now, following on from the post-GFC allocation of responsibility for financial stability, and for the manipulation of micro and macro-prudential instruments, a far wider allocation of non-traditional operational functions to Central Banks. It has been akin to the opening of Pandora's Box.'

[106] ibid. [107] ibid.

[108] The 'extend and pretend policies' when it comes to sovereign debt 'management' (restructuring) cannot hide a few uncomfortable truths. The ECB may have to take losses. Memories of the LDC crisis in the 1980s and the lost decade in Latin America cast a long shadow on the current situation in some euro area member states—it took years for the Brady plan to replace the misguided Baker Plan. Where you draw the dividing line for loss-sharing arrangements and who provides what sort of support are key issues yet to be solved.

[109] See Tucker (n 2) 37.

and expansion of the money in circulation (macro support, open market operations).

Despite the difficulties to differentiate between illiquidity and insolvency in a crisis, illiquidity does not automatically mean insolvency. In the words of Tom Baxter: 'Illiquidity is always the harbinger of insolvency; but not every illiquid financial firm is, or will become insolvent'.[110] And lending to well capitalized profitable banks that become victims of irrational panics is at the very core of why LOLR is so important for the functioning of the financial system.

Since LOLR is the most effective 'fire-fighting' tool for the authorities, restricting *ex ante* the ability of the authorities to act may be misguided. What we need is a clear legal framework that sets out LOLR policies and procedures in advance *ex ante*, but leaves ample discretion to act and establishes adequate accountability *ex post*. Flexibility and speed are essential. Constructive ambiguity must be abandoned.

However, clarity should not entail inelasticity. Flexibility—encapsulated in the exercise of discretion—is needed when the next crisis arises in order to respond to problems. Decisions will need to be made under pressure often without accurate information.

It is easy to criticize central banks and their actions as lender of last resort *ex post*, but in the midst of the crisis, and given the unpredictability of events, the inability of legislators (eg, in the US) to approve emergency legislation in a timely fashion, and the lack of accurate information about valuations and the soundness of financial institutions, central banks acted with the flexibility that was required to stop the fire from spreading. They were no ordinary times. Under huge pressure, central banks attempted through their liquidity assistance policies to re-establish confidence when market conditions were extremely fragile; the criticism in this regard of whether the Fed was independent or not in the pursuit of financial stability during the crisis somewhat misses the point. The priority then was to stop the fire. Legislators have since been rewriting the fire regulations.

Moral hazard must be fought in good times. In a situation of a financial collapse, it is not the right time to talk about moral hazard. Notwithstanding the critique of the bailout of AIG, we must acknowledge that that the global financial system has evolved since the LOLR theory was first presented by Thornton and Bagehot.

Today's interconnectedness of financial institutions and markets and the nature of funding markets suggest that support should be granted without

[110] Baxter (n 54).

unnecessary restrictions against collateral to solvent financial institutions to counteract the risk of contagion, the run on the markets.

This chapter has focused on national arrangements for LOLR. There are, however, important additional international implications, which I hope to turn to at some future date.[111] We need to think outside the boundaries of national law to find solutions to the challenges we face.[112]

[111] From an international perspective, the US should not forget the benefits of 'enlightened self-interest'. The US dollar remains the reserve currency par excellence (a privilege that could change in future; lest we forget the challenges coming from regional initiatives in Asia and Latin America and the law of unintended consequences). Regional networks based on the US dollar swaps include the Chiang Mai Initiative Multilateralisation and the BRIC's Contingent Reserve Arrangement. (See eg, Camila Durán, 'The International Lender of Last Resort for Emerging Countries: A Bilateral Currency Swap?' (2015) Global Economic Governance Programme Working Paper 2015/108 <http://www.globaleconomicgovernance.org/geg-wp-2015108-international-lender-last-resort-emerging-countries-bilateral-currency-swap> accessed January 2016). The World looks to the Fed for the provision of dollar liquidity (See eg, Stephen Cecchetti, 'Towards an International Lender of Last Resort' BIS Papers No 79, September 2014, 131–36). And this can be a real challenge.

In a speech in 2013, Mark Carney spoke about the provision by the Bank of England of liquidity in currencies other than sterling: Carney (n 45). He pointed out: 'As markets evolve, banks and markets here may need backstops in other currencies in our time zone before business opens for the Federal Reserve and after it has closed for the Bank of Japan. Although the Bank of England can supply limitless quantities of sterling, we rely on other central banks for access to their currencies. In response to the crisis, a network of swap agreements between advanced economy central banks was established giving us the ability to provide a range of currencies to UK-based institutions. This network of swap lines should not necessarily be limited to the G7 economies. In June, the Bank of England signed such an agreement with the People's Bank of China, reflecting the growing international role of the Renminbi to include branches of Chinese banks in our broader policy of openness to hosting foreign wholesale banking activities.'

[112] The issue of foreign currency liquidity has been raised by Madame Christine Lagarde, IMF Managing Director, in the context of emerging markets: 'IMF Head: Emerging Markets Need Safety Net' *Financial Times* (London, 12 January 2016) <http://www.ft.com/fastft/2016/01/12/imfs-lagarde-emerging-markets-need-stronger-safety-net/> accessed January 2016. Camila Durán has advocated in a paper in 2015 the establishment of a multilateral hub for facilitating currency swaps. See Camila V Durán, 'Avoiding the Next Liquidity Crunch: How the G20 Must Support Monetary Cooperation to Increase Resilience to Crisis' (2015) Global Economic Governance Programme <http://www.globaleconomicgovernance.org/avoiding-next-liquidity-crunch-how-g20-must-support-monetary-cooperation-increase-resilience-crisis> accessed January 2016. The point has been reiterated in a recent book, *The End of Alchemy: Money, Banking and the Future of the Global Economy* (Little Brown 2016), by Mervyn King, where he calls not only for the reinvigoration of the IMF but also for a permanent system of swap arrangements under which central banks lend to each other in whatever currencies they are needed to address short-term liquidity shortages. Mervyn King, as John Plender points out in his review of the book, that Bagehot's famous dictum is out of date because bank balance sheets are much larger and have much fewer liquid assets than in the nineteenth century. Central banks are thus condemned in a crisis to take bad collateral in the shape of a risky, illiquid assets. King suggests replacing the LOLR by what he calls a 'pawnbroker for all seasons'. John Plender, 'Uncertainty Principles' *Financial Times* (3 March 2016) <http://www.ft.com/cms/s/0/e40af84c-e081-11e5-8d9b-e88a2a889797.html>.

Index

Milton Keynes UK
Ingram Content Group UK Ltd.
UKHW021024140124
435995UK00003B/10

9 780198 777625